ACHIEVING ENVIRONMENTAL STANDARDS

Second Edition

MIKE GILBERT
and
RICHARD GOULD

FINANCIAL TIMES
PITMAN PUBLISHING

FINANCIAL TIMES

MANAGEMENT

LONDON · SAN FRANCISCO
KUALA LUMPUR · JOHANNESBURG

*Financial Times Management delivers the knowledge,
skills and understanding that enable students,
managers and organisations to achieve their ambitions,
whatever their needs, wherever they are.*

London Office:
128 Long Acre, London WC2E 9AN
Tel: +44 (0)171 447 2000
Fax: +44 (0)171 240 5771
Website: www.ftmanagement.com

A Division of Financial Times Professional Limited

First published in Great Britain 1998

© Financial Times Professional Limited

The right of Mike Gilbert and Richard Gould to be identified
as authors of this work has been asserted by them in accordance with
the Copyright, Designs and Patents Act 1988.

ISBN 0 273 63100 4

British Library Cataloguing in Publication Data
A CIP catalogue record for this book can be obtained from
the British Library.

This publication is designed to provide accurate and authoritative
information in regard to the subject matter covered. It is sold with the
understanding that neither the authors, BSI nor the publisher is engaged in
rendering legal, investing, or any other professional service. If legal advice or
other expert assistance is required, the services of a competent professional
person should be sought.

The publisher, BSI and the authors make no representation, express or implied,
with regard to the accuracy of the information contained in this book and
cannot accept any legal responsibility or liability for any errors or
omissions that may be made.

1 3 5 7 9 10 8 6 4 2

Typeset by Northern Phototypesetting Co Ltd, Bolton
Printed and bound in Great Britain by
Biddles Ltd, Guildford and King's Lynn

*The Publishers' policy is to use paper manufactured
from sustainable forests.*

ABOUT THE AUTHORS

Mike Gilbert played a key role in the development of BS 7750 and has since managed BSI's International Training business, was a director in the Quality Assurance Division and is now Managing Director, BSI Quality Services Europe. He has remained a strong and committed supporter of environmental improvement through standards, systems and certification programmes.

Richard Gould is an environmental specialist with BSI. He has a PhD on the environmental impacts of air pollution, and during the past 15 years, has worked throughout the world on many aspects of environmental management. As a writer on the environment, he has contributed to *New Scientist*, *The Times*, the *Guardian* and *Environment Business Magazine*.

CONTENTS

PART 4

PART 5

PART 6

PREFACE

ENVIRONMENTAL MANAGEMENT SYSTEMS – SAVE MONEY – SAVE THE ENVIRONMENT

In 1992, I wrote the first edition of *Achieving Environmental Standards* in response to requests to provide 'how to' help for organizations wanting to use new environmental management system (EMS) tools and techniques. These were seen to be a new, systematic and effective, way to improve an organization's environmental performance through root cause analysis and the development of practical, manageable solutions, with two key benefits:

- saving the organization money – reducing waste, better control and less risk
- improving the environment – reducing emissions, waste and materials.

The first edition sprang from the immense and growing body of knowledge about environmental management, quality systems use, auditing protocols and the publication of BS 7750 – the world's first environmental management systems standard.

Since then, a great deal has happened. For a start, environmental issues have grown in importance – so much so, that phrases such as *global warming*, *sustainable development* and *ozone depletion* are common.

Also EMS standards have evolved; BS 7750 has been withdrawn and replaced by an international standard BS EN ISO 14001, based on BS 7750. This standard has made a profound, global impression – over 2500 firms worldwide are now registered to ISO 14001 and more are being certified every day. Furthermore, ISO 14001 is now an accepted core element of systems required by the European Union's Eco-Management and Audit Scheme (EMAS).

These developments drove a demand for the second edition of *Achieving Environmental Standards*, with two major changes. First, the design of the book follows the structure of ISO 14001 and includes sections on the requirements of the EMAS Regulation and Scheme. Second, the original book included case study material from the pilot scheme of BS 7750. The new edition includes new and expanded case studies because readers said that they not only found these most useful, but we have learnt far more about the benefits and practical issues of implementing a successful, effective system.

The case study material was written and researched by the second author, Rick Gould, who also contributed new material to other sections of the book. As well as being a writer, he has over 15 years of international experience of environmental research and management, and thus brings real-world experience to the new edition. It has been a delight working with Rick.

We both hope that you will find this book as useful as the first edition. It provides guidance on implementing EMS and how to get the best out of the changes that this may bring. The EMS is a tool which can help your organization operate more effectively and efficiently. An effective and efficient organization wastes less, and, as many environmental problems are caused by waste, its reduction can lead to a win-win situation; both the environmental and your bottom line can benefit.

ACKNOWLEDGEMENTS

Innumerable people have given their time and help for this edition, and we are extremely grateful for their generosity. In particular we should like to thank the following companies and organizations for allowing us to describe their environmental management systems within the case study material: Brake Linings Ltd; British Standards Institution; British Telecom plc; The Body Shop plc; Du Pont (UK) Ltd; Camborne Fabrics; Elmwood College; the Environment Agency, UK; the US Environmental Protection Agency; Environmental Resources Management Ltd; ETAC Ltd; Fenland Laundries Ltd; Formosa Plastics Corporation USA; Hewlett Packard Ltd; London Borough of Sutton; LSI Logic, Inc; March Consulting Group; Schlumberger Gas Ltd; Shotton Paper Company Ltd; UK Waste Management Ltd; Vauxhall Motors Ltd.

Rick Gould wishes to thank his family for their patience during the many evenings and weekends he spent writing the new material for the second edition, and Mark Barthel of BSI for advice throughout the preparation of the book. Lastly, special thanks must go to Helen Bennett for her skills as a researcher, editor and administrator.

PART

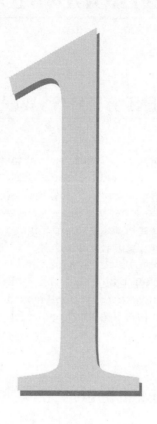

1

1

INTRODUCTION

MANAGEMENT SYSTEMS SAVE YOU MONEY

One year after the launch of ISO 14001, well over 2000 organizations had registered to this voluntary standard, while several hundred had registered to the related Eco-Management and Audit Scheme (EMAS). The interest in formal environmental management systems (EMSs) is growing dramatically.

At first this can seem odd. After all, there is no law which says that an organization has to take an interest in an EMS programme based, for example, on ISO 14001. Like the quality standard with which ISO 14001 shares a common ancestry, this is a voluntary system which costs time and money to implement. So why are thousands of organizations taking such an interest in formal, registered EMS?

Put simply, evidence shows that if you implement an EMS, then your organization will save money, improve its environmental performance and reduce its risks of environmental prosecution, giving your organization a new competitive advantage.

EMS and its role in sustainability

ISO 14001 and EMAS are relevant because of a concept called *sustainability*. Sustainable development, defined by the World Commission on Environment and Development, has become accepted by politicians and industry leaders as a guiding philosophy. It ensures that the use of environmental resources to meet current needs is managed so as not to damage those resources for future use.

This means living on the earth's income rather than eroding its capital. It means keeping the consumption of renewable resources within the limits of their replenishment. It means handing down to successive generations not only man-made wealth (such as buildings, roads and railways) but also natural wealth, such as clean and adequate water supplies, good arable land, a wealth of wildlife and ample forests.

Applying sustainability

Applying the concept of sustainable development is difficult! It sets new environmental performance requirements for society and industry that bring change in many ways, from the domestic use of bottle banks to national decisions on policy and investment. Environmental requirements for industry arise as pressures from outside or as opportunities to achieve benefits from inside. Whether a large company or a small company, the opportunities and potential benefits are great and the risks of non-compliance equally high.

Yet the practice of meeting performance requirements is not a new one for industry, it strives to meet customer requirements all the time. To help it meet these requirements, industry uses quality system standards as management tools to act as a benchmark and establish appropriate practices and procedures to assure success. In meeting the new environmental performance requirements, whether for products or organizations, industry needs *new* benchmarks to demonstrate their progress, through an environmental management systems approach based on ISO 14001 or EMAS.

These models of good environmental management can be applied by any organization, and like the quality systems approach, assured success in this area is becoming an important consideration in the business development plans of many organizations, supporting the progress towards the sustainable development goal.

The principles of sustainable development involve integrating environmental criteria into economic practice to ensure that the strategic plans of organizations, while satisfying the need for continuing growth and evolution, conserve nature's 'capital' for the future. Applying the principle implies living within the carrying capacity of existing eco-systems. This will require a change in many aspects of society and commerce. It is not only about air pollution, ozone depletion, water conservation, raw material use and waste management; it is also a truly international issue, affecting cross-border transactions, trade, finance and political agendas.

The role of industries which operate on an international basis is therefore the key to a constructive approach to achieve the sustainable development goal. Industry influences the source of raw materials, the manufacturing and distribution processes, the consumers' responses and the methods of waste disposal through their activities. A proactive lead from industry to find positive incentives to change and improve environmental performance would mean opportunities for less legislative control, a healthier communication process with the community and ultimately a sustainable industrial and social future for us all. This is where defined standards of environmental management conformity can help.

Systems approaches

The quality concept has led to a revolution in many organizations to meet the need to show customers that their organization's internal quality management system has the capacity to produce products and services that meet the purchaser's specified requirements. As a result many organizations seek certification to defined, international, quality system standards – ISO 9000. An assessed and certified quality system capability provides a 'badge' that signifies an attained level. Quality-assured status is now a growing requirement across all sectors of commerce and services worldwide applying to over 150 000 companies.

This quality management approach requires a cyclical system illustrated by the 'improvement loop' in Figure 1.1.

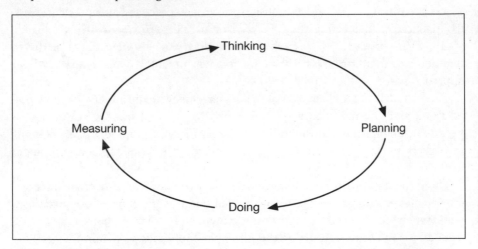

Fig. 1.1 The improvement loop

An organization must *think* about what its goals and targets are and how they might be achieved, must *plan* in more detail how to reach them, must *carry out* its plans, and must *measure* not only how successfully they have been carried out, but also whether the background situation has changed, in order to think and plan for the next phases of its activities.

Imagine, then, an international standard that provides a method for assured environmental management system performance, using an approach parallel to quality management. Although not a panacea or a gateway to sustainable development, the existence of an environmental management system along the lines of ISO 14001 or EMAS, provides for the integration of environmental criteria into an organization's performance at all levels.

Being generically related to other management systems, it could be integrated into the organization's whole system and not cause the upheaval attendant on the implementation of a new programme. It would be a help, not a hindrance.

The benefits of certificates and external registration

A supporting certificate provides external visibility and assurance of the organization's commitment and performance, providing market differentiation for those who meet the criteria and a 'badge' as an incentive or reward for those who meet the requirements. Being a voluntary scheme, it provides industry with a self-regulatory basis for continual improvement in environmental performance through the audit and review process. Being independently assured by a third party provides internal and external confidence in performance.

Environmental performance pressures

Organizations today are under many pressures to manage and improve their environmental performance, such as having to comply with more stringent legislation and to satisfy customer demands. The drivers are powerful and diverse and do not appear to be receding.

The UK, for example, demands improved performance through legislation such as the Producer Responsibility Obligations (Packaging Waste) Regulations, 1997, the Special Waste Regulations, 1996, the Environment Act, 1995 and the Integrated Pollution Prevention and Control Directive (IPPC). New legislation is increasingly taking an integrated approach – modelled on the UK's innovative Integrated Pollution Control (IPC) systems – and uses the principle of 'the polluter pays'.

For example, during late 1997, the UK's Environment Agency brought successful prosecutions against several companies which had polluted watercourses, killing thousands of fish for several kilometres in some instances. In every case, the companies responsible for the pollution were not only fined heavily, but also had to pay the legal bills of both sides, plus the costs of cleaning up the rivers and streams to restore them to their former states. In every case, the expenses of cleaning up the pollution dwarfed both the legal expenses and the costs of preventing the pollution which would have been involved, had the companies chosen prevention instead of cure.

Waste management regulations in the UK – such as the Duty of Care Regulations, which require producers of waste to take responsibility for spent materials from cradle to grave – can have significant financial penalties that far outweigh the direct costs of a system failure. These can include withdrawal of consent and business closure.

Against this background, Best Practicable Environmental Options (BPEO), Best Available Technology (BAT), Environmental Impact Assessments (EIA) and Economically Viable and Best Available Technology (EVABAT) are beginning to place the legislators' interests into the company decision-making processes.

Consumers, and this includes purchasers in the supply chain, are exerting pressure on companies to provide more environmentally appropriate choices. Major companies are questioning not only the environmental performance of the products they purchase, but also that of the organization which makes the product. For example, without prescriptive legislation, the use of CFCs as propellants in domestic products almost disappeared in a two-year period as a direct result of pressure from consumers and pressure groups.

Banks, insurance companies and shareholders exert pressure. Insurance companies require higher premiums for companies with poor environmental performance records and will not insure some environmental risks because of the extensive liabilities incurred. Shareholders now have options to join 'Green Funds' where the investment criteria include the commitment to environmental 'clean technologies', waste minimization or other aspects of good environmental performance.

Peer pressure can also be a significant factor. It means that current operating activities should meet the needs of present stakeholders (shareholders, employees, customers and communities) without compromising the ability of future generations to meet their needs.

Environmental performance: benefits

The factors which 'cost' organizations environmentally, whether through loss of business, large fines, higher insurance premiums or negative publicity, are called 'negative' motivators. However, there is a positive side to improving environmental performance – the 'positive' motivators.

The concepts of reduction, re-use and recycling are not just slogans thought up by environmentalists. Application of such concepts can bring real cash savings to any organization. Reduction of energy consumption and waste within an organization saves money. Many companies have successfully run energy management and waste minimization programmes, and produced staggering savings which can significantly boost profitability.

As waste removal and landfill gets more expensive, the less there is to be taken away, the less the costs incurred will be. Re-use of packaging can reduce waste and save on purchasing costs. Re-using water resources is proving financially beneficial for some companies, particularly now that water metering is pricing water use at a more realistic level. Recycling materials and products can save money. Companies have discovered that proper management of paper, cardboard and metal wastes can generate a small income rather than incur a cost for removal of waste materials. The benefits for organizations can be great.

In addition, the implementation programmes that support such initiatives can change the way the company operates permanently. Such an approach to business change provides a powerful tool to harness the energies of management and staff to change the organization from within. However, although many large companies are reaping benefits from improved environmental performance, large businesses also rely on smaller businesses, and they are using their purchasing power to influence their suppliers. Suppliers therefore, must change. Indeed the ability of smaller organizations to change can exert powerful influences if properly directed. The metaphor of the 'motivated minnows' versus the whale is still true. Imagine the speed of turn you see in a school of fish changing direction, compared with that of the whale. These are the benefits to be derived from motivating many small organizations to change.

One such benefit is the ease and speed of communications and response to changes of management direction – an ability to respond to customer needs at a level where responsibility for action and the action itself exist. Feedback from small businesses in the early EMS programme however, indicated other problems:

- *Financial:* While there is a recession on why bother? Survival is the priority; there is a high cost of capital; the playback is long term; we have low profit margins and this poor bottom line, together with limited assets, makes us a poor lending risk when there is little finance around.
- *Resources:* Resources are limited in terms of manpower, technical knowledge and influence, therefore we need off-the-peg solutions.
- *Image:* Small organizations are unable to exploit the good PR that comes from such a project.
- *Advice:* Practical support and not theory is needed and the cost of expertise (consultants) is perceived to be high.

Of all businesses in the UK, 96% employ fewer than 20 people. They employ over a third of the private sector workforce and produce nearly a quarter of the total UK turnover. So it is vitally important that ways are found to aid small businesses in practical progression towards better environmental management. The lessons to be learnt are very clear. Even if at this time they are mainly the lessons of 'big business', they can be extrapolated by the smaller business. After all, our experiences in improving the quality of the environment show how important the behaviour of small business is. Rick Kelly, former head of the scientific services department of the Greater London Council (GLC), draws a parallel with cleaning up the River Thames. It took many small companies changing their actions in little ways to make a difference. The engineer on the shop floor was as vital as the director on the board. One large company changing was not enough.

There is a parallel here with the quality approach that will be clear throughout this book: the need to focus on the small things to improve the overall picture, whilst retaining sight of the big picture at the same time. 'Big business' concepts must be made to work for the benefit of small organizations. What is needed to help them is a simple, systematic approach to achieve the required environmental management standard. Integrated management systems offer the possibilities of greater efficiency and greater buy-in among employees, leading to a more effective, more profitable business.

Changing criteria for success

In simple terms, for many organizations resolving the environmental issue is a major factor in determining a successful future and continuing profitability. Whereas price has always been one of the principal motivators of purchasers' choice, increasingly the 'environmental priority' of the product *and* the manufacturer are likely to be deciding factors in purchasing decisions. How can you assess the overall environmental performance to arrive at a conclusion that this company is OK and that another company is not? Who can make such judgements and what will be the implications on passing or failing? The solution for many organizations is to look at the way management performs as the yardstick.

ABOUT THIS BOOK

The approach in this book follows a similar pattern to the quality loop. It provides a model programme for an organization to use in *thinking* about, *planning, implementing* and *measuring* change in the way it meets environmental performance standards. As a 'model' it is intended for use by any organization, large or small, commercial or non-commercial.

We have assumed you are in the role of the environmental programme manager, charged with developing and implementing a programme to achieve a defined level of environmental management. In this case you are following ISO 14001 and EMAS as the model and, using the four steps, *thinking, planning, doing* and *measuring* achievement. All businesses are unique. Therefore, the model is designed to be generic, although the implementation tools that are used allow management to ensure that the contents of the management system are relevant to, and owned by, the managers in the organization.

We aim at simple solutions, focused on clearly identified problems that are relevant to the global environment issues *and* to your business. Energy management, waste control and reduction, reuse of materials and recycling, will figure, but the policy objectives and targets will be your own.

Along the way we will identify objectives at each stage, outline a method of achieving the objectives, and illustrate the text with practical examples. Because this activity is primarily an internal, management-led communication programme, the success or failure of the communications is key. Communications in the workplace are based on the relationship between people, leaders and followers. The book, therefore, will have regular hints and tips on communications. Most importantly, we have included case studies from companies and organizations which are either registered to a formal EMS, or are actively pursuing registration.

2

WHAT IS AN EMS?

THE PRINCIPLES OF ENVIRONMENTAL MANAGEMENT

Many national and international organizations established and promoted guidelines and principles for good environmental management. These include the International Chamber of Commerce (ICC), the Business Council for Sustainable Development (BCSD), the Confederation of British Industry (CBI), the Coalition for Environmentally Responsible Economies (CERES), the Chemical Industry Association (CIA), the chemical industry's Responsible Care® programme and the European Petroleum Industry Association (EUROPIA). There are a number of common elements in these guidelines, all of which typify a systems approach to environmental management:

- A *policy* statement that indicates the organization's overall commitment to the improvement of environmental performance, including conservation and protection of natural resources, waste minimisation, pollution control and continual improvement.

- A set of *plans and programmes* to implement the policy throughout the organization, including the advancement of the programme through suppliers and customers.

- The integration of the environmental plans into the day-to-day *operation* of the organization, developing innovative techniques and technologies to minimize the impact of the organization on the environment.

- The *measurement* of the environment management performance of the organization against the plans and programmes – auditing and reviewing progress towards achieving the policy.

- The *communication* of information, education and training to improve understanding of environmental issues – publicizing aspects of the environmental performance of the organization.

All of these elements combine to provide a systematic and structured management approach to environmental performance which is the subject of this handbook.

This systematic approach can be illustrated by showing the organization as a tiered structure: executive management at the top, making strategic decisions and setting *policy* (thinking); middle management, interpreting the policy into specific *objectives and targets* (planning); and operations staff, implementing the plans to achieve the objectives through *operating procedures* (doing). Activities are implemented, controlled, verified and *measured* to achieve the plans. The progress towards achieving the policy is audited to assess progress, and executive management review the progress in setting new or revised targets (thinking), as shown in Figure 2.1.

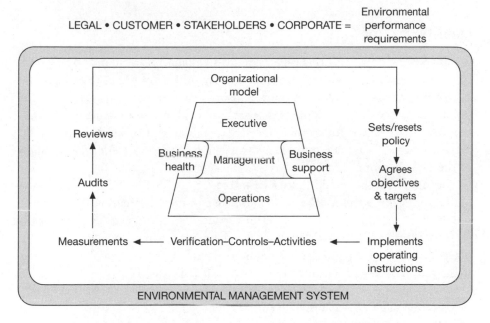

LEGAL • CUSTOMER • STAKEHOLDERS • CORPORATE = Environmental performance requirements

Fig. 2.1 Diagrammatic representation of environmental management system related to a business model

These principles have been linked to established management practices, quality systems standards and related programmes of continual improvement for organizations that are committed to sustainable development.

MANAGEMENT SYSTEMS

How do you currently manage sales, purchasing, expenses, tax, personnel, product design and performance? You do not leave these to chance: you would not survive in business if you did. So you take control, you define the requirements and put a system in place to meet them. *Product* requirements, set by the customer, can be addressed by a quality system. Your system has management procedures in place to establish responsibilities, set targets, deploy resources, educate and train staff, monitor performance, audit the system, review and make changes to stay on track.

You can extend your management system to address the environmental issue. What will be new, however, is the focus applied to elements within the system.

The setting of *standards* for such management systems is also not new. Such a standard, or model system, exists with the international standard ISO 9000 for products and services.

Quality systems

Quality system concepts bring aspects of quality management to bear on all areas of the management of an organization. Quality in this context is the concept of *conforming to specified requirements*. A quality management system is the related policies, practices and procedures that are used to direct an organization's activities towards products (or services) meeting specified requirements. In ISO 9000, these are focused on the requirements specified by the *purchaser* of the products of the organization.

The international standard, known in the UK as BS EN ISO 9000, offers a model for quality systems that is often used in contractual situations between the purchaser and supplier of a product or service. Registration to the standard is used to assure a buyer that a supplier has the necessary management systems in place to deliver, consistently, the required standard of the product or service. Registration is carried out by independent bodies like the BSI.

Worldwide, more than 150 000 organizations are registered as having quality systems that meet the requirements of ISO 9000 parts 1, 2 or 3, while in the UK, there are over 25 000 firms registered.

Organizations that implement a programme to achieve registration to ISO 9000 audit, often change the organizations' management systems to ensure full compliance with the ISO 9000 specifications. This need for change in the way an organization is managed means that strong leadership is essential to success in implementing such programmes.

Total quality management

Total quality management (TQM), supported by BS 8750, takes the process of quality management a step further. Focusing beyond the quality management systems necessary for product or service delivery, TQM provides guidance for management philosophy and practices that aim to harness all the resources of an organization in the most effective way to achieve the objectives of that organization. It provides management tools that can be used to improve every part of an organization, whether directly or indirectly focused on products or services.

Total quality management programmes, like the use of the European Foundation for Quality Management (EFQM) business excellence model, Baldrige criteria and the balanced scorecard, change the corporate culture. A TQM organization's management system concentrates on analyzing and refining *every* internal process and practice to become focused on customer-orientated measurements where the customer is the 'final arbiter' of an organization's effectiveness and efficiency. The 'customer' is the recipient of a product or service, either inside the organization (e.g., staff, other departments), or outside the organization, e.g., customers, shareholders or the community.

A key feature of the total quality management approach is the continual analysis, measurement and improvement through the quality loop which is illustrated in a simplified form in Figure 2.2. You can enter the circle anywhere, either *thinking* about a new way of working, *measuring* an existing process, *planning* for improvement or just *doing* things differently. The key thing is the 'never ending' search for improvement.

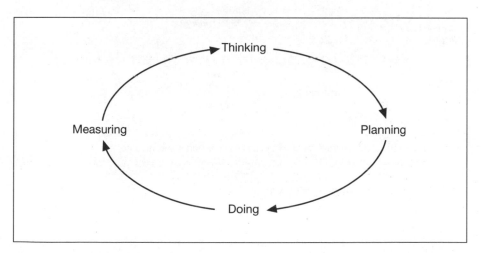

Fig. 2.2 The continual improvement loop

Think about what the goals are, the targets to be achieved, the route to be taken and the measurements to track success. Whether you are aiming at zero defects in a production process, no billing errors, or discharge rates within a specified limit, this can only be achieved through the activities in the organization. How will this be done?

Planning is the step to design the activities and processes to achieve the goal. Who will have to do what, and by when in order to achieve the goal? What resources, skills and expertise are needed? What have we got? Is there a requirement for new resources, training and other steps?

Doing is the implementation of the plan or process. Striving to achieve simple, repeatable steps that bring the product, service or process into effect in an effective and efficient manner.

Measuring is the key to assessing the effectiveness of the *doing* stage. It assesses results and focuses on the areas for improvement. It leads to further thinking and refinement of the system. Do we need to do anything? What needs modifying or changing? What new measurements should be in place? The target is a constant 'honing' of the process to achieve even higher standards of performance, aiming at 'zero defects'. But we know that in life, things are not perfect. We can aim at a goal of 'zero defects', but as we approach milestones along the way, we will see we are 'off-course'. This is normal. The quality loop allows us to make changes to re-direct ourselves towards the target, through taking corrective action (*see* Figure 2.3).

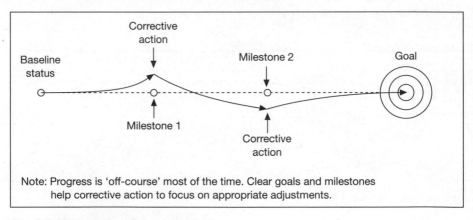

Note: Progress is 'off-course' most of the time. Clear goals and milestones help corrective action to focus on appropriate adjustments.

Fig. 2.3 Milestones and corrective action

Another way of looking at this pattern is the Kaizen (small steps) approach (*see* Figure 2.4). This encourages organizations to constantly review and improve small aspects of performance between major changes in performance standards and goals. It requires everyone in the organization to participate in a positive way to improve the business performance – reducing the impact of major process changes.

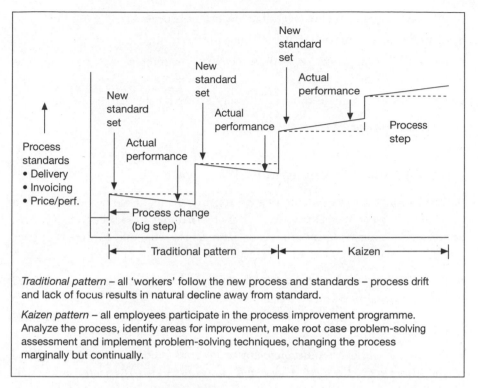

Traditional pattern – all 'workers' follow the new process and standards – process drift and lack of focus results in natural decline away from standard.

Kaizen pattern – all employees participate in the process improvement programme. Analyze the process, identify areas for improvement, make root case problem-solving assessment and implement problem-solving techniques, changing the process marginally but continually.

Fig. 2.4 Traditional and Kaizen patterns

ENVIRONMENTAL MANAGEMENT SYSTEM STANDARDS

The environmental management system standards approach brings together three concepts:

- Everything we do in business has some impact on the *environment*.
- *Management systems* control everything we do in business.
- Standards can be set for *environmental management systems*.

The environmental management system is the means to control and improve the environmental performance of the business. It is the mechanism to ensure that you have in place the necessary controls to *understand* the environmental performance required; to *measure* your current environmental performance against that requirement; to *identify* where areas for improvement exist; and *implement* the improvement plan through controlling and tracking your critical activities to achieve the desired results. *You* require the environmental management system to be:

- fully integrated into your overall management processes;
- contributing to improving overall company performance;
- recognized as appropriate by those people most interested in your environmental performance;
- respond to the issue of 'thinking globally, acting locally'.

Using ISO 14001 or EMAS does this.

Environmental management tools

Before looking at the elements that go together to make up a comprehensive environmental management system, it is useful to understand other management tools used for improving environmental performance that may form part of your integrated environmental management system.

- **Products:** There are schemes for labelling products that meet predetermined environmental performance criteria, established through a product *life-cycle analysis*, e.g., batteries that are mercury free. The UK has a scheme under the EC Eco-Labelling Regulation.
- **Projects:** There is a requirement for major construction projects to undergo an *environmental impact assessment* procedure. This is enacted under UK planning laws promulgated by the EC Directive on environmental impact assessment.
- **Sites:** Many organizations have used a form of audit to assess activities that have an environmental impact. Thus *environmental auditing* is quite common in the petroleum and chemical industry sectors where, because of the nature of the product, processes and complex regulations, management requires close control of environmental performance.

Environmental auditing has been defined as:

> A systematic, documented, periodic, and objective evaluation of how well environmental organization, management and equipment are performing with the aim of helping to safeguard the environment by (i) facilitating management control of environmental practices; (ii) assessing compliance with company policies, which would include meeting regulatory requirements.
>
> *International Chamber of Commerce*

The role of standards

There are standards for all of these management tools to ensure effective implementation: standards against which products are to be tested to acquire an eco-label (established by the relevant competent body managing the scheme); standards for the scope, the process and the technical content of environmental impact assessments (established by the regulators); and standards for environmental auditing practices and procedures (established by industry and consultant trade associations). One of the benefits of having standards is that they provide a common basis on which to compare the performance results of different products or systems. Standards can be used inside an organization to self-assess compliance with a requirement and they can be used by those outside an organization as a benchmark of good practice – an important factor when public information about the environmental performance of an organization is accepted as key to a sustainable development philosophy.

A model or standard for environmental management systems, therefore, provides a useful tool for an organization to use in controlling its environmental performance effectively and providing a basis for external recognition. Furthermore, a standard on environmental *management* systems that relates to the existing standard in quality systems (ISO 9000) would provide an *integrated* approach that would allow organizations to demonstrate both a product/service performance and an environmental performance compliance capability. This is the basis for ISO 14001: A specification for environmental management systems. This standard establishes a generic model for any organization that is compatible with the requirements of ISO 9000 quality systems, but separate from it, to allow its independent application and assessment.

ISO 14001 provides a general, or generic, guide to good environmental management systems practice that is internally auditable and externally assessable.

ISO 14001 does not identify the specific environmental performance criteria expected in any particular company or industry sector. The issues faced by a large chemical company are not those faced by a small printing works, tannery, local authority or hospital. For industry, therefore, it may be appropriate to relate ISO 14001 to own-sector environmental performance issues. Such guidance could provide help in two areas:

- to those inside an industry about the issues to address in the policy and practices of the organization; and
- to those outside the industry who wish to assess the implemented system against the standard and a model of good practice that is relevant to that industry.

The provision of industry-specific guidelines

In setting environmental performance targets within the organization, therefore, you will want to ensure that these are relevant to your industry and the standard.

You will want to ensure that your response is consistent with the current, and possible future, requirements of the Environmental Protection Act (EPA) and, for example, the Integrated Pollution Control (IPC) schedules within it.

IPC introduced the concept of BATNEEC, 'the best available techniques not exceeding excessive cost', intended to ensure that there is a cost-effective benchmark of good environmental performance within industry sectors. ISO 14001 therefore recognises the possible types of waste produced by industries and their physical form. An assessor examining the environmental management system of an organization in these industry sectors might reasonably expect that such recognized industry issues would form a prominent place in the environmental performance targets.

Elements of the environmental management system

One of the environmental management tools discussed earlier was the environmental audit, which helps target management effort. The audit does this by identifying areas where environmental performance is failing to achieve the required standards and recommends management actions to correct the situation.

If it is possible to define the shortcomings in a management system that addresses environmental issues, is it also possible to define what such a system *should* look like? What elements, activities, practices or procedures should be established within a system for managing environmental performance?

The principles of management system standards we looked at earlier, led to the development of the international standard ISO 14001, together with related standards for assessment and registration.

THE CYCLE OF REVIEW AND IMPROVEMENT

What are the elements?

ISO 14001 is described in more detail in *Appendix 1*, but broadly, the elements of the standard include:

- *Commitment* from the top of the organization is key to the success of the application of an environmental management system.
- An *initial environmental review* which establishes the benchmark of environmental performance, the primary areas of environmental effect and the opportunities for improvement.

- A statement of *environmental policy* which summarises the organization's commitment to and direction for environmental performance management.

- *Methods for understanding the requirements: environmental effects procedures,* including tools to analyze the environmental impacts of the organization's activities to ensure that the system was focused on the critical areas for consideration:

- A *cradle-to-grave analysis* which identifies the environmental issues related to the manufacture of product, from the procurement of raw materials through the manufacturing process and on to the use and disposal of the product.

- A special approach to projects and the *environmental impact assessment* of other major decisions within the organization, prior to the commitment to a course of action.

- An *environmental management cascade* which identifies environmental issues throughout the organization, involving all business activities and staff.

- A method for identifying the *regulatory and other interested parties' requirements* to be met by the organization in its activities, leading to the setting of environmental objectives and targets throughout the organization.

- *Environmental quality system* – a supporting quality system to ensure that the environmental performance objectives and targets set as a result of the effects analysis and the regulatory requirements are met. The system includes:

  (a) A system audit and review procedure to ensure that the environmental quality system and related environmental performance are meeting the specified requirements.

  (c) A reporting method to inform those with an interest in the organization's environmental performance of the achievements that have been reached.

The TQM feature of the systems approach in ISO 14001 is that it promotes a continual improvement through a cyclic process of reviews and action (*see* Figure 2.5).

With all of these elements in place, adequately documented and implemented to a recognized standard, the organization should be assured that the required environmental performance is being met.

The principal elements of ISO 14001 are also a recognized part of the EMAS regulation, which *Chapter 4* outlines in more detail.

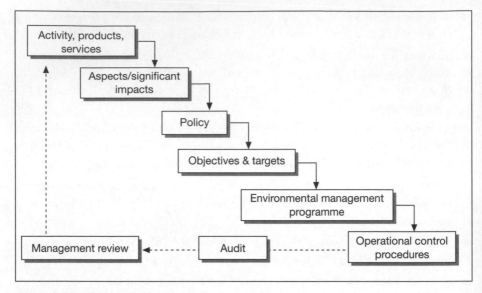

Fig. 2.5 The EMS improvement cycle

Checklist

? *Have you established a reading list of material to establish a base-line knowledge?*

? *Have you reviewed the environmental impact of the organization's activities at the high level?*

? *Have you looked at the current management system status in relation to quality systems or other quality programme approaches?*

? *Have you read through the environmental management system standard ISO 14001?*

Schlumberger – an integrated approach

This company uses a systems approach to managing several elements of its organization, and then integrates them into one management system. This approach has one objective – profitability. Schlumberger's logic is that a company exists to supply a product or service, and make a profit by doing so. A quality system, for example, identifies *fitness-for-purpose* and so provides a customer's requirements. A health and safety system ensures that the workforce remains in its best condition to fulfil this need, while an environmental management system reduces waste, which means lowered overheads. Combine this with a system of operational management which keeps employees involved and motivated, and the result is a highly efficient and profitable way of working.

When meeting a customer's requirements, every part of this process has aspects of health and safety, fitness-for-purpose, potential environmental impacts and production-operations. Therefore the company has a system which includes the requirements of the standards ISO 9001, ISO 14001 and the guidelines of BS 8800 – the new British Standard on health and safety management.

3

FINANCIAL AND LEGISLATIVE BENEFITS

> ## Objective
> This chapter looks at the different driving forces behind an environmental management system (EMS), allowing you to focus on the benefits. These benefits are financial and regulatory as well as environmental.

SO WHY HAVE AN EMS?

Organizations adopt an EMS, or similar programmes such as Responsible Care, for two reasons; either because their customers force them to, or because they perceive a benefit in doing so. So what are these benefits? In simple terms, they are:

- **Financial:** An EMS means less waste and greater efficiency. Implement an EMS effectively and you will save money. Furthermore, many banks and insurance companies give preference to organizations with reduced environmental risks.

- **Markets:** Customer demands and trends such as 'green consumerism' are driving a demand for products and services with better environmental profiles.

- **Legislation:** Organizations with an effective EMS have fewer environmental incidents, reduce the risks of breaking the law, and get on better with the regulators.

- **Community and employee relations:** Many organizations say that their workforces have embraced environmental management enthusiastically, and that they have a better relationship with their local communities.

The following sections examine some of the major benefits in mo
ing at financial benefits, waste minimization and legislative issues.

BENEFITS OF AN EMS: THE BOTTOM LINE

Environmental management saves money. In fact some companies have saved enormous amounts, which they have re-invested in new initiatives which save more money and produce further environmental benefits. Some cynics suggest that these must have been wasteful companies to generate such savings, yet there is ample evidence to show that this is not true.

There are many efficient and profitable companies which have focused on issues such as energy efficiency and waste minimization long before anyone even thought of an EMS standard or scheme. So how do such companies benefit further from the systems approach? According to one company, before it implemented an EMS, it would look at an issue such as energy efficiency or effluent treatment in isolation. So projects were discrete and while they generated savings and environmental improvements, the company focused on isolated areas at the exclusion of the entire operations. The EMS changed this, making the company more aware of how different operations interact, and gave its management insight into new areas or issues where further improvements could be made.

For example, during a two-year period after implementing its EMS, the company reduced its electricity consumption by 90%, water use by 23% and effluent produced by 33% per kilo of material produced.

In the UK, Vauxhall Motors has benefited from enormous savings since successfully implementing an EMS. Its energy and water-use costs have fallen by at least 5%, generating payback periods of less than one year. Furthermore, the reduction in waste produced means that the company has cut its annual landfill charges by nearly 50%, amounting to £75k each year. Meanwhile, across the Atlantic in the USA, integrated circuit manufacturer LSI Logic has saved millions of dollars since implementing an environmental management programme (*see* Table 3.1).

Most companies typically recover their implementation costs within two years, many within one year. Schlumberger in the UK states that its payback period was just six months, and those were generated by a 15% reduction in energy costs during the first year after implementation. If these savings were considered in the same way as other investments and returns, then payback periods from six months to two years translate to annual returns on investments ranging between 200% and 50%. Schlumberger performed even better the following year, more than tripling the savings.

Table 3.1 Environmental management programme

Issue	Benefits
Savings	Protecting the earth is the right thing to do; it also makes good business sense. LSI Logic has implemented several programs that have benefited the environment and saved the company over $2 million.
Environmental management systems	LSI Logic has developed an environmental management system that conforms to ISO 14001 standards. All environmental regulatory requirements are monitored to ensure compliance. Environmental goals are established to go beyond compliance in the areas of toxic and hazardous material minimization, pollution prevention, water and energy conservation and solid waste reduction
Elimination of CFCs	In 1993, LSI eliminated chlorofluorocarbons (CFCs), the leading chemicals linked to the depletion of the ozone layer, from its manufacturing operations. At LSI, CFCs were mainly used for cleaning flux from semiconductor packages. The company eliminated CFCs in its fab operations by switching to water-soluble fluxes, water-based cleaning systems and other non-CFC technologies.
Chemical and hazardous waste reduction	LSI has significantly reduced its use of hazardous manufacturing chemicals such as sulphuric acid, photoresist and phosphoric acid, saving the company $1.2 million. This was accomplished through operational improvements, process changes and recycling of chemicals. The company has reduced its total volume of hazardous waste by 88 percent since 1987. LSI has eliminated the use of ethylene-based glycol ethers – chemicals that have been linked to potential reproductive hazards – to ensure worker safety. In 1996, LSI Logic joined an Environmental Protection Agency program that aims to reduce perfluorocarbon (PFC) emissions by chip makers. This program, called "PFC Emission Reduction Partnership for the Semiconductor Industry", is designed to reduce emissions of such global warming gases to the earth's atmosphere.
Recycling	LSI recycled 317 tons of material, including paper, plastics, cardboard and metals, in 1996. Located throughout the company are bins for recycling white paper, computer paper and mixed paper such as newspapers and magazines. In the cafeterias are containers for recycling glass and aluminium. The company also uses recycled paper in its janitorial supplies, product data sheets, employee publications and other collateral material. In addition, LSI is a member of the Environmental Protection Agency's (EPA) "WasteWise" program, a voluntary effort to reduce municipal solid waste through recycling, waste prevention and purchasing recycled products.

Table 3.1 (continued)

Issue	Benefits
Energy-efficiency	By switching to more energy-efficient lighting such as motion-detectors and low-energy fluorescent bulbs, LSI has reduced its lighting costs by 30 percent. LSI is a member of the EPA's "Green Lights" program, which aims to reduce air pollution through the use of more energy-efficient lighting. In addition, LSI uses a computerized climate control system in several of its facilities, cutting energy usage in those buildings by 25 percent.
Commute-alternative programmes	In co-operation with RIDES for Bay Area Commuters, LSI provides a ride-matching service for its Bay Area employees who are interested in carpooling. The company also participates in the Bay Area Air Quality Management District's "Spare the Air" program. Employees are notified a day in advance via electronic mail when high air pollution levels are expected and are encouraged to carpool to work.
Awards	LSI Logic has won several awards for its environmental performance. In September, 1997, for example, LSI Logic's Gresham, Oregon, campus was recognized by the Business Recycling Awards Group (BRAG) for exemplary efforts toward waste prevention and recycling. According to Gresham Mayor Gussie McRobert, LSI Logic has "one of the best commercial waste-reduction programmes in the region" and "serves as an important model for other businesses."

Source: LSI Logic www site

Waste minimization

Waste minimization is another key way in which an organization can save money, whether through process optimization or resource-use efficiency. Many organizations have implemented a system of waste minimization without going for EMS first off, but the two systems go hand-in-hand. 'Waste minimization is a good starting point for an EMS, and an excellent foundation for implementing a system based on ISO 14001 or EMAS. Both use the same cyclic approach based on monitoring, targeting and improvement, and they complement each other,' says Nick Storer of the UK's March Consulting Group, which has worked on several waste minimization and EMS programmes.

'The strategy behind waste minimization is to reduce waste at source. In other words, you try to make sure that you do not make it in the first place, by looking at all your inputs, outputs and losses. Then you determine ways of optimizing your process to maximize your outputs for minimal inputs and reduced losses. Quite often, you can make substantial reductions in waste for little or no financial investment, and a systems approach is a good tool to identify where you can act,' adds Storer.

THE REGULATORY FOCUS

At the moment, there are no environmental laws which state that your organization has to have an EMS. However, there are three good reasons to consider an EMS for legislative purposes:

- **Improvement:** Your environmental performance is likely to improve. One ISO 14001 registered plastics manufacturer in the USA, for example, has reduced the number of environmental incidents by 50% since implementing its EMS. Its relationship with its regulators has also improved.

- **The new IPPC Directive:** In Europe, companies will soon have to comply with the requirements of the new Integrated Pollution Prevention and Control Directive (IPPC). In simple terms, this is a hybrid of the UK's Integrated Pollution Control (IPC) system, waste minimization and management systems. Analysts and environmental commentators have noted that the most effective way to meet the requirements of IPPC will be through EMS implementation.

- **Reduced risk:** Fewer environmental incidents – such as accidents and emergencies – mean less chance of prosecution. And if things do go wrong, then there is evidence that judges consider an EMS to be a mitigating factor when assessing penalties.

A regulator's view

The UK's Environment Agency places an enormous emphasis on integrated approaches to environmental management and regulation, as well as the benefits of risk analysis as a regulatory and management tool. The Agency has taken a keen interest in EMS for two reasons.

First, the Agency considers that sites with an EMS pose less risk. The Agency has developed a methodology of risk analysis for its regulated sites. Known as Operator Performance and Risk Appraisal (OPRA II), this methodology grades a regulated process on the basis of how much risk it poses to the environment. A site with a high risk will merit more visits and control. Table 3.2 shows how an Agency inspector assesses the performance of a process operator, and a comparison of this table with the requirements of ISO 14001 shows that an operator which has a well-developed EMS will have a much higher performance rating. There is a similar table for assessing environmental hazards and risks.

Second, the UK's Environment Agency feels that an organization implementing an EMS should consider regulators as stakeholders and external interested parties. For example, the Agency has objectives concerned with environmental protection – such as the greenhouse effect – but such issues are not currently regulated. So the Agency would like to be consulted on such issues because it has

Table 3.2 UK Environment Agency's Guidelines on quantifying an Operator Performance Appraisal (OPA) (OPRA II)

Attribute	OPA of 1	OPA of 3	OPA of 5
1. Recording and use of information	Limited or non-existent monitoring or records. No evidence of use of information. Failure to record all data required by authorization.	Information available as required by authorization. Records used in process management.	Recording and assessing environmental information to higher level than specified in conditions. 100% records kept available, copies submitted promptly to inspector. Information used to high level in process management. Use of information in public communications. Information systems audited regularly.
2. Knowledge and implementation of authorization	Registration/authorization unavailable. Operator not aware of legal requirements. Significant outstanding relevant improvement programmes.	Key personnel aware of/have access to main authorization details, and understand main requirements, including BPEO/NATNEEC.	Current registration/authorization displayed or immediately available, and relevant staff fully aware of registration/authorization conditions and residual statotory requirements. No significant outstanding improvements. Compliance audited regularly.
3. Plant maintenance	No coherent maintenance programme, taking no account of environmental effects and dependent solely on breakdown. No priority assigned to environment-critical items. Plant operating requirements not defined, haphazard maintenance procedures. High frequency of breakdown/ maintenance-related incidents. Equipment performance deteriorates significantly between maintenance activities.	Formally developed maintenance programme based on appropriate industry standards, which takes into account environmental effects of breakdowns and maintenance-related releases.	Advanced and regularly audited maintenance programme, placing priority on environmental effects of brfeakdown and maintenance. Plant maintenance procedures clearly defined and followed. All critical equipment and operating parameters monitored and maintained accordingly. Low frequency of breakdown/ maintenance-related releases. Maintenance programme ensures equipment environmental performance does not deteriorate significantly.

Table 3.2 (continued)

Attribute	OPA of 1	OPA of 3	OPA of 5
4. Management and training	Ineffectively staffed, inappropriate skills, poorly defined reporting structure and no clearly identified responsible person. Personnel not aware of consequences of releases. Little or no training on process or environmental issues.	Plant effectively staffed with well-trained, competent personnel who are aware of consequences of releases. Controlled by responsible person at all times. Formal training programme.	Advanced training in place, involvement of senior management, availability of replacement staff at all times, emergency/abnormal conditions allowed for. Staff receive broad training, refresher courses, further education encouraged. Training process audited thoroughly. Commitment to environmental performance demonstrated within management and policy.
5. Process operation	No (or poorly written) procedures/ instructions. Operation of plant haphazard, changes not fully controlled. Frequent process deviations/near misses.	Effective operating procedures available and implemented. Adequate control of process operations, shift handover and non-routine operations. Limited process deviations/near misses.	Fully documented, up-to-date and comprehensive procedures and instructions are in place, audited and being followed. Process operation well controlled. Rare process deviations/near misses. Procedures identify environmental effects of operations.
6. Incidents, complaints and non-compliance events	Repeated (>5/year) notifications and incidents causing complaints, or one or more serious incidents. Failure to comply with improvement notices. Enforcement action by Agency was necessary.	Fewer than three minor incidents and no serious incidents in last year. Full compliance with improvement notices. No more than one strongly worded letter from Agency.	No reportable incidents or justified complaints about the process in last year. No action taken by Agency, no strongly worded letter sent to operator.
7. Recognised environmental management systems	No certification or verification to recognized standards for environmental management systems.	Process environmental management system has ISO 14001 or EMAS.	Process environmental management system is certified to ISO 14001 and verified by EMAS.

Source: EA

28

important and valuable contributions to make to environmental management in general, in addition to its regulatory duties.

Elsewhere, other environmental regulators are following the Agency's lead and examining the relationship between compliance with environmental legislation and the use of EMS. At the end of 1997, for example, the California Environmental Protection Agency was co-ordinating a programme to look at the effect of EMS on regulatory compliance, and to this end, it was developing a matrix system similar to the UK's OPRA II.

Waste minimization is another area where the Environment Agency has sponsored projects and helped companies towards EMS and pollution prevention. Such projects and inputs help companies to improve their environmental performance and decrease their chances of breaking the law. This strategy of co-operation and pollution prevention benefits everyone, so it is worth talking to the regulators at an early stage of implementation. Bob Payne of Brake Linings Ltd reinforces this. 'It is important to build up a good, honest relationship with your regulators and let them know what you are doing at an early stage. Our Environment Agency has taken a keen interest in our EMS, especially as it has improved our environmental performance and minimized waste.'

CASE STUDY

Waste minimization and EMS – financial and environmental benefits

The UK has developed several waste minimization clubs, where companies pool resources and information for mutual benefit. Within these, a central organization usually leads the club while the companies within it will provide some of the funding. In return, they will receive technical support and guidance from a select group of leading consultancies who are solutions providers in waste minimization.

There have now been several of these waste minimization clubs, all have produced substantial financial savings and environmental achievements for the companies within them. The projects have achieved these savings by tackling the causes of waste – and its reduction or avoidance – at source,

Project Catalyst in the northern UK was the largest of these clubs, involving 14 participating companies and running for 16 months. The project was managed by a consortium of three consultancies – March Consulting Group, Aspects International and WS Atkins (the lead consultant) – while the UK Department of Trade and Industry (DTI), the BOC Foundation for the Environment and the participating companies provided funding.

Project Catalyst was an enormous success, identifying hundreds of opportunities for cutting emissions to air, discharges to water and waste transferred to land. The project identified potential financial savings of almost £9 million per year for the participant companies; of these, about 30 % involved no investment, while ▶

▶ around a third had a payback period of under one year. Technically, the project implemented these savings as follows:

Good housekeeping: 19%
Recycling and reuse: 23%
Product modifications: 3%
Technology modifications: 55%

Waste minimization has both environmental and financial benefits. The former included the potential to reduce landfilled waste by 12 000 tonnes per year, a decrease of 1.8 million tonnes of liquid effluent and a reduced water-demand of over 1.9 million cubic metres. Not only did the results demonstrate the value of a regional waste-minimization club, but the project also catalyzed many operational and managerial changes. Many of the companies in the project have now implemented EMS, thus demonstrating the way that EMS and waste-minimization projects are complementary.

THE ECO-AUDIT
MANAGEMENT SCHE

BACKGROUND TO EMAS

The European Commission (EC) developed the eco-audit and management scheme (EMAS) in response to a perceived need for environmental accountability and public access to information within the Member States of the European Union (EU). It aims to encourage the use of environmental management systems.

The European Commission started work on an environmental auditing initiative in June 1990, circulating the first discussion paper in the autumn of that year. A long period of development, involving a number of drafts, then followed. The regulation was finally formally adopted on 28 June 1993. During the development period, a number of modifications were made, including changing the name from 'eco-audit' to 'eco-management and audit scheme' now abbreviated to EMAS. Figure 4.1 shows the co-development of EMAS, BS 7750 and ISO 14001.

Although the EC introduced it as a regulation, participation in the scheme is voluntary. The use of an EC regulation avoids the need for national enabling legislation in Member States, ensuring that exactly the same text will be followed in them all, and that there will be a common implementation timetable. The regulation came into effect in July 1993, and the scheme then became operational in April 1994. The EC will review it in 1998.

On submission of the Environmental Statement, verified by an independent, accredited Environmental Verifier, the Competent Body will issue a Statement of Participation, entitling the participant to use the scheme logo. Various forms of statement will be used, to cover single or multisite registration, in one, some or all of the Member States.

The EC designed EMAS as a tool to evaluate and drive improvement of industry's environmental performance, doing so on a continuous basis and to provide

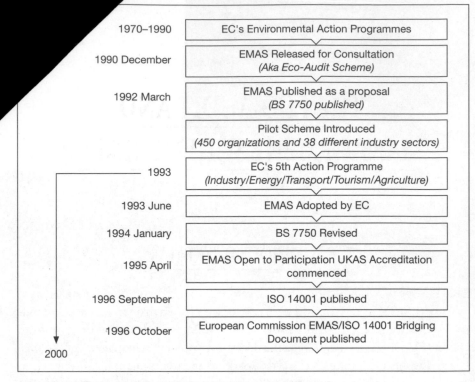

1970–1990	EC's Environmental Action Programmes
1990 December	EMAS Released for Consultation *(Aka Eco-Audit Scheme)*
1992 March	EMAS Published as a proposal *(BS 7750 published)*
	Pilot Scheme Introduced *(450 organizations and 38 different industry sectors)*
1993	EC's 5th Action Programme *(Industry/Energy/Transport/Tourism/Agriculture)*
1993 June	EMAS Adopted by EC
1994 January	BS 7750 Revised
1995 April	EMAS Open to Participation UKAS Accreditation commenced
1996 September	ISO 14001 published
1996 October	European Commission EMAS/ISO 14001 Bridging Document published
2000	

Fig. 4.1 Co-development of EMAS, BS 7750 and 14001

public information on industry's environmental performance. The scheme does not provide standards of environmental performance.

The EMAS cycle follows the generic systems approach (*see* Figure 4.2). When compared to ISO 14001, it is broadly similar and follows the same circuit of review, policy, planning, action, audit, action and review. There are minor differences between the two EMS, which are outlined in Table 4.1.

These aside, EMAS differs from ISO 14001 in five principal ways.

- In ISO 14001 there is more emphasis on the system as a tool for environmental protection, and compliance with the requirements of the system to maximize environmental protection. In EMAS, the emphasis is on environmental protection itself, rather than the system.
- EMAS requires an Initial Environmental Review as an assessable component of the system.
- EMAS requires an Environmental Statement as a public declaration of the organization's environmental profile.
- EMAS requires compliance with environmental legislation, whereas ISO 14001 requires a commitment to comply.

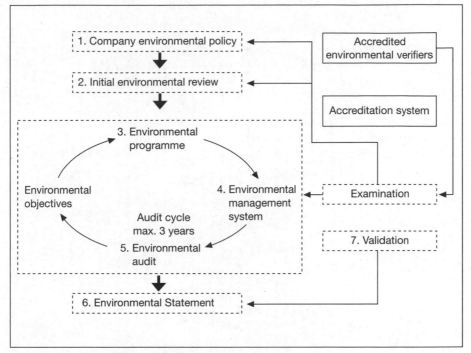

Fig. 4.2 Generic systems approach of the EMAS cycle

- Registration to EMAS requires a process called verification. An external assessor will have industry-specific expertise to verify the various components of the EMAS system in place. This verification process, for example, could include calculations to check whether an organization's mass-balances and emissions data are correct.

Eligibility

The initial scheme applied only to industrial activities as defined below. At present, non-industrial sectors can apply EMAS on an experimental basis only; however, at the end of 1997, the EC was revising the EMAS Regulation to encompass a wider range of sectors, such as those in services. The initial scheme applied to:

- mining and quarrying
- manufacturing
- electricity, gas and water supply
- recycling, treatment, destruction or disposal of solid and liquid wastes
- local government (UK only)

Table 4.1 A more detailed comparison between ISO 14001 and EMAS

Standard	ISO 14001	EMAS
Origin	A national standard	Introduced by means of an EC Regulation
Location	Applies anywhere in the world	Applies across the whole of the European Union
Application	Can apply to the whole organisation or ring-fenced, discrete companies within a site	Applies to sites
Sector	Open to any sector, activity or service	Restricted to industrial activities and local government
Activities	Open to some non-industrial activities, eg transport, local government	Non-industrial activities can only be included on an experimental basis
Systems approach	Focuses on organization's implementing systems, compliance with the system and continual improvement	Focuses on environmental improvement at a site and providing of information for the public
Initial review	Initial Environmental Review recommended but not a specification of the standard	Initial Environmental Review mandatory and assessable
Policy	Environmental policy commitment to continual improvement of environmental performance and compliance with legislation	Environmental policy commitment to continual improvement of environmental performance and compliance with relevant environmental legislation
EMS audits	Environmental management audits concerned with the assessment of compliance with the environmental management system	Environmental audit assesses the performance of organisation management systems, processes and factual data
Frequency of audits	Frequency of audits not specified but every procedure must be audited at least annually	Maximum audit or audit cycle frequently specified at three years
Public declaration	Only environmental policy must be publicly available	A presentation of the environmental policy, programme and management system made publicly available in the statement
Disclosure	Management decide as to how much other information to disclose	Public environmental statement and annual simplified statement including factual data on environmental performance essential
Third-part certification	Third party certification necessary for registration	Third party verification essential
Verification	Through auditing	Verification duties detailed and systems specified for who conducts verifications and supervises these activities
Advertising	Advertising not specified	Advertise site participation through Statement of Participation
National registration	No national registration body, but certifiers are regulated by national bodies	Government assigned national Competent Body controls registration of sites

EU countries can introduce a registration scheme for particular sectors – for example, the UK has introduced a scheme for local government – but if there is no relevant sector scheme, then a site cannot become registered.

Another feature is that individual sites within a company appliy to join the scheme, not the organization as a whole. The site can be anywhere within the European Union.

Participation

EMAS specifies the area, criteria and issues that must be covered in each stage. Once the organization has completed all these actions, it can seek external verification. Before it may apply for site registration, the organization must satisfy accredited environmental verifiers that the organization has satisfied all the Regulation's criteria.

After this process, the organization may apply to a competent body for registration. In the UK, this body is the Department of the Environment, Transport and the Regions. The organization must submit a validated environmental statement and a fee and, if successful, the site is placed on the scheme's register.

Every year, the organization must publish a simplified environmental statement. Within three years following registration, the company must submit another validated environmental statement and registration fee. The competent body will then re-evaluate the site's inclusion on the register.

A site can lose its registration in one of three ways:

- If the organization does not submit a validated environmental statement within the specified time.

- If the competent body learns that the site no longer complies with the requirements of the Regulation.

- If a regulatory authority informs the competent body that the site does not comply with environmental legislation. The competent body can then suspend registration; the competent body can reverse the suspension once the organisation has remedied the non-compliance and set up procedures to ensure that it does not happen again.

KEY DOCUMENTS

The Initial Environmental Review (IER)

The IER is an assessable part of EMAS, and the regulation specifies the scope of its contents. The scope includes the following issues:

- legislative requirements
- history of prosecutions/non-compliance with laws
- potential environmental effects
- discharges to air
- discharges to foul sewers
- discharges to storm-water
- landfill issues, e.g., which wastes go to landfill sites
- incineration
- waste
- energy (each process)
- noise
- odours
- product use
- raw materials
- eventual disposal
- transport.

The environmental statement

The environmental statement must include a description of the site's activities, an assessment of all significant issues, and a summary of data on:

- waste generation
- air emissions
- effluent discharges
- consumption of raw materials
- consumption of energy
- water use
- noise

- other significant environmental effects
- environmental factors which affect environmental performance.

The statement must also include the site's environmental policy, details of the environmental management programme, the date for the submission of the next statement, and the name of the Accredited Environmental Verifier. The environmental statement has to be available publicly

TRANSITION FROM ISO 14001 TO EMAS

While developed at the same time, requirements of the EMAS scheme and BS 7750 were different. So in 1994, the revised version of BS 7750 was modified to make it as compatible as possible with EMAS, with the main difference being the externally validated public environmental statement. Many companies in Europe and the UK implemented BS 7750 with the intention of subsequently meeting the requirements for registration to EMAS. With ISO 14001 superseding BS 7750, the EC has now accepted EN ISO 14001 as a key component and precursor to EMAS.

An EMS based on ISO 14001 is now seen as an appropriate foundation for EMAS, and the two EMS systems continue to converge. There is now a *bridging document* which the EU has prepared to assist users of EN ISO 14001, 14010, 14011 and 14012 move to EMAS.

This bridging document aims to:

- Identify areas where EMAS establishes some EMS and auditing requirements which are not specifically covered by the EN ISO 14000 standards and guides.
- Identify and highlight those areas where the agreement of elements of the EN ISO 14000 series of standards and the requirements of EMAS are not obvious.
- Identify key EMAS requirements outside the scope of the EN ISO 14000 series of standards and guides – the public statements.

CASE STUDY

London Borough of Sutton

The award-winning Council of the London Borough of Sutton (LBS) is committed to environmental management, and the Council decided to go for EMAS registration as a demonstration of its commitment, as well as the desire to benefit from the savings and environmental assets that an EMS brings. The Council was the first local authority in the world to gain EMAS registration, and it serves as a model for others to follow. Now, following its example, more than half the local authorities in the UK have expressed a serious interest in EMAS.

Monitoring and targeting resource use and waste production is a core element of Sutton's system. For example, since the first sites were registered in 1995, the consumption of energy for oil, gas and electricity in all Sutton Council's properties, excluding housing, fell by about 8 million kWh between 1992 and 1996, to just under 60 million kWh, while the Environmental Services building consumed 2% less energy in 1996 than in 1995. In terms of waste, Sutton's Environmental Services are estimated to have recycled or composted 23% of their waste in 1996: a 5% increase from 1995.

5

COMPARISON OF ISO 14001
AND ISO 9001

A COMMON BACKGROUND

When the BSI drafted BS 7750, it used the experience it gained when developing BS 5750. The BSI saw that the cyclic systems approach within BS 5750 could be readily adapted to managing environmental performance. BS 5750 was extremely successful and its subsequent adoption by ISO as ISO 9000 has resulted in a worldwide take-up of quality systems.

BS 7750 and ISO 14001 which succeeds it were designed to have a great deal in common with ISO 9001/2/3. However, there are also some significant differences, and these are best illustrated by explaining the core roles of the standards.

- **ISO 9000:** quality systems. The driving force behind ISO 9000 in an organization is the customer or client. A customer has a need for a product or service, and this is defined by certain parameters. ISO 9000 provides a model to assure the customer that you can meet those parameters and demonstrate this through independent assessment.

- **ISO 14000:** This is a series of environmental management standards. By analogy, the environment could be seen as the customer with specific requirements, many of which are fulfilled through regulations. The standard ISO 14001 provides a model systems framework which enables an organization to meet those requirements, and demonstrate that capability through independent assessment.

The ISO 9000 series and ISO 14001 are organized according to the cycle shown in Figure 5.1.

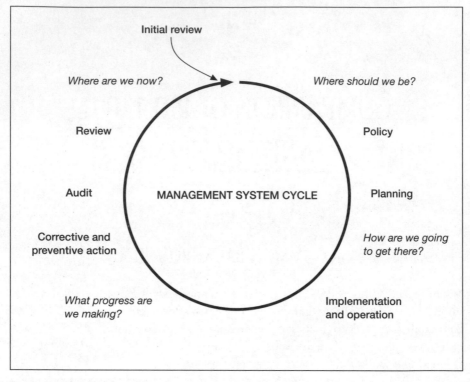

Fig. 5.1 The generic cycle of a management system

Extending the systems approach to ISO 14001

Figure 5.1 represents any cyclic, systems-based management system such as those based on the ISO 9000 series. ISO 14001 extends the systems approach from ISO 9001 to include the following elements:

- the organization has to establish environmental policies, programmes and management systems
- the organization must integrate environmental management into overall management systems
- the organization must systematically and periodically evaluate the performance of the policy, programme and system
- the organization must continually improve its EMS.

Systems audits

One of the key areas common to both quality and environmental management systems is the approach to auditing. ISO 8402 defines an audit as:

A systematic and independent examination to determine whether quality activities and related results comply with planned arrangements and whether these arrangements are implemented effectively and are suitable to achieve objectives.

Common key elements of an audit

An audit is an independent assessment, making use of checklists and procedures, and verifies conformance by looking for objective evidence. ISO 9001 and ISO 14001 have specified requirements, requiring an organization to analyze what it does, develop a documented system to manage its processes, and then implement the system to achieve the necessary control.

Types of audits common to ISO 9000 and ISO 14001

There are three basic types of audit, which are first party, second party and third party. Briefly, a first party audit is an internal audit, a second party audit happens when the customer is an auditor and the supplier is the auditee, while a third party audit is typically carried out by an independent party, such as the BSI, who maintains a register of organizations that have been successfully assessed.

The procedures and standards for EMS auditing evolved from those for QMS auditing, and these are outlined in Table 5.1.

Table 5.1 Guidelines for auditing

ISO 1011/1	Guidelines for auditing quality systems, pt 1, Auditing
ISO 1001/2	Guidelines for auditing quality systems, pt 2, Qualification Criteria for quality systems auditors
ISO 1011/3	Guidelines for auditing quality systems, pt 3, Management of Audit Programs
ISO 14010	Guidelines for Environmental Audits
ISO 14011	Guidelines for Auditing EMS Systems
ISO 14012	Qualification criteria for environmental auditors

Table 5.2 compares ISO 9001 and ISO 14001, and from this, it can be seen that there are many elements in common.

This commonality – especially since the inception of the health and safety systems guide BS 8800 – allows companies to integrate their management systems.

Table 5.2 Comparison between the ISO 9000 series of standards and ISO 14001

ISO 14001:1996		ISO 9001:1994	
General requirements	4.1	4.2.1 1st sentence	General
Environmental policy	4.2	4.1.1	Quality policy
Planning			
Environmental aspects	4.3.1	—	
Legal and other requirements	4.3.2	—[1]	
Objectives and targets	4.3.3	—[2]	
Environmental management programme(s)	4.3.4	—	
	—	4.2.3	Quality planning
Implementation and operation			
Structure and responsibility	4.4.1	4.1.2	Organization
Training, awareness and competence	4.4.2	4.18	Training
Communication	4.4.3	—	
Environmental management system documentation	4.4.4	4.2.1 without 1 sentence	General
Document control	4.4.5	4.5	Document and data control
Operational control	4.4.6	4.2.2	Quality system procedures
	4.4.6	4.3[3]	Contract review
	4.4.6	4.4	Design control
	4.4.6	4.6	Purchasing
	4.4.6	4.7	Control of customer-supplied product
	4.4.6	4.9	Process control
	4.4.6	4.15	Handling, storage, packaging, preservation and delivery
	4.4.6	4.19	Servicing
	—	4.8	Product identification and traceability
Emergency preparedness and response	4.4.7	—	
Checking and corrective action			
Monitoring and measurement	4.5.1 1st and 3rd paragraphs	4.10	Inspection and testing
	—	4.12	Inspection and test status
	—	4.20	Statistical techniques
Monitoring and measurement	4.5.1 2nd paragraph	4.11	Control of inspection, measuring and test equipment
Non-conformance and corrective and preventive action	4.5.2 1st part of 1st sentence	4.13	Control of non-conforming product
Non-conformance and corrective and preventive action	4.5.2 without 1st part of 1st sentence	4.14	Corrective and preventive action
Records	4.5.3	4.16	Control of quality records
Environmental management system audit	4.5.4	4.17	Internal quality audits
Management review	4.6	4.1.3	Management review

[1] Legal requirements addressed in ISO 9001, 4.4.4

[2] Objectives addressed in ISO 9001 4.1.1

[3] Communication with the quality stakeholders (customers)

Schlumberger Gas

This company is located in Stretford, Manchester (UK), and is part of the multi-national Schlumberger Industries Corporation. The Stretford Plant has manufactured domestic and commercial gas meters since the 1920s. It now makes other types of meters and offers related services.

The company was ISO 9000-certified in 1987, and has refined and simplified its QMS since. When the company decided to implement an EMS, it knew that it could implement an effective system very quickly by exploiting the lessons it had learnt from its QMS experience. Their initial aim was to have a system which could manage resources and waste more effectively, provide a framework for legislative compliance, improve process efficiency and save money.

The approach worked, because the system was independently certified about six months after starting work, and paid for itself in another six months through the savings it generated. As a part of a wider programme, ISO 14001 was the second stage in developing and implementing a totally integrated management system, which came on line in October 1997.

Schlumberger's EMS consists of three elements; a policy statement, a formal organisational element, and a dynamic element. Many components of the formal element were similar to those in ISO 9000, such as Management Review, Systems Audits, Training, Structure and Responsibility, Document Control and Operational Control. The degree of cross-over was so significant, that many of the procedures for ISO 9000 were adapted to ISO 14001 with just a few word changes.

For those parts of ISO 14001 not covered by the ISO 9000 system, Schlumberger emphasises the importance of addressing each requirement in the simplest, most practical way, bearing in mind that the purpose of any business is to generate profits, and that any formal management system should support that.

6

MANAGING CHANGE

Objective

The objective of this chapter is to show that implementing an EMS is a *programme* of change. This chapter:

- outlines what a change management *programme* requires and covers
- outlines how to manage change
- contains a checklist

THINKING ABOUT THE IMPLICATIONS

Before you embark on the programme of improving your environmental performance through a management systems approach, let me ask you a question, 'Are you serious?' The question has to be asked of yourself and the senior management of your organization because in answering positively, you will need to accept the full implications of the approach.

The environmental management systems improvement programme is one of *change*. It will, if properly followed through, re-examine the value judgements made in the organization at all levels. It will result in setting new objectives for *all* the business units, managers and staff, which will need to be supported by consistent beliefs, values and motivation throughout the business. So if you are not serious and do not accept the implications of change, *do not start*. A half-hearted attempt to 'be green' while changing nothing about the way things are done in the organization will fail, with the loss of credibility, resources and morale in the process. If you *are* serious, welcome to the start of the environmental road that has no ending.

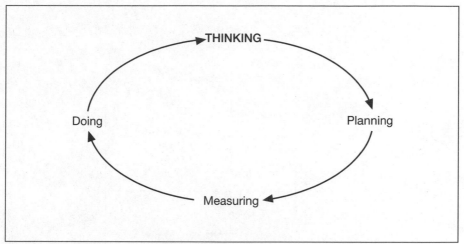

Fig. 6.1 The 'thinking' part of the improvement loop

WHY CHANGE?

A changing world

We live in a fast-changing world, where change has become the rule rather than the exception. However, all change is not the same. Planned and comparatively predictable change (e.g., a commuter's twice-daily change of location) is easier to cope with than uncertain change (e.g., marriage, divorce, moving house, new children and the death of loved ones) where individuals are unsure as to the outcome of the change, and its impact on their lives, roles, relationships and so on. The process of change is aptly illustrated by the change house shown in Figure 6.2. Change, and the success that flows from change, often leads to complacency. This itself decreases awareness and can dull the responses necessary to cope with external influences, which in turn leads leads to denial that a change is needed. When external factors force change in a situation, confusion results. The only option is to make change happen and manage the results – avoiding complacency.

The need for business organizations to change

A business can be described as the planned co-ordination of activities in order to achieve desired goals. In order to survive, a business must adapt and evolve.

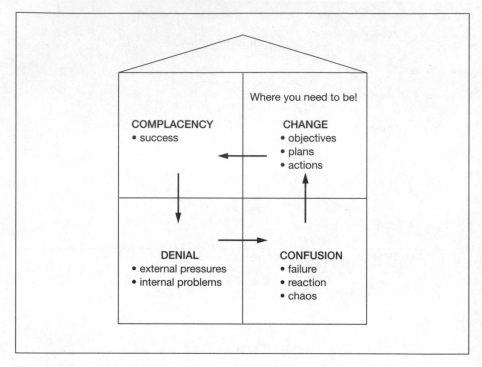

Fig. 6.2 The change house
Source: Ashridge Management Training

The evolution of a business often mirrors that found in living organisms:

● developing from a simpler to a more complex form
● adapting to internal and external pressures and opportunities
● expanding, growing and perpetuating itself
● shrinking or dying.

Kanter, in researching organizational change, concluded that organizations could be either integrative or segmentalist. Integrative and innovative organizations succeed in adapting and coping with change, while segmentalist organizations that resist change fail.

Integrative organizations were characterized by an entrepreneurial spirit and change was the norm. Change was embraced as an opportunity rather than as a threat. People worked with overlapping territories, often uncertain authority and open channels of communication. Change, not tradition, was the culture that staff were committed to. Such organizations were also successful in the marketplace.

Segmentalist organizations were culturally anti-change and concerned with compartmentalizing events. Change was perceived as a threat to the neat, structured and tidy world. People were discouraged from pursuing pet projects, rarely thought beyond their job descriptions and infrequently consulted different specialists (who might challenge their perceptive positions). Reward was based on ability to do the last job, not on capacity to do the next one. These organizations tended to do less well or fail.

Faced with a request for change in environmental performance, individuals and groups, inside the organization, will question whether it is necessary. There needs to be clear reasons:

- Business benefits – we will be more profitable.
- Legal and other requirements – we will not have a licence to operate otherwise.
- Environmental aspects and impacts – it will significantly change the environment.
- Changing stakeholder expectations and priorities – our customers, shareholders, and staff expect it.

An initial key to success is getting commitment which is covered in more detail in *Chapter 9*.

A SYSTEMS APPROACH

Change management in a complex organization can be simplified by using a systems approach, which shows that:

- an organization exists in an environment
- it has inputs, processes, and outputs
- feedback loops exist.

Inputs can include finance, people, technology, energy, materials and information. Processes exist to create goods and services. Outputs are finished goods, services, and losses (unprofitable by-products).

In reality the organization has multiple sub-systems – e.g., different divisions – which interrelate in positive and negative ways. All can be simplified to this system. To manage change, the change facilitator needs to look beyond system boundaries and examine the relationships of change in one area to the function of another – and there needs to be a clear, achievable objective that you will know when you have got there.

THE REQUIREMENTS FOR IMPLEMENTING CHANGE

Implementing the environmental management system (your goal) will need support from top management, not only in the form of attitude, but also of resources. These resources include human resources, specialized skills, technology and financial resources, while the implementation programme requires the right people, with the right equipment, brought together at the right time, with the right budget to do the job effectively.

Obstacles to effective change

Capacity

The success of the EMS implementation programme lies in the ability of the workforce to implement the organizational changes required to improve environmental standards. In order to encourage an active and participatory approach, managers must consider the *capacity* of staff to effect change. Communication and the analysis of training needs reveals gaps in people's abilities to make the changes necessary to achieve the new situation.

Consistency

There is nothing more frustrating than to be encouraged to change the way we carry out our day-to-day activities, only to find that the changes we propose are inhibited by others in the organization who do not appear to have the same message about the need for change. Having consistent messages, values and motivation throughout an organization will reduce the likelihood that such a situation will occur.

Leadership

Those at the top of the organization hold the key to making changes. Organizational hierarchies mean that often those who 'own' the business processes (i.e., senior managers) have less awareness of the impact and effectiveness of these processes than do the staff whose function is to make them work. If the management approach is *not* to encourage change, because to do so challenges the authority of the management, then ineffective processes often continue to operate even though the operators know they can be improved.

Fear

The 'fear factor' is work. Table 6.1 shows how the process knowledge usually operates within organisations.

Table 6.1 Management tiers with respect to process ownership and practice

	Process ownership	Process practice
Senior management	HIGH	LOW
Middle management	MIXED	MIXED
Operations staff	LOW	HIGH

The understanding of management has led to the movement of 'empowerment' in management training today. Empowerment encourages staff to make change happen and to accept their individual roles in making the processes work by contributing to process design and taking ownership for the quality of work they see in front of them. Empowerment means removing the 'fear factor' of being caught doing things wrong.

The 'fear factor'

The root of the 'fear factor' is the fear of the unknown and it can seriously affect the ability to change of any organization. It is essential to eradicate the 'fear factor' in change management if you are going to succeed in implementing your EMS programme. You want to encourage good performance from staff in areas which are unfamiliar to them. Your staff must gain confidence and knowledge in those areas. Reduce the fear of the unknown and the fear of failure at the outset and you are more likely to succeed in your objective. The fear of failure is the key – do away with this and people will respond to change enthusiastically.

You can reduce the 'fear factor' in many small ways at the lowest level in the process, but to allow that to happen you have to start at the top and displace the current paradigm of 'management knows best'. Managers have to start to see themselves as enablers, setting goals and objectives and supporting the staff in implementing them. The manager is the person who removes inhibitors to progress and does not create or support them. An education programme will go through a number of phases to achieve this: from awareness and consciousness, through understanding and agreement to implementation and ownership.

THE LEVELS OF CHANGE

The implementation of an EMS can be reduced to three stages: agreement on the present situation; agreement on the future direction in the form of the objectives and targets; and the EMS as the change mechanism.

Jane Laffan divides training and communication for EMS implementation into a formal and an informal system. The formal system includes the implementation and operation, checking and corrective action elements of the standard. The informal system uses workforce interest in global issues to encourage their active participation in the EMS programme.

The mechanisms used to achieve change, as shown in Figure 6.3, are largely human resource issues.

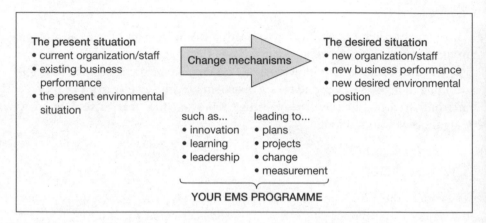

Fig. 6.3 The human resource issues in implementing change

The present situation will be a reflection of what is actually happening now and how the organization is responding. The initial environmental review provides this information. Communication and the analysis of training needs will have revealed gaps in the ability of people to deliver the changes deemed necessary.

The change programme will cover leadership and communications, the plans and action, that follow make the change to where you want to be. The audit and management review process will confirm your achievement.

STRATEGIES FOR MANAGING CHANGE

There are three main strategies for managing change; the *rational*, the *coercive*, and the *normative*. In practice you will need to use a variety of approaches, because your business culture and the particular situation, will dictate which style pre-dominates and which tools are most effective. This strategy will change from site to site, function to function, and shift to shift. Information – in the right form at the right time – is a crucial component of managing change, while the aim remains to integrate the EMS seamlessly into the way that an organization works. So how do these three change strategies work?

The *rational* approach assumes people are reasonable, and emphasizes a logical explanation for the need for change, based on *empirical* evidence. An organization using this approach assumes that it can guide people to make sense of the data and accept the changes necessary to improve the situation.

The *coercive* approach is different. This is a hierarchical approach, where subordinates have little choice but to accept the instructed change. Sometimes, to move into change 'mode', this control and command approach is essential.

The *normative* approach focuses on the need to change to achieve new standards of performance, through training, and the benefits of change are highlighted for both the individual and the organization.

Sometimes you will need to coerce, sometimes rationalize and usually use the normative approach to attain the EMS standard you desire.

The three levels of change

Promoting change and motivating effectively needs to work on three interrelated yet discrete levels; *individual*, *group* and *organizational*. The individual level in an organization consists of a collection of unique individuals. They will have their own values, beliefs and motivations. Individual change can be achieved, for example, by providing the right information or by modifying behaviour through rewarding desired actions. The group level exists throughout organizations and a different tactic is needed to change groupings. You can, for example, design the group systems to make them more effective, while at the organizational level, understanding how the organization works allows both management and the workforce to match their needs to organizational systems.

As a result of change, some people will benefit in some ways and perceive themselves to be winners. Some people will be, or feel themselves to have been, disadvantaged in some way, and will perceive themselves to be losers. The important thing to note is that people's perceptions can be changed, so that everyone feels that they have benefited from the implementation of the EMS.

Force field analysis

One tool to do this is known as 'force field analysis', which many organizations have used successfully to define the roles and interactions of groups, whole organizations or specific situations. It is a powerful technique to analyze the forces that may help or hinder change and the subsequent management of that change.

A force field analysis is based on an examination of the driving forces in any situation. A change, the pressure to change, strategy might suggest that results can be achieved by increasing the driving forces, but in practice this can increase resistance in an organization. Reducing the strength of *resisting* forces can have a much more effective influence on change. Communicating with staff and developing a participatory approach is a positive way to reduce resistance and develop an adaptive learning capacity in the organization. In such cases, it is also important to consider your organization's culture, because it will differ from one place to another, or even between sections within the organization. Some people prefer to be led, whilst others will need to be given ownership of the new elements of a changing system, so that they feel in control of what is happening.

Researchers have found that in simple terms, there are six change drivers, which are:

- **Communication**: provide full information about environmental management and why it would be valuable. The information should flow in all directions within the organization.
- **Involvement and commitment**: early involvement is vital if change is to be owned by staff and they are to become committed to it.
- **Economic incentives**: if resistance is rooted in fear of loss of earnings, security or promotion prospects, then the situation will need clarification.
- **Bargaining**: often the way organizations work in practice. The interests of workplace representatives and management may conflict and concessions may be necessary if acceptance is to be gained.
- Threat or opportunity? Change may be accepted as a normal organizational process or it may not. Presenting the benefits from changes will help its introduction and lessen resistance.
- **History**: an organization which ignores its past loses both its history and even its future.

For any situation, consider which of these six drivers might contribute to changing the equilibrium – either for or against the desired change.

How to do force field analysis

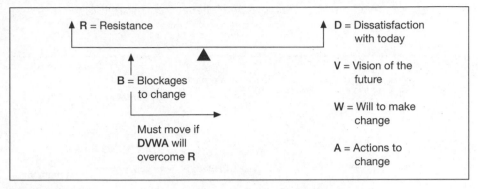

Fig. 6.4 See-saw

- Draw a see-saw on a flip chart. Now build up the following picture:
- Put the letter 'R' for 'resistance' on one side.
- On the other side add:
- A letter 'D' for 'dissatisfaction'; 'V' for 'vision'; 'A' for 'action' and 'W' for 'will'.
- Explain that for balance to shift, D, V, A and W must outweigh R.
- Finally, add a letter 'B' for 'block' to the 'R' (resistance) side.
- How might the 'block' be moved towards the other – 'change' – side to shift the balance?

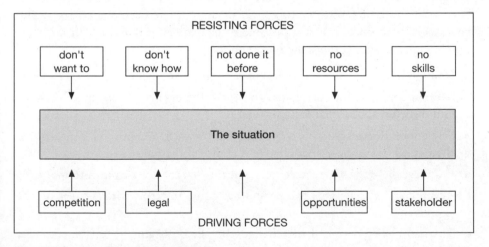

Fig. 6.5 Construction of the force field

Force field analysis (*see* Figure 6.5) reveals the dynamics of the change process, including any possible blocks. Neither removing these blocks, nor increasing the driving forces will, in themselves, promote change (*see* Figure 6.6).

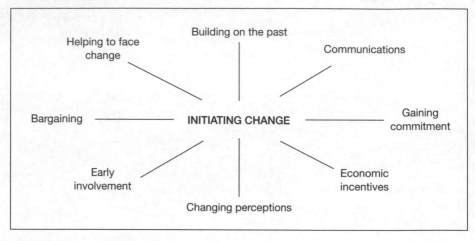

Fig. 6.6 The change procedure

The transitional process and resistance to change

People's responses during the change process can be mapped as in Figure 6.7. The transitional process has several stages.

The response can apply to individuals, groups or organizations. People (or groups, or organizations) do not necessarily progress through accepting change at the same rate. It is possible to get 'stuck' somewhere on the curve, or to slip back more than once. It is not possible to manage everyone through the same psychological stages at the same rate. The stages are:

- **Immobilization:** people resist the change and are rooted in 'old' belief systems.
- **Minimization:** actions are taken to negate the change. There may be shock and disbelief about what is happening.
- **Self-doubt, depression:** this is the first stage towards acceptance. It means that the person has realized that change is really on their agenda too.
- **Enquiry:** the stage where acceptance begins – what does it mean to me?
- **Acceptance:** at this stage the person has come to terms with what is on the agenda.
- **Testing:** having accepted the change, the person begins to test out the new position from their own perspective.

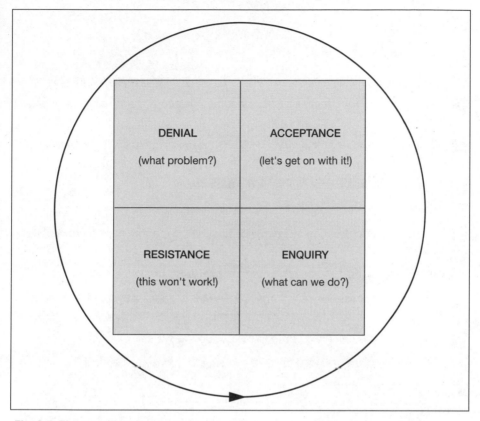

Fig. 6.7 The transitional process

- **Search for meaning:** the implications of the change are now being assimilated into the person's active consciousness.
- **Internalization:** the last step in the transition. The change has now become 'normal practice' and is no longer challenging or a discomfort.

The key thing to remember is that change will only be sustainable if people's perceptions are challenged and shifted.

Checklist

☐ *Am I clear about my objectives?*

☐ *How open can I be? Which elements of the process are for public disclosure?*

☐ *What is the power structure? Lines of communication. The official and unofficial systems.*

☐ *What are the language and norms? Make sure you match these for effective communications.*

☐ *What is the predominant culture of the organization?*

☐ *Where will my efforts pay off? Select target areas carefully.*

☐ *Who is discontented? These people can become excellent internal champions of change.*

☐ *Who are the rivals? Those with counter positions to protect.*

☐ *How can I access the 'silent majority'? The neutrals are potential agents of change.*

☐ *What resources can I find? Inside and outside the system.*

☐ *What action plans are needed? And can/should I devise these alone?*

PART

7

PREPARING FOR THE
PLANNING PHASE

Objective

The objective of this part of the book is to set the scene for the overall programme. Think about the investment requirements, the management issues, and the outline plan.

Now that you understand more about environmental management system standards, you need to understand the nature of the change that is required, the organization's capacity to make the change effectively and the steps to implementation.

THE INVESTMENT REQUIREMENTS

Quality is free, and there is no doubt that in the long term, investment in improved quality systems does pay for itself in reduced costs and lower risks of failure. Similarly, many examples have shown that the investment in *environmental* quality programmes brings real benefits in energy, waste and resource savings and reduced risk of legislative breaches. The investment required is in the areas of:

- management resource;
- time allocation;
- training; and
- financial investment.

The management resource is:

- The allocation of a senior *management* representative to oversee the programme as part of his or her responsibilities. He or she will act as the project owner and director, responsible for policy and other strategic issues.

- You may allocate responsibility for implementation to a *project manager* who will implement the policy that has been agreed at a senior level.

- In addition, all managers will need to commit resources to learning and communicating the new approach.

All staff will have to devote *time* to learn the new challenges and invest in planning improvements as the cascade of information throughout the organization takes place. Time must be taken to attend the awareness and implementation workshops and to follow up on the activities subsequently identified.

Training will be a requirement for all the staff to help them become aware of the issues and to equip them with new skills to resolve the issues in their day-to-day work routines.

Some *financial* resources may be required if you propose to employ outside resources for some of the initial environmental review activities. Financial investment may be required as a result of your investigations to achieve identified improvements in activities or business processes. These will be costed as any proposed business investment, and assessed on their merits. As an example drawn from the BSI pilot programme, a small business working group identified a potential 100 hours' consultancy time and 750 hours' 'company time' spread out over a 12-month programme.

THE MANAGEMENT ISSUES

One of the steps advisable at this early thinking stage is to check that the organization is capable of making the changes necessary to achieve the new goal, and to assess the organizational skills required to carry it out. This 'coherence check' (see *Testing a Company's Power to Implement* by W. Paul Krasse and Ed de Sa Pereira) will provide information you need before you start the planning process of your project. All the business elements of the organization must be checked, but in particular the *skills* available within it, as these will enable you to understand where the main inhibitors to progress may lie, and plan to deal with them.

A report is needed to summarize the overall status of the organization's capacity to accept the proposed change management programme.

Achieving an integrated system

One way of looking at an organization as an entity is to break it into its elemental parts. This has been done in the past by McKinsey using a seven-element approach. The alliterative technique of the 7-S helps us to understand the importance of the linkages between *all* the elements in an effectively functioning business organization.

The elements of the 7-S model are shown in Figure 7.1. Each element needs to be weighted to meet the needs of the shared purpose and the other elements, to create a balanced management system.

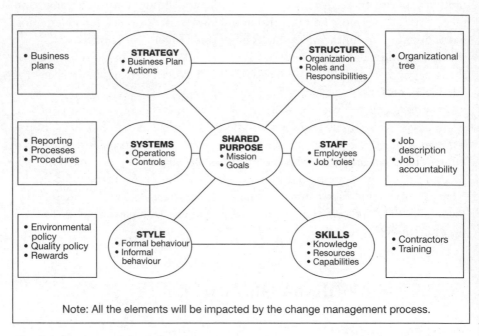

Fig. 7.1 **Elements of the 7-S model**

- **Shared purpose** captures the goal or mission of the organization.
- **Strategy** comprises the business plans of the whole and parts of the organization to achieve the shared purpose.
- **Structure** identifies the integrated roles and responsibilities for parts of the business.
- **Systems** comprise the business process, practices, procedures or activities that result in outputs towards the business goals.
- **Staff** are the people in the organization, their status and areas of activity.

- **Skills** are needed to implement the shared purpose, either provided by staff or outside resources.
- **Style** is the way managers and staff behave and use time, and are recognised and rewarded by the organization.

All the elements of the 7-S model need to have appropriate consideration when designing, developing or analyzing organizations in order to make changes. One of the common causes of failure when organizations implement changes is the lack of integration between the business elements during the change process. We are all familiar with different scenarios:

- A new accounts system or a new ordering system is introduced, but the staff are inadequately trained to bring their skills up to the necessary level for maintaining the system. The system is then criticised for failing when the answer may lie elsewhere.
- A company sets out a new strategy but fails to change the internal styles and reward systems to reflect the new direction. The organizational reward system may still be encouraging behaviour to meet the needs of the old values.

As the manager responsible for implementing the environmental management system, you are introducing a new strategy that will require an overhaul of *all* the business elements, but not necessarily fundamental change. You will assess and adapt the 7-S model to meet your circumstances.

- **Shared purpose:** to include improved environmental performance as a common goal of desirable behaviour, captured in the policy.
- **Strategy:** to ensure that environmental performance criteria are integrated into the business plans of the whole and parts of the organization.
- **Structure:** to ensure that environmental performance roles and responsibilities are defined and allocated.
- **Systems:** to ensure that the day-to-day practices and procedures implement the environmental performance standards, and track performance for reporting.
- **Staff:** to ensure that appropriate staff are identified to enable the smooth implementation of the environmental procedures.
- **Skills:** to equip staff and have access to the necessary skills required to implement the environmental procedures.
- **Style:** to ensure that managers reflect the environmental performance standards in the way they behave, use time, and reward their staff.

When an organization makes changes to all of these elements – and the changes are integrated in consistent support of the shared values – then you will have high confidence of achieving your goal.

The 'coherence check'

The 'coherence check' consists of a review of all the elements related to your organization, but with particular focus on just two: the **strategy** and the **skills**. The review of *strategy* is to understand the current direction of the organization, and to relate that to a changed strategic approach that includes environmental management as a new consideration. The review of *skills* is to understand the capacity of the organization to achieve the transition. Without the relevant skills being available, a focus on other elements may fail if the staff are inadequately trained to accept and implement the changes required.

So you must now arrange a series of interviews with the senior managers, using the 7-S model to discuss the current status of:

- the business activities;
- existing business development plans;
- the possible implications of the introduction of environmental management systems;
- the availability of skills to facilitate the transition; and
- other business elements that have particular relevance.

The result will be a composite picture of the current business, the overall strategic direction of the organization, and the areas of concern in implementing the environmental management system. Interpretation of those results should allow you to focus on the terms of reference of the project – what you are going to do, what you are not going to do; the general timescale, costs and resources available; the priority of the project; and the scope of your responsibilities.

THE PROJECT QUALITY SYSTEM

As project manager, you will need the freedom and authority to make decisions about project resources, and actions by others you are dependent upon.

It is important to clarify these responsibilities as a part of the project documentation, and the most appropriate way of approaching this is to develop a project quality plan. This will contain a number of elements that you must document and to which you must obtain agreement, namely:

Objective: Agree the mission, scope and extent of the project activities: e.g., 'to implement an EMS on XYZ site, by 31 March.'

Strategy: The overall plan to achieve the objective; from initial review to audit and assessment, the major activities mapped out.

Dependencies: What you are dependent on to achieve the mission; e.g., the project team, resources, commitment, staff and systems.

Deliverables: What you will deliver in achieving the mission; e.g., workshops, communications, system documentation, audit results and a registration certificate.

Procedures: The detailed procedures to be developed for implementation; e.g., checkpoints, reporting, detailed timetable and instructions for participants.

Measurements: What will be measured to track progress; against plan, workshop satisfaction, resources.

Change control: How changes to the project plan will be implemented; what change control procedures or error correction will be necessary.

An outline of these elements of your project in a single document will assist you in clarifying the position of the project and the roles and responsibilities of the key participants.

THE OUTLINE PLAN

A project must have:

- unambiguous completion criteria (you will know when you have finished);
- unambiguous success measurements (you will know how well you did it!);
- a definite life span (a start and an end); and
- a defined organization (who is doing what).

The completion criteria will be conformity to the environmental management system standard ISO 14001. The success measurement will be the assessment of compliance to the standard through the internal audit, and external certification. The timescale will depend on the organization's size, complexity and activities, as well as its capacity to change. The 'organization' will include definition of the roles and responsibilities of the senior management representative, the implementation project manager and the project implementation team, the new roles for staff and managers at a generic level, and any additional specialist resource.

Programme phases

The programme will have the several phases:

1. Management review and approval.
2. Planning and set-up.

3. Initial review.
4. Awareness through line management.
5. Implementation through line management.
6. Project review.

Management review

Management review is the presentation of the 'coherence check' and agreement to the scope, resources and criteria of the project.

Planning and set-up

Planning and set-up is the phase of bringing together the implementation team, confirming the mission and detailed programme development workshop.

Initial review

The initial review is a formal review of the environmental risk, opportunities, strengths and weaknesses.

Awareness programme

Raising awareness is achieved through the design and implementation of a presentation for cascading information through the organization.

Implementation programme

The implementation programme is achieved through the implementation workshop. This is designed to involve discrete business units, departments or functional managers with common reporting lines. They will be encouraged to review their current business activities in the light of the requirement to address environmental management issues. Implementation workshops are reviewed in greater depth later, in *Chapter 17*.

Project review

The project review is the activity to assess the completeness of the project and the attainment of the project goals. It will include self-assessment and initial audit results. As an example, a small firm in an early BSI EMS pilot showed the following steps:

Initial review (8 weeks)	Familiarisation/fact finding/data collection.
Policy formulation (4 weeks)	Scope/ethos/focus/style.
Systems set-up (12 weeks)	Manual/procedures/training.

System implementation (28 weeks)   Primary and secondary procedures/operational control.

Systems auditing (16 weeks)   Training EMS auditors/in-house verification/external mock certification/QA check.

The total programme ran for some 52 weeks with phases overlapping.

Checklist

[?] *Have you considered the investment requirements and explored the potential inhibitors?*

[?] *Have you carried out the 'coherence check' and report?*

[?] *Have you analyzed the skills which define the organization's capacity to change?*

[?] *Have you identified which decisions are yours and who else you need agreement from?*

[?] *Is everyone committed?*

[?] *Have you a complete picture of the organization?*

Communication hints

◆ Embark on a brief but comprehensive 'listening campaign'.

◆ To get a picture of the 'state of the art', attend seminars, read papers including ISO 14001, ISO 14004 and EMAS, documents and books, talk to your peers and competitors, use professional bodies, your trade association, your national standards' organization and environmental and business NGOs.

◆ Tell everybody all the time about the importance of the work. Do not understate the involvement and commitment that is required. Treat the programme as a serious, professional project that has significant implications on the future of the business.

CASE STUDY

Formosa Plastics Corporation, USA

FPC USA was the first chemical manufacturer in the USA to have all its sites certified to ISO 14001. It all began in August 1995, when the Corporate Environment, Health & Safety (EH&S) Department proposed the goal of ISO 14001 registration to the company's Executive Vice-President, and the senior management quickly granted approval. Then the Corporate EH&S Department quickly commenced plans to gain plant-level support for the initiative.

The initiative was led by John Pastuck, Manager of FPC Environmental Services. 'Our goal was to develop a single, consistent EMS which worked effectively for each of the plants', he says.

There were two steps leading to the implementation of the system. First, EH&S staff held a series of meetings with senior plant managers and EH&S managers at each facility, where Pastuck's team described the potential value of an EMS based on ISO 14001. He says that a good sales technique is critical at this stage, to engage the co-operation and enthusiasm of all staff, and adds that he sees the following benefits as the most compelling:

- potential for cost savings
- potential competitive advantages
- improved performance in compliance
- improved relationships with local communities and regulatory officials
- enhanced auditing programmes.

Pastuck adds that having lived through the headaches and distractions caused by compliance issues – which divert resources from the core business – plant managers and EH&S manager agreed that an alternative, proactive, quality-based management system would add value to their operations.

The second stage was to make sure that everybody involved in the project knew and understood what ISO 14001 meant, before Pastuck's department could finalize a strategy for getting registration by December 1996. So Corporate EH&S co-ordinated an ISO 14001 two-day training programme in November 1995, with some help from BSI. The first day covered the ISO 14001 standard and the process of registration, while Day 2 was a working session to discuss current systems, operational issues, and to finalize a strategy for implementing the EMS. Then FPC USA began implementation in earnest.

8

ISO 14001: FREQUENTLY ASKED QUESTIONS AND SOME ANSWERS

1. Does it help to have ISO 9000? Is it an essential prerequisite?

ISO 14001 was designed to 'stand alone'. You do not need ISO 9000 certification as a prerequisite. The approach to ISO 14001 uses the same concept of a structured quality system, but is set up to assure specified environmental performance goals. Organizations that have ISO 9000 find it relatively easy to extend their management systems to address the ISO 14001 requirements. Many of those approaching ISO 14001 directly find the structure and approach well presented and 'good common sense'.

While researching this book, the authors interviewed a wide spectrum of companies and only came across one which was registered to ISO 14001 first. However, having done that, the company saw the benefits of a systems approach to quality as well as environmental management, and so proceeded to get ISO 9002.

2. How do you obtain management commitment from an environmentally disinterested board?

First, follow the advice of Tony Wright of Schlumberger and tell them what they want to hear – that an EMS will very probably save them money and make them more competitive. This applies to most organizations.

Then take some time to analyze current issues in the organization – particularly financial issues related to waste and energy use – and assess potential savings. Check if the customers are thinking environmentally. Assess the potential risks for loss of business. Check if new or planned legislation may have an effect on the organization's activities. Assess the potential threats of non-compliance. If, when you present your findings, you get a 'nice but we don't have the time or resources' response, it's time to draft out your CV!

3. How do you put a boundary around the list of regulations? Won't it be huge?

All organizations need some process to ensure that they stay within the law. It may be by using professional experts, consultants or qualified staff, or by using documentation and continuous professional training programmes. The standard requires documentation *relevant* to the environmental aspects of your activities. This means important consents, planning consents or restrictions, discharge limits and regulations that require a specific or particular response over and above day-to-day compliance.

4. How do you put a boundary around the environmental aspects and impacts analysis? Isn't this endless and therefore impossible?

The use of the word 'aspects' sometimes makes you feel it means all the possible consequences of any behaviour. After all, everything we do has some environmental effect – even breathing. The key factor here is the test of *reasonableness*. What would be reasonable in the eyes of those outside the organization?

The initial 'scan' around the organization can ask function, business and departmental managers to self-assess overall aspects and identify those as 'significant' against predetermined criteria. Ways of limiting the extent of an aspects analysis vary depending on the problem. It can be where your product ceases to be identifiable – if it is used in another process or changed by the next process.

There is no hard and fast rule. The authors never like giving an 'it depends' answer, but in this case it is true. Ask yourself, 'Is it reasonable for the particular tool being used, e.g., life cycle analysis, to stop here?' Should it continue to the next step in the process? What happens if the store has a fire, the chemicals were combined, or the aluminium sulphate was placed in the wrong tank? Where does the water waste go, the solid waste end up? Is my contractor properly authorized and registered?

5. How do you identify a significant issue?

The standard focuses on significant issues to limit the objectives and targets to relevant and achievable goals. In particular, it focuses on two factors related to the activity: product and process. Do they relate to global issues? For example:

(a) ● Global warming: energy use or 'greenhouse' gas emission;
   ● Resource depletion; waste minimization and sources of materials and choice;
   ● Pollution: discharges, emissions and waste streams.
(b) How significant are they within the operation?

If you are in manufacturing, issues may be related to CFC phase-out, or energy and waste streams at high level; however, if you are a fencing contractor, in addition to material supply source, you may well consider the choice of wood preservatives you use in your business.

6. If the manual is going to contain all the information on how I run the business, won't it be huge?

In a word, 'No'. Schlumberger's Environmental Manual was just 12 pages long. If you have no other management manual, at first sight the requirement seems daunting. The intent however is to bring together in one place all the key elements of the systems you use so that you, your organization and third parties can see that you have a comprehensive system. It is a place to put unique documentation like a policy statement and an organization roles and responsibilities diagram. It is not the place to repeat the documentation on the *Control of Substances Hazardous to Health (COSHH)*. The manual should *signpost* where other documents are to be found and who the owner or maintainer is. In this way it can be readily seen that a process exists, and where it can be found and who owns and uses it.

One of the misconceptions about documentation is that is has to be like the word itself – big. However, focus on the military approach and ask yourself, 'What do people need to know to do their jobs?' Don't, for example, fall into the same trap as a well-known, blue-chip engineering consultancy which wrote a 27-page procedure for internal communications when setting up its ISO 9001 system.

7. Objectives and targets sound fine, but you don't really expect detailed quantification, after all some things can't be measured?

Statisticians will tell you that most things *can* be measured. The goal is to put some measurement on all the significant activities and processes, even those you feel today have not been measurable. Some companies create measurement scales or estimates drawn from available data on a simple, empirical scale to set a baseline and start to *measure for improvement*. The key is to establish a measurement system and then improve both the process being measured and the measurement system in the light of the information gained.

8. Can my organization comply with ISO 14001 for part of the organization (main production processes) to satisfy a third party, without applying it to its own in-house activities?

No. One of the critical elements for success in the approach to environmental management under ISO 14001 is the 'whole organization' requirement. It encourages a more holistic approach to the issue, because that is the only way to address some of the environmental issues we face. It does allow the definition of 'organization' to go down to a small level, including a site, but not to separate a process from the organization that supports it.

9. *Training raises many questions. Do I really need to run a new training programme? What should be the main learning points in the education plan? What is the most effective approach?*

All the organizations interviewed during the research for this book said that training was the most critical aspect for the success of the EMS, once senior management had committed themselves to it. In simple terms, the EMS project is doomed unless people within the organization know what to do.

There is a need for a training programme to make people aware of the issues. Then, if you want to do things differently, you will need to involve them in applying that awareness to their jobs. The main learning points are suggested in *Chapter 10*. There are benefits in integrating the environmental training into the main company programmes, providing the specific learning points are addressed in the revised content.

10. *How do you make the environmental policy statement public?*

Some companies use the annual report, and others make special arrangements including publicly available documentation. Many, for example, are using the Internet to promulgate their policy statements. The critical point is that everyone in the organization knows the policy exists and can refer to it.

11. *Where does the initial review stop? This could be an endless activity like the effects analysis.*

The main aim of the initial review is to identify those areas that the EMS should focus on. The SWOT analysis format will provide the overview to highlight the areas necessary for inclusion in the policy and that will require more detailed analysis under the environmental effects analysis.

A simple rule is that the more time spent on the review means less time on the planning phase of ISO 14001.

12. *How do I commit my organization to continuous improvement when many of the environmental effects are governed by mechanized processes difficult to improve without substantial investment?*

The focus of ISO 14001 is *continual* – and not continuous – improvement, a conscious committee decision. Compliance does not require improvement everywhere in the organization every day. It does require a continuing programme of improvement that, over a period of time, demonstrates that a reduced burden is being placed on the environment. Today, it may be improvements in energy management; tomorrow, in waste minimization; in six months, a planned investment will reduce water usage. One change may result in an increase in, say, gas consumption, with a decrease in electricity consumption. This may provide an overall improvement in environmental performance as part of a continual improvement programme.

13. My company is very busy trying to survive in the middle of a recession (or the middle of a rapid growth situation). Where do I find the resources and time to implement an EMS?

This is a common point. However, Vauxhall Motors was affected, like many other industries in the early 1990s, by the recession when they started their EMS, yet pushed ahead anyway and succeeded despite lean times. Lack of time and resources are the most frequently cited reasons for doing nothing, and familiar to those responsible for the quality programmes in many organizations. As quality guru John Deming said, 'You don't have to do this, survival is optional!' Try to make the programme relevant to you and your position. Focus on the small steps, and progress by integrating the activities into the day-to-day business of your organization. Reward those who deliver real benefits to the bottom line. Whether you are struggling or very successful, improved profitability is worth the investment.

14. What happens if I don't achieve my objectives and targets? Will I lose my certificate? What about the bad publicity?

There is a risk that failure to achieve objectives and targets in a significant way may result in deregistration and, consequently, bad publicity. Such an approach should reflect the value of the registration and the credibility of those in the scheme who do achieve their targets.

Experience with quality systems assessment shows that appropriate recognition of system failure, followed by subsequent corrective action does not jeopardize registration. However, persistent breaches would be viewed differently. It is specified in the Eco-Management and Audit Regulation (EMAS) that any breach of legislation will result in deregistration, through links between the legislators and competent body.

15. How should I carry out audits? Should I use internal staff or must I use consultants?

There is no 'must' about the use of external consultants for system design or internal audit. Consultants provide resources that would otherwise not be available in an organization. They can also provide a broader perspective with their wider experience. Internally trained staff have more knowledge about your business than an external consultant and you retain the skills within the organization.

Qualifications for assessors/verifiers calls for independence from the organization being assessed. This usually means an assessor from an appropriately accredited body. However, EMAS indicates the individual verifiers could be internal, providing they are independent of the business area being assessed, and are suitably accredited.

16. How will assessment and certification work? Will this be by my ISO 9000 assessor or by a new organization with all the attendant extra costs?

As skilled as your ISO 9000 assessor may be, experience in environmental auditing has shown that he or she is unlikely to be competent in areas specific to environmental performance, methods of measurement, testing, and legislation. The skills needed for an audit team to assess an EMS effectively are:

- system assessment skills
- environmental skills
- industry skills.

Industry skills are necessary to ensure that appropriate issues are being considered by the EMS in relation to the standards of your specific industry. These skills can be obtained by training staff experienced in other skills or by team building.

17. What does 'abnormal working conditions' mean?

Unlike an accident, incident or emergency conditions which are uncontrolled, 'abnormal working conditions' refers to activities that are controlled but occur infrequently. Because they are unusual occurrences, risks of system failure may be higher and special actions may be needed to ensure the environmental policy and practices are not put at risk. Examples include start-up and shut-down procedures wherever people are unfamiliar with the routines and standards expected, or where the systems are untried and untested, and refurbishment or construction activity.

18. What should be the scope of 'emergency plans'?

Emergency plans should be established as a result of a formal risk assessment procedure to identify, in a structured manner, those anticipated risks within the organization. Some eventualities have a higher probability than others. These should be planned for, including discussions with outside agencies.

However, major incidents like Flixborough, Piper Alpha and Exxon Valdez show that the consequential events beyond the first, possibly predictable, event can have far-reaching consequences. The incident and accident management systems therefore need to have flexible responses but clear roles and responsibilities in terms of communications, actions and reporting. Lessons from such events can then be learned quickly and passed on to reduce future risks.

19. We are only a small company. Doesn't ISO 14001 only apply to big companies?

No. The key issue is environmental significance and criticality. Remember that significance depends as much on the local environment as it does on the processes that an organization uses. While researching this book, Richard Gould visited registered organizations ranging from a huge multinational with over 135 000 employees and an annual turnover greater than the GDP of many countries, to a tiny manufacturing outfit with 12 staff. People used to say the same thing about ISO 9001, but organizations registered to ISO 9001 range from two-person outfits to those employing several hundred thousand.

20. We are a service company. Doesn't ISO 14001 only apply to manufacturers?

No. It is a framework for improving environmental performance which can apply to any type of organization. Those interviewed for this book included several service organizations, such as local government.

21. What is the connection between EMAS and ISO 14001?

ISO 14001 can be seen as the systems framework for EMAS. There are many common elements, and an organization registered to ISO 14001 can progress to EMAS by doing a few additional things, such as:

- Having an assessable initial environmental review which conforms to the required format.
- Producing a publicly available, comprehensive report known as an *Environmental Statement*.
- Having the environmental performance verified by an accredited independent expert – like the BSI.

22. What is the cost of implementing ISO 14001, using the cost of ISO 9001 as a baseline?

BSI's experience from clients has shown that implementation costs are about 1.5 times the cost of ISO 9000, and it is about the same to register and maintain the

73

system. Many certifying bodies now offer integrated continuing assessments to reduce the cost and time impact.

23. Can you ring-fence parts of an organization? Supposing you have some pretty difficult issues to deal with, such as an old, on-site power station? Can you exclude this first?

No. You can ring-fence discrete parts of an organization, but not components within each part. A good example is Du Pont in Northern Ireland. Their site has two main businesses – Kevlar® and Lycra®. Each of these businesses is being registered independently, as they are discrete, autonomous businesses on their own sites within a much larger site.

24. How do you get an EMS to work? What would be your top tips?

- Do not invent a new system, but make sure that the EMS dovetails with your existing systems. According to Sony UK's experience, unless the EMS is integrated within the existing ways of working, then it is likely to fail.

- Empower people with ownership. Let them look after procedures. Get them to do things and ask for their ideas. People feel important and motivated if you ask them for their inputs, even if you choose not to act on their suggestions.

- Keep the system as simple as possible. Don't over complicate things, and focus on what people need to know.

- Focus on savings to engage the commitment of senior management.

- Do not underestimate the power of awareness and the importance of training.

25. How quickly can a company get registered after deciding to implement a system?

Camborne Fabrics of the innovative Interface Group did it in 12 weeks. In the next two years their EMS helped them to save about £350 000.

9

OBTAINING THE COMMITMENT
AND ESTABLISHING THE TEAM

> ### Objective
> To raise awareness of the environmental issues which affect your organiza-
> tion and make a specific proposal for action, addressed to a senior man-
> agement level.

IN THIS CHAPTER

At this stage you have established a core of information about environmental
issues generally, a basic knowledge of the environmental standards you wish to
implement and a picture of your organization's readiness to develop and implement an EMS standard strategy. You now need to acquire agreement at board
level to proceed, including agreement on the scope of the plan and the resources
needed to build the implementation team, agreement on the timetable of implementation, and of course, a project plan (*see* Figure 9.1).

It is a requirement of ISO 14001 that the top management of the organization
define and review the environmental policy at regular intervals in order to maintain their commitment to environmental management. Otherwise the decision-
making processes, resource allocation, priority setting and business
measurements (to name a few), without which you will not achieve the integrated environmental management system you desire, will not work for it. So
how do you get that commitment? Whose authority do you need?

The communication impact matrix (*see* Figure 19.1 in *Chapter 19*, page 184)
is important in designing the communications process correctly to achieve the
desired output. In this case the on-going objective is to raise *awareness* of the

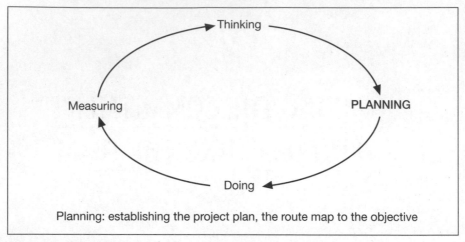

Planning: establishing the project plan, the route map to the objective

Fig. 9.1 The 'planning' part of the improvement loop

issues at senior management level and obtain agreement to specific proposed course of action.

RAISING AWARENESS IN YOUR ORGANIZATION

Raising awareness is done through two steps in this plan. Firstly a formal presentation is made to executive management to obtain approval for the programme design and give the authority to act; secondly, having established the project team and carried out the initial review to 'benchmark' the current environmental performance, a presentation is designed to be cascaded by line management prior to the implementation workshop activity.

What information is likely to interest senior management?

- Recent environmental court cases, relevant to the organization's activities and the implications on its liabilities.
- Recent or planned environmental legislation that directly or indirectly will affect the organization's activities.
- Inquiries or pressure from customers and consumers that may impact future profitability.
- Industry or community 'peer pressure' that may identify threats or opportunities.

Having collected your information to raise awareness, you may now make a more formal presentation to the board on the way forward.

PLANNING THE PRESENTATION

Book yourself on to the agenda of a relevant management executive meeting and plan your presentation. You could entitle the paper *Environmental Management Standards: an issue for us?*, or whatever is relevant to you with your knowledge of the business. Consider what the desired outcome of your presentation is. Not only awareness and understanding, but also the commitment to a course of action. If you want agreement you must be firm about the four Ps: *position*, *problems*, *possibilities* and *proposal*.

You must put a firm *proposal* to the executive team. The senior managers will know that there are choices to be made – in which direction should the organization go, how far, how fast and with what resources? As with any project such *possibilities* must be explored. To agree to explore the options suggests you have made a clear *problem* statement – one that is relevant to the organization's profitability, image or legal status. The problem will need to be put into context if it is to have meaning to the senior management team, and this is the position statement which should introduce the presentation.

The proposed running order therefore is as set out below.

Position

Where are we now? What are the outside events that may affect your organization? Consider:

- legal background
- stakeholder interests
- insurance
- customers
- corporate drivers
- community or peer pressure
- banks
- staff
- competition.

What is the internal status of your organization? Points to address include:

- environmental performance
- incidents
- staff awareness
- finance

- accidents
- risks
- management skills
- resources.

Include also highlights of current environmental performance; existing management system status; *Control of Substances Hazardous to Health (COSHH)*; occupational health and safety issues; investment programme; projects; initiatives.

Problems

Why should your organization bother to improve its environmental performance? The presentation should highlight:

- what we know/don't know
- the lack of cohesion and direction
- lack of recognition or priority
- products/services not being developed
- the failures that exist
- cost of failure
- savings not being taken
- recognition of opportunity.

Your organization also has the opportunity to change its culture, to introduce or reinforce its drive for quality.

Possibilities

- Do nothing: in the light of the above, is it business as usual? Then what?
- Do everything! Do what? What are the priorities? What should be invested? What will the impacts be?
- A balanced, cost-effective solution, which will be appropriately managed to a measurable conclusion, e.g. registered compliance to ISO 14001 or EMAS in a given timescale.

Proposal

The seven steps towards achieving environmental management standards:

1. Obtain executive commitment today to set up the necessary project team, resources and organization.

2. Carry out an initial review of the company's status and report back to the board.

3. Establish an outline environmental policy and obtain executive approval.

4. Establish a detailed action plan, for awareness and implementation of the policy, and obtain approval.

5. Communicate the plan through 'awareness' presentations.

6. Implement the plan, through 'implementation' workshops.

7. Measure the success of the plan and the improvement in environmental performance.

At this point you must become the 'active listener'. Although the champion of the proposal, in the end it is the task of the executive managers to make the decision. They have to 'own' it. They will discuss, probe and dig to see if you have done your homework and that your facts are correct, and be particularly interested in the predictive part of the presentation – 'What if the EMAS scheme does not prove essential? 'What if the environmental issue goes away?', 'How do you know this will become a major issue?'. You must answer these questions honestly. You will not always know the answer, and an 'I don't know, but it seems to me that ...' answer is usually the best approach.

You must be flexible in responding to ideas about changes to the plan providing they still meet the objective, but be firm. You must not compromise on the impact the plan will have. The executive managers must be fully aware of the implications and accept them. It is a management change programme and *will* have significant impact.

Once you have the authority to proceed you can now establish what activities must take place and set up a team to undertake these activities.

ESTABLISHING THE PROJECT ACTIVITIES

To implement the requirements of the project you will need to be aware of the activities which will have to take place. Table 9.1 shows the activities and the stages at which they will be employed in the EMS implementation programme. You will notice that some of the activities address more than one requirement, e.g., the implementation workshop. Management meetings are needed to agree scope, programme, policy, status and future action plans of the EMS. These can be specific meetings or extensions of existing management meetings. The choice depends on your view of the most appropriate route that will achieve success.

Awareness presentations are needed to set out the position and direction of the programme. Interactive sessions help to share the current state of knowledge and to introduce the problems that will be faced. No attempt is made in this stage to develop solutions; every attempt is made to highlight the benefits in pursuing the policy of improved environmental management.

Table 9.1 The activities needed for the EMS implementation programme

Requirement	Activity
Management policy	Management meeting
Organization and personnel	Awareness presentation Implementation workshop Performance planning Job objective setting
Environmental effects	Implementation workshop Performance planning EMS documentation
Programme	Implementation workshop
Management manual and documentation	Implementation workshop
Operational control	Implementation workshop
Records	Implementation workshop
Audits	Self-assessment exercises EMS audit
Reviews	Management review meeting report

Implementation workshops are needed to develop the response at a departmental level. Interactive sessions are used to explore the activities to be implemented and the contribution that each department can make to the business goals. Implementation workshops can also explore the areas where activities and procedures can be changed to meet the environmental performance challenges.

Self-assessment exercises can be used to allow managers and staff to measure their progress in implementing the EMS. An environmental management system skeleton must be documented to provide a framework for departmental activity and to analyze practices and procedures. The contents of the framework is provided by each department through the implementation workshop.

Job objectives are needed to define the roles and responsibilities for staff who manage or perform work related to the environmental policy, objectives and targets.

Performance plans are needed to set specific achievement objectives for those who perform work related to the environmental policy.

EMS audits are needed to assess the compliance of the system with the standard's requirements so that the management activities and procedures meet those requirements, and so that the system elements are effective in meeting the environmental standards requirements.

Management review meetings are needed to monitor progress and performance and to establish an improvement programme related to the current EMS. Registration activities need to be managed to obtain and maintain a certificate for an accredited registration body.

The implementation workshop is the main tool for establishing the departmental environmental management system as it will be part of the common skeleton that you provide. It may be that your organization already has a documented quality system in place that provides a local framework for objectives, practices and procedures. In that case you will be adding to the contents of that system, to ensure integration of the EMS into the existing management system. The EMS then becomes a 'thread' running through the organization. It is tied into the day-to-day activities, practices and procedures and is integrated into the reporting, objectives setting and rewards systems. The EMS, therefore, will be just as simple, or as complex, as your current organization.

ESTABLISHING THE PROJECT RESPONSIBILITIES

To illustrate the typical structure of the project approach, the roles and responsibilities are as follows.

- *Executive management*: The senior management body in the organization – the board or committee responsible for running the organization – owns the environmental policy, programme and review procedures.
- *Management representatives*: Members of executive management responsible for the implementation programme, through the EMS project manager.
- *EMS project manager*: Line manager responsible for implementation of the project plan, leader of the project team.
- *Project team*: Project support team drawn from all parts of the organization. Each represents a department or function to ensure ownership and co-operation throughout the organization.
- *Line managers*: Managers responsible for discrete areas of activity or process within the organization. Responsible for the performance management of

others, and they will need to identify environmental co-ordinators or representatives in their area of control.

- *Departmental environmental co-ordinators*: Responsible to a line manager for understanding, co-ordinating, supporting and representing the department in activities related to the project programme.
- *Internal auditors*: Staff trained in audit skills, to support the internal and external EMS audit activities. These may be departmental environmental co-ordinators, or other staff. When auditing they must be independent of the area under review.

ESTABLISHING YOUR PROJECT TEAM

The project team is key to implementing the communication and workshop programme. The team should be drawn from the management departments and staff groups. The project team is the main resource for getting the message out to the people on the ground, your local 'champions'. Who should be in your project team and what should they be responsible for?

An important member of the team is the *environmental programmes manager* who is responsible for delivering the project, i.e., you. You are likely to provide the secretariat and general co-ordination activities. You will need a chairperson who is the executive sponsor or *management representative*. (This may still be you in a small organization!)

You will need a representative from each *line management function* – from the production, manufacturing, maintenance, marketing research and administration departments. You must have a representative from each function, even if the manager's initial response is, 'This does not apply to me!'. All parts of the business have some environmental impact, and all aspects of the business interact with one another, so you will need full participation if the change management programme is going to be successful,.

If you have a *quality programmes* manager responsible for the ISO 9000 programme, you will need his or her support to integrate the requirements into the existing documented systems. If you have staff programmes for education and communications, you will also need the support from these departments to help design and integrate the messages in your organization's training and communication.

The next step is to develop a coherent plan of action that is 'owned' by your team members. To do this, you will develop and involve them in a workshop to establish a common view of the goal and the critical factors to succeed in achieving the goal.

Checklist

? *Have you planned your presentation to obtain agreement with the senior management? Position, problem, possibilities and proposal.*

? *Have you established support for your plans at the highest level of the organization?*

? *Have you considered the relevant environmental issues that will provide interest for your senior management?*

? *Have you checked the activities for each part of the programme?*

? *Is your team complete with representatives from each key function?*

CASE STUDIES

Schlumberger

Tony Wright from Schlumberger has a wide experience in implementing management systems, having started with quality, and moved on to manage those for health and safety and environment. He is experienced in encountering walls to initiatives, so he has two tools for getting the motivation of the company staff and its management. 'Management are concerned with managing businesses, and businesses have one important function; to make a profit. If they do not make a profit, then they cannot do anything else for long. Therefore I focused on the financial benefits of management systems right from the start, and then everything else follows on from there', he says.

Second, keeping people motivated is a challenge, so he exploits current trends. 'While people are generally resistant to change, they are also interested in new things, so I keep everyone absorbed by spicing up the management system. The Internet and intranets, for example, are flavour of the month at the moment, so we are exploiting these IT technologies to engage people in the systems', enthuses Wright.

Elmwood College

According to John Salter, Environmental Manager and Lecturer in Horticulture at Elmwood College, 'Commitment of staff and students towards environmental improvement was the single most important factor in determining the success or otherwise of implementing an EMS.'

At the College, the initial impetus came from the students themselves. A group of horticulture students had to do an environmental audit of the College as part of their Current Issues Unit. While doing this, they generated an interest in a number of improvements, such as a recycling scheme for waste paper and aluminium cans.

Top-level commitment is also critical, and Salter suspects that the environmental initiatives would have not gone beyond this if the Principal of the College was not wholly supportive of the EMS project. Without this drive from the top, it is unlikely that the Board of Management would have approved the funding and resources for implementing the EMS.

10

ACTION PLANNING:
A TEAM WORKSHOP

Objective
The goal is to obtain agreement on the detailed action plan for implementing the EMS to the chosen standards

You have agreement at high level to implement the overall programme, but now you need support across the company from the people who will be responsible for seeing it through.

The managers in the organization, therefore, need to have a voice in the plan to implement the changes. This is done through representation or the project team, and it is important to establish consensus for the project plan with the team members, so that they feel they 'own' it, when reporting back to their constituencies.

CREATING A PLAN WITH THE PROJECT TEAM

The first stage is to bring together the *project team* members. It is essential that the team has an agreed mission which should not be just the goal itself, but also identification of the activities necessary to achieve the goal and the priorities of those activities. The team must also have secured the allocation of resources to meet those activities. The critical success factor (CSF) technique is the best method to use to reach a consensus on the mission statement and the activities that will be necessary to achieve the mission. A successful project plan can be attained through a CSF workshop.

The critical success factors

The objective of the workshop is to enable a team of people with a common goal to agree what the priority activities are, and therefore where resources should be focused. It does this by introducing the concept of CSFs, which help identify key actions in a positive and co-operative way. The approach has been successful in helping teams plan projects, improve departmental business processes, functions and organizations.

Critical success factors provide a link between the mission, which is clear, unequivocal and measurable, and the activities necessary to achieve the mission. The mechanism employed is based on a consensus approach. After that, analyzing and agreeing the activities to achieve the CSFs is (relatively) painless and becomes a (comparatively) straightforward exercise.

For the factors to be 'critical' in importance, there must not be too many of them. Indeed, if there are more than eight, they begin to stray into a general statement of wishes. By keeping the number of factors to eight or less, we can be confident they really matter.

Each CSF must be precisely focused on one element. It is not sufficient to say, 'We must have senior management support and the skills necessary to implement the programme.' This statement incorporates *two* CSFs which may both be critical but which may require different activities to implement them.

Each CSF must be fundamental to achieving the mission and each must be a *measurable* achievement or an 'achieved state'. For example, if your mission statement is:

> 'To establish an environmental management system in [company name] by [date] that meets the requirements of ISO 14001 and/or EMAS.'

then the statement, 'We must have senior management commitment to the programme' is a CSF because without senior management commitment the mission will fail. It is measurable because you will know when you have achieved senior management support.

So set up a meeting of the project team to develop the CSFs and the action plan. Attendees will be *all* the team – all the members must be present. If they are not available, change the date. One of the key factors for success in this kind of exercise is consensus from all the participants, so do not hold the meeting without everyone there.

A TECHNIQUE FOR DECIDING THE PROJECT PLAN: A CSF WORKSHOP

Step 1: Agree the mission

A 'mission statement' is a brief statement of one or two sentences summarizing what members of the team are jointly going to do. That sounds easy, but experience shows that what you may think you have agreed is not the goal that the others in the team have in mind. Sometimes 'hidden agendas' appear at this stage. This is just as well; clear them up now and be prepared to listen and react to comments and suggestions until the mission is agreed. It must be by consensus, but of course it has to be in line with your terms of reference. Get this wrong and all the rest of the activities that follow will be wasting resources.

Step 2: What are the dominant influences on the mission?

Hold a ten-minute brainstorming session to answer this question. Anything and everything that could influence the achievement of the mission can be mentioned. The usual rules apply.

The material which results from the brainstorming session forms the core from which you will draw out the CSFs. All the dominant influences have implications on the mission, but as you examine them, some will be more critical than others. The dominant influences can be grouped under the categories of the 7-S model (see *Chapter 7*, page 60) to ensure an even spread of factors.

Brainstorming rules

- 10–15 minutes at the most, briskly led.
- Everybody should contribute, in orderly fashion, but you can 'pass'.
- Anything can be said, no matter how lateral it may appear!
- Nobody can challenge or question other contributions.
- No more than two word concepts – not a speech!
- Keep track of ideas on a flip chart.

Step 3: List the CSFs

You now use the brainstorming material to identify the CSFs. The team knows the mission and has an idea of the dominant influences that affect the achievement of the mission. From that you can list the factors critical for success. Remember that the list should not exceed eight essential points if the exercise is to be successful, each starting with 'we must' or 'we need'.

Take a point from the dominant factors and see what was meant by it. How critical does the team feel it would be to the achievement of the project? Develop a sentence that best captures the 'achieved state' to be desired. Keep working at it until the team agree, by consensus, that the sentence is right. This is your CSF. Then take another dominant influence and repeat the process. Do not fall into the trap of adding 'just one more'. Keep pressing the team to choose the really *critical* factors among all the things that could affect the mission.

An alternative method is to divide a flip chart into eight boxes and then place the dominant influence of similar themes into a particular box (*see* Figure 10.1). Such a technique avoids the left-over syndrome. For example, using this method would mean that all the items relating to training and educational skills would appear in a single place.

1. ● Skills ● Competent ● Able	**2.** ● Money ● Equipment ● Resources
3. ● Change ● Willing ● Able to shift	**4.** ● Leadership ● Top down drive ● Goals set
5. ● People keen ● Commitment ● Want to …	**6.** ● Plan ● What? ● When? ● Who?
7. ● Objectives ● Targets ● Standards	**8.** ● Roles ● Responsibilities ● Who does what

Fig. 10.1 The eight-box technique

Example

(from Brunel University's workshop group establishing CSFs)

Brunel management programme: Eco-Audit and environmental management systems

Mission: 'Putting in an EMS to meet ISO 14001'

Critical Success Factors

1. We must have an appropriately skilled team.

2. We must have a resource plan to meet the mission.

3. We must have open minds to accommodate change.

4. We must have a 'TEB' (totally enthusiastic boss).

5. We must have committed 'GOGs' (guys on the ground).

6. We must have a plan.

7. We must establish performance standards and targets to aim for.

8. We must identify roles and responsibilities.

Other CSFs might include the following:

- We need to ensure that our staff are trained to understand the implications of the company's environmental policy, objectives and targets.

- We must ensure that the environmental programme is integrated into the day-to-day practices and procedures to be effective.

- We must demonstrate market advantage from our proposed investment in improved environmental performance.

- We need to establish an effective quality system to monitor and continually improve the implementation of the environmental management systems standards programme.

As a quality check, you can go back to the 7-S model in *Chapter 7* to check for completeness, but do not be surprised if one or two elements are thought not to be critical. It may be that skills, ownership and planning are key right now, and that style and systems are seen to be less so. Your original *coherence check* (*Chapter 7*, page 62) will probably have confirmed that.

Step 4: Decide on the action to be taken

You now have a group which agrees the mission, and the critical factors necessary to achieve the mission. From here it is a relatively straightforward step to decide on the actions necessary to achieve the CSFs.

On a separate flip chart write the CSF across the top of a page. You need four columns: action, owner, date and measurement.

Action: Define an activity which is necessary to achieve the CSF. You can brainstorm the activities if it helps. Check with the group that you have all the actions necessary to achieve the CSF.

Owner: Acceptance of ownership implies taking responsibility for implementing something. You might experience unwillingness to accept ownership but the team has agreed that certain things need to be done, so identify the owner whose role in the organization best fits the task in hand. For example, if the task is an issue of communication, then ownership should be the responsibility of the representative of the communication department. If it is a training issue, the training department's representative has ownership. Make sure the tasks are shared out so that everyone is interdependent on each other to succeed – this helps later on. Do not take all the actions yourself. You are the project manager, not the entire team, so share the ownership.

Date: It is no good having an open-ended action to be implemented. You need to know when the action needs to be completed and set a date. Be careful to set reasonable targets: too far ahead and jobs never get done; impossibly short and you lose credibility.

Measurement: You will all need to understand the completion criteria for the task. It needs to be relevant to the subject, but it can be fun. If gaining executive management approval to the plan is an action, a documented minute will do. However, gaining approval from the training manager for the workshop plan might be measured by a blue rosette! Employ techniques that will lighten the meetings and make them worthwhile and fun to attend.

Now you have a plan for one CSF, go through the rest. You will find the first a bit slow to do, but as you progress a momentum gathers and it leads you through the last CSFs quickly. Record the actions to be taken for each CSF, alone with the owner, date and measure in a table such as that shown in Table 10.1. You will also find that some actions appear on more than one CSF. This is to be expected, and repetition of such an action indicates that it is probably a critical activity.

Step 5: Consolidate the results into a comprehensive action plan

You should now ensure that the actions are clearly noted by the team participants. Your job is to take away the results and consolidate them into a comprehensive action plan for the team, in a form that they can present back to their

Table 10.1 Allocation of owner, date and measurement for CSFs

Action	Owner	Date	Measurement
Draft plan for review	Project Manager	1 January	To agreed criteria
Senior management review and comment	Departmental representatives	1 January	Response, 3 March
Revised plan to senior management	Departmental representatives	14 March	Documented
Present plan to senior management meeting for approval	Project Manager	21 April	Minuted
Publish and communicate	Project Manager	28 May	House Magazine

sponsoring departments. This is the core of the project plan you have set out to achieve. Like all plans, however, it is only as good as the information presented. To keep it current and relevant as a control tool you need to track progress against the plan and adjust it whenever things slip or accelerate. The team will then regard the plan meetings that you will hold as essential.

Checklist for successful projects

? *Terms of reference must be clearly established:*

- *What is the desired outcome?*

- *Who is responsible for what?*

- *What are the criteria for decision-making?*

? *The project manager must have an appropriate balance of responsibility and authority to achieve the desired outcome.*

? *The project must be supported by a team with an appropriate balance of skills and resources.*

? *All the team members must have clear objectives.*

? *There must be a plan to achieve the objectives.*

? *A tracking mechanism should monitor the progress to the plan:*

- *Where are we?*

- *Where should we be?*

? *A control mechanism should be in place to change the plan should it be necessary.*

- *What needs to be done?*

- *Who is responsible?*

- *How will you know it has been done?*

? *There must be a communication process to keep everyone informed of progress.*

Communication hints

◆ The output from this workshop provides material to report to the executive management team on the agreed way forward. Use the opportunity to reinforce the mandate you have been given to clarify the actions that now have the support of their nominees.

◆ If you have an in-house newspaper or magazine, use some of the material to publicise the project start-up, the project team members and the outline of the plan to begin the awareness process.

◆ Ask your project team members for confirmation that they have reviewed the material with their own area of responsibility to ensure the messages are getting back to the line managers.

11

THE INITIAL
ENVIRONMENTAL REVIEW

Objective

The goal is a report that will be presented to the project team and executive management. This report describes the organization's environmental setting, risks, liabilities, obligations and baseline performance. The report will assist the project team in developing the CSFs by establishing a plan to implement the EMS. It will also provide data for communications, and measurements for tracking progress in the future.

Figure 11.1 highlights the 'doing' part of the improvement loop.

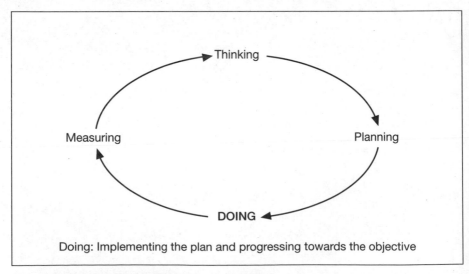

Doing: Implementing the plan and progressing towards the objective

Fig. 11.1 The 'doing' part of the improvement loop

ISO 14001 REQUIREMENTS

ISO 14001, unlike EMAS, does not formally require an organization to carry out an initial environmental review. However, ISO 14001 does require an organization to understand its baseline environmental performance. Therefore an assessment of an organization's environmental baseline which covers its strengths, weaknesses, opportunities and threats is an essential starting point to building an EMS.

It is noteworthy that when the authors researched this book, they did not encounter one organization which had skipped the initial environmental review (IER).

A benchmarking tool and a roadmap

This chapter describes the purpose and content of an initial environmental review (IER). It describes how to conduct an IER, which issues to address, how to present the results, and what to do with the results of the review.

The IER determines the baseline of an organization's environmental risks, and its performance in managing those risks. The IER is the first stage of any effective EMS, because it not only establishes a starting point, but also drives the Environmental Policy, and provides the information and initial data for the awareness presentation. More importantly, the IER is the foundation for the most important and demanding parts of an EMS – the evaluation of environmental aspects and impacts. In short, an IER tells you where you are on the environmental map, and then gives you pointers for the future direction of your evaluations and management programme.

So look upon the IER as a tool which will help you culture your embryonic EMS. Once you have discovered your baseline, it will help you to design the awareness presentation to be cascaded throughout the organization, and set the agenda for the implementation workshop programme. This is the key to integrating the environmental management system into your company management system.

A TOOL TO GENERATE AWARENESS

The awareness presentation will be designed by you, for use throughout the organization by you and/or the project team members. A suggested outline of the presentation is given at the end of this chapter.

The implementation workshop (*Chapter 17*) is an interactive activity carried out with a manager and his or her subordinate team, which may be a board, a management team or a manager and his or her reporting staff. The IER is often referred to as the 'searchlight sweep' around the organization in order to highlight those areas where more detailed analysis will be required. It is the first of the environmental audit type of activity. It is a structured, systematic programme but not designed to test on assertion or measure against a standard. It is a fact-finding review of the whole organization.

Note: Because the term *environmental audit* has so many different uses, it is not used by ISO 14001. The standard refers more precisely to the *initial review, environmental management system audit* and *environmental management system review*. All of these are a form of environmental audit. The standards ISO 14010, 14011 and 14012 describe auditing in more detail.

The product of this stage of the implementation procedure is a report which will recommend actions for improvement. The process of the IER is to look at *all* the aspects of the organization. Where relevant it should extend beyond the business boundaries to look at suppliers, purchasers and the product life cycle. The report which results from the review will provide guidance on the areas of significant environmental impacts, so it must consider all parts of the organization and all activities. The report should contain the following elements:

- An appraisal of current environmental policies and practices.
- The environmental setting of the organization, so that you can establish the risks.
- A simple input-output analysis to define the processes, their regulatory requirements, and any by-products with environmental impacts.
- An appraisal of past, current and future performance.
- An outlook on environmental issues and implications.
- A SWOT analysis – the strengths, weaknesses, opportunities and threats.
- A PEST analysis – political, economic, social and technological issues.

THE SWOT ANALYSIS TECHNIQUE

This technique analyzes strengths, weaknesses, opportunities, and threats of the whole organization.

Internal strengths and weaknesses

Strengths

The strengths are those areas of system control or performance that are positive. For example, having: ISO 14001 and ISO 9000; a strong pollution control process; new plant or equipment; non-contentious products or services; high levels of skill; a committed senior management. These are areas to build on in developing and moving forward.

Weaknesses

These are areas where system control or performance appears at risk: where practices, procedures or processes indicate some opportunity for failure. Some examples might be: breaches of legal compliance; the risk of significant exposure should a failure occur; poor materials management; the use of hazardous processes with inadequate controls; a lack of operating instructions; a lack of emergency plans; a lack of clarity in the ownership of the process. These are areas that the action plan will focus on.

External opportunities and threats

Opportunities

These are areas where new actions or initiatives may bring benefits. For example, the introduction of: new products; new services; new processes; skills training; management leadership programmes; links to product quality; links to total quality management (TQM). These will need to be followed up in the action plan.

Threats

These are risks which may not be clearly apparent but which may damage the short- or long-term development of the organization. Examples could be: changes in market circumstances; new laws being developed; the effects of changes in consumer demand; the effects of change in supply sources; social or community pressure; or stakeholder risk assessments by banks or insurance companies. These may need policy formulation before actions are implemented.

A PEST ANALYSIS

In addition to the SWOT analysis, a PEST analysis can also help you to know and understand the strategic implications for your organization. Each item is outlined as follows:

- **Political:** the situation controlled by the local, regional, national or international governments.

- **Economic:** It is harder to invest in recessions. On the other hand, EMSs have proven financial benefits by saving money for an organization. Tools such as energy audits and waste minimization can all save you money.

- **Social:** Demonstrating your commitment to a continual improvement may be a key to your success or even survival in business.

- **Technological:** Changes in technology can offer new opportunities for products and services. Formal EMS also encourages greater degrees of environmental control through the EVABAT concept (economically viable application of best available technology).

CONDUCTING AN IER

The key to carrying out an IER is to treat the activity as a project. Like all projects it should comprise the stages described in Table 11.1.

Table 11.1 The phases of the IER

• *A thinking phase*	Define and agree the scope and objectives; set unambiguous completion criteria
• *A planning phase*	Define a schedule; plan your organizational requirements, resources, methods, roles and responsibilities
• *A doing phase*	Implement a gathering information programme; evaluate and report within a specified time frame
• *A reviewing phase*	Agree the actions arising from the report

There has to be a plan to get from the start to the finish of the review. It should be designed to achieve the objectives and laid out clearly and unambiguously. A tracking mechanism is needed to monitor progress towards the objective and a control mechanism is required to change the plan if there is a problem.

Defining the scope of the review puts a boundary around the assessment. Decide where you will go and where you will not. For example, are you reviewing the whole company, the whole of site X, or the whole life cycle of product Y? Agree an outline timetable and the measurements for completion.

Setting objectives ensures that the team is focused on what it will produce and when, so that effort goes only in the area required.

Defining the schedule and planning your organizational requirements, resources, methods, roles and responsibilities sets out how the project will be carried out. What people, finance or equipment do you need?

Implementing the information-gathering programme provides you with the raw data you will need for the review. Assess the data and put the results into an initial report. Be careful to stay on programme.

Agreeing the actions arising provides you with a follow-up procedure to implement the report.

Scope and objectives

Agree the objectives and limitations of the assessment. Which parts of the business have a priority or are likely to be the focus of the review? Is there a time constraint? What are the expectations at the completion of the project? What resources are available?

In discussion with the team, agree who will be the core personnel to carry out the review. You may choose to delegate this to a small sub-team of two to four people who can have access to all areas of the company. Ensure that team members have the right levels of expertise. For example, have they project skills, technical skills and process knowledge?

Schedule and resources

Plan out the resources available against the areas to be assessed, so that all the team members know who is responsible for what. Having mapped out the programme, get all the team together to discuss and agree the way forward.

IER: MEETING AGENDA

Introduction and background:

- the project scope and objective
- the plan of work
- who is doing what
- how it will be done
- communications – in the team and outside the team
- report plan.

It is useful to providet each team member with a 'role data sheet' so that each

Activities	Weeks									Ownership
	1	2	3	4	5	6	7	8	9	
Scope	XX									FB
Schedule and resources	XX									All
Checklists	XX									MH
Questionnaire	XX									MH
Communicate	X	XXX								TO
Action										
Management			XXX	XX						MH
Area 1			XX	XXX						FB
Area 2			X	XXX						CG
Function 1				XXX						FB
Function 2				XXX						CG
Data Collation	X	XXX	XXX	XXX	XXX	XX				MH
Draft report					X	XX				MH
Reporting										
Team review	XX			X	X			X		All
Management	X	X			XX			XX		All
Executive								XX		MH
Follow-up										
Urgent items						XX			XX	TBA
Agree action plan									XX	All

Fig. 11.2 Initial environmental review – example plan

98

knows precisely what they are to do and where they are to do it. For some areas you will have to define how to obtain the data – the methodology.

Interviews will form the main source of information. Talk to key personnel about the operations and activities. Checklists allow you to ensure that all the information from the interviews is in a common format.

Interview checklist

? *Indicate your 3–6 main activities.*

? *What are the objectives?*

? *Who or what are you dependent upon?*

? *What is the output?*

? *What are the environmental effects of the organization's activities?*

? *What are the levels of energy use, waste, discharges or emissions?*

? *What raw materials, paper, transport are used?*

? *What are the legislative issues?*

Questionnaires can be very useful. Use a telephone interview if the data are critical and the contact remote.

In other areas, you are looking for data on consents; energy bills; existing practices and procedures; measurements; reports inside the organization; guidance from trade associations or consultants' reports; and documentation from regulatory authorities.

To ensure that you get the support you need from all the staff, let them know clearly in advance about the activity and the possible contacts and interviews. Bring the team together at regular intervals during the review to compare progress against the plan. Follow-up and be willing to change the plan if a new area or direction seems valid as a result of the interim meeting. An example of such a plan is shown in Figure 11.2. The aim is to ensure that all main activities have a place in the programme and that each activity has an owner and can be allocated an appropriate amount of time and resources.

Action

You are now ready to go out and gather the data you have identified as necessary. Implement the plan; fill in the questionnaires; carry out the interviews; and track down the data you need.

Conducting the IER can be divided into ten phases. Briefly, these are:

- **Questionnaires:** sending out a questionnaire to determine the baseline data.
- **Site location:** describing the location of the site and its environmental sensitivity.
- **Process analysis:** doing a simple process analysis to determine an organization's input, outputs and by-products. You can also include LCAs during this stage.
- **Regulatory analysis:** analyzing which laws, regulations and Codes of Practice apply to each process.
- **Performance analysis:** benchmarking your environmental performance for each process.
- **EMS fitness test:** does your organization have an EMS already in place? If not, then see which elements of the EMS exist. Systems for managing quality and health and safety, for example, are good foundations for many parts of an EMS.
- **SWOT analysis:** using the results of the previous stages to determine the strengths, weakness, opportunities and threats.
- **PEST analysis:** an analysis of political, economic, social and technological issues.
- **Recommendations:** setting pointers for the Environmental Policy and the direction of the EMS.
- **Reporting:** the project team then summarizes its findings in a report, and presents these findings to the senior management.

These are covered in more detail as follows:

Questionnaires

In *Appendix 4*, there is an example of a pre-survey questionnaire which AIG consultants send to an organization before doing an environmental audit. Quite often the people who complete these questionnaires leave a great deal of them blank. However, this can be just as valuable as lots of information, because a missing answer can tell you a great deal about potential risks and liabilities. It can also tell you which areas you should focus on when doing the review.

For example, suppose that an organization stores lots of liquid chemicals within unbunded enclosures, and the site is next to a river which connects to an estuarine nature reserve. Then suppose that the questionnaire shows that the organization knows very little about its drainage systems. This is potentially an area with a very high environmental risk.

Locality

The potential for a process to have an environmental impact depends on four things. These are (i) the process, (ii) the extent of that process, (iii) the sensitivity of the receiving environment and (iv) the way in which the process is managed. We explore this idea in more detail in the *source-pathway-sink* concept, which is covered in *Chapter 13, Environmental Aspects and Impacts*.

Of these four factors, environmental sensitivity is the most important. Many people are surprised to discover that a particular process can be totally insignificant or represent an enormous environmental risk depending purely on local sensitivity. So what determines this sensitivity?

Anything in the locality which is affected by your activities is known as a *receptor*. When examining the site, start with a detailed map of the area and look for sensitive receptors such as residences, schools, hospitals, farms, nature reserves and watercourses. Remember that the air and soil are also receptors.

Underground: Out of site, out of mind?

Do not forget that ground underneath the site can also be sensitive. It may contain a groundwater resource, and if the soil between this groundwater and your site is permeable, then this is classed as extremely vulnerable to contamination. So as well as maps of surface features, have a look at maps of the locality's geology and hydrogeology.

Historical liabilities

It is also important to look at a site's history, because it might reveal some environmental liabilities. Has the site been used industrially for a long time? If so, who used it, and for what purposes? Historical maps sometimes reveal old landfills, redundant underground storage tanks and previous activities which could have left a legacy of contaminated land. These are factors which modern maps do not always reveal.

Process analysis

An input-output analysis is a good way to quantify the processes on a site. Figure 11.3 shows a black-box representation of a process. In this, raw materials are the inputs, finished products are the outputs, and the by-products are known as *losses*. These losses are noise, liquid effluents, energy losses, air pollution and solid wastes.

In a coatings process, for example, the inputs could be paints, bicycle frames and solvents. During the process of painting, the solvents evaporate and disappear up a chimney into the air. So the output in this case would be the painted bicycle frames, while the solvents represent the losses. And these organic solvents might then react with sunlight and nitrogen oxides to produce photochemical ozone, which is a destructive gas.

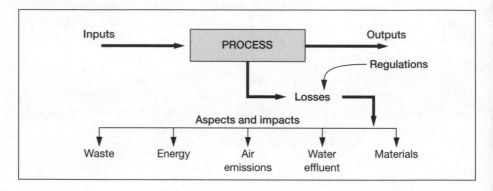

Fig. 11.3 Simple input-output model

Environmental regulators commonly apply laws and limits to these losses, so one approach in the IER is to create a matrix of processes, their effects and the regulations which apply to them. Using the black-box approach in Figure 11.3, take a look at the following issues:

- a map of the site indicating which areas are used for each process
- the site drainage plans – are they up to date?
- energy management and use
- raw material, suppliers' performance and impacts
- regulated processes, such as those controlled by air quality regulations
- transport and distribution
- best environmental option analysis
- waste management, disposal compliance, composting and recycling
- suppliers' performance
- water quality, water use and discharges
- product design and assessments
- packaging materials.

Legislation and regulatory requirements

Using your matrix of processes and activities, draw up a list of the laws, codes of practice, standards and regulations which apply to them. Don't forget to consider future legislation as well as current issues. This could include the forthcoming IPPC Directive. In particular, use the following items as a checklist:

- current legal obligations and consents
- future regulations
- European influences
- product legislation
- communications with regulators
- marketplace legislation
- waste controls.

Environmental performance

The next stage is to assess your environmental performance, and there are three levels to this. First, there is a type of performance based on a so-called *command-and-control* system, such as environmental regulation. Industries, for example, often have emissions limits for air pollution, so in this case, the performance would be based on the extent of compliance. Second, performance can be based on issues which are not directly regulated, or the organization might be well within compliance, but certain processes could have significant environmental impacts. These include energy consumption, resource use and waste minimization.

The third level of performance is based on public perception. There could be aspects of the organization, for example, which neither management nor regulators consider to be even remotely significant, but the public (as receptors to the site) perceive as otherwise. Particular issues to consider are:

- records of monitoring and measuring, e.g., air emissions, effluents
- energy efficiency over several years
- waste production and minimization
- public perceptions
- any prosecutions, Enforcement Notices or cautions
- complaints
- awards for environmental initiatives
- existing EMS programmes, formal or otherwise

- investment plans
- environmental management strategy
- liabilities and assets
- insurance and indemnities.

Elements already in place – the EMS Fitness Test

The consultancy Environmental Resources Management (ERM) has an adept manner of distilling complex issues into tangible packages. One of these is the EMS Fitness Test, whereby ERM's consultants analyze an organization's existing management systems to determine which elements of an EMS are already in place. If any do exist, then to what extent do they comply with the standard? ERM uses the Fitness Test to perform a Gap Analysis, which they then use to focus the development of the EMS.

The BSI uses a similar benchmarking system in its EMS Implementation Course (the source of much of *Chapter 6*), whereby an organization assigns a score for each element which the standard addresses. Such benchmarking systems usually follow the format of the ISO 14001 Standard, and cover the following issues:

- environmental management practices and procedures
- environmental policy
- environmental strategy
- communications
- environmental systems
- environmental responsibilities
- training and skills base
- procurement policy
- project assessments
- environmental records
- environmental audits
- materials and equipment supplies
- environmental reporting
- environmental reviews
- contingency plans
- progress actions plans
- emergency planning and emergency response training
- communication strategy.

The site visit

While a significant amount of the IER will include desktop research and interviews, the most important part of the review is the site survey. Have a look both on the site and outside it, so that you can appreciate the perspective of the receptors. Carry a camera and take plenty of pictures, as these are often extremely effective in the report. The kinds of things you should look out for include:

- evidence of housekeeping standards
- control of storage areas
- enclosures for liquid containers
- areas for managing waste
- emissions points to air
- effluent discharge points
- the locality and the different receptors.

Reporting

Before the data starts to come in, prepare the report structure and format. This will allow you to allocate the data as it comes in into the right sections for summary analysis. A typical report framework includes the following:

- executive summary
- introduction
- site description
- site history
- environmental setting
- process descriptions
- regulatory issues
- environmental effects and issues
- EMS elements
- performance analysis
- focus on significant effects
- recommendations and conclusions.

Gather all the data from the team as it is generated. Check that it makes sense, is factual and accurate. Review any areas of serious concern with the manager of the area to allow him or her the opportunity to start any remedial actions immediately.

When you write the report, there are some good rules of thumb to follow. First, think about the who the readers are, and focus on what they need to know. All the salient points should be in the executive summary and conclusions, as senior management often read only these parts of the reports.

Second, use tables, figures and pictures, as these can depict a lot more than several hundred words.

Third, do not be judgemental. The report should state *facts* which are supportable by evidence. Summarize your conclusions and propose recommendations for action where there is a clear way forward. Wherever possible identify what the problem is, and what should be done to initiate improvement actions. Do not provide a solution, but indicate a direction to be taken for a solution to develop. Identify the ownership of the problem and the resources and timetable for resolution. Suggest relevant standards for achievement or models as examples and any other information that is relevant. If areas need further investigation that will take you outside the scope of the review, identify them and include them in the recommendations for further action.

Discuss the findings with the team to ensure that there is a common understanding of the issues, criteria and priorities, and with the managers and those who participated in the review. Your objective on publication of the report is that there should be no surprises.

The presentation to the executive environmental policy team should be preceded by forwarding a copy of the report for review. This can be followed by individual meetings if the results are likely to be contentious. Formally present the report at the executive management meeting. Use a summary set of OHPs and talk for no more than 15 minutes. The talk should cover:

- what the scope was;
- how it was done;
- thanks for co-operation;
- conclusions in full;
- recommendations and an explanation of the priorities.

Allow time for discussion of the recommendations and ensure that a clear direction is given. There can be several outcomes of the meeting:

- the agreement and acceptance of all the recommendations;
- the agreement and acceptance of most of the recommendations but a modification of the time and resource effort that will be needed to implement the recommendations;
- the non-agreement and rejection of the recommendations, but approval to undertake more review work (this is acceptable, but you should obtain clear terms of reference for the new programme);

- the non-agreement and rejection of the recommendations and a refusal to undertake more review work (project completed – if you have managed to achieve all the project objectives, then well done!)

Follow-up

Assuming you have been successful in achieving agreement on progress so far, you must now implement the follow-up programme. The first steps are to ensure that any areas where urgent action was recommended are acted upon immediately. The second is to publish the report, or a summary of it, as part of the awareness communication programme. This provides a powerful launch to the initiative, and the facts and figures usually make fascinating reading. Then invite the owners of the actions that have been approved to a meeting to kick off the second phase of the implementation plan. This meeting will result in the establishment of policy, the setting up of a management organization, the definition of roles and responsibilities and so forth.

Checklist

? *Have you a clear scope for the review, and is it appropriate for your objectives?*

? *Has the team participated fully in the programme design?*

? *Have you addressed the key issues?*

- ◆ *Corporate and business issues:* policy; practices; procedures; training; environmental auditing; environmental labelling; employees; banks; insurance; shareholders; transport; regulations; stakeholders; local community.

- ◆ *Operational issues:* health and safety; acoustics; COSHH; accidents; incidents; emergency plans; quality management;

- ◆ *Environmental issues:* air (CO_2; global warming; pollutants; CFCs; Halon; acid rain); water (supply quantity; supply quality; effluent discharges; conservation); waste (reduction; reuse; recycling; packaging; paper; minimization); energy (power; lighting; fuels; efficiency); nature (resources use; raw materials; habitats; site management).

? *Does the SWOT analysis address all the management issues?*

? *Does the report identify highlights as well as problems and deficiencies?*

? *Does the report identify the resources and outline programme for implementation?*

Communication hints

◆ Try to be as open and informative as possible on the exercise. You will want to share this information with the staff in the organization when you introduce the awareness issue so try to let them know what's coming and when.

◆ Be specific about the source of the requirement, e.g., EPA 1990 Schedule 1 and Schedule 2.

◆ Remember to build on existing practice, e.g., COSHH. You are not trying to re-invent the wheel.

◆ Use a variety of information-gathering techniques. There are all types and styles of user out there. Some prefer the interview, others the questionnaire. Asking the question in a range of ways improves your response.

◆ Provide an executive summary in the report for those who are too busy to read the whole report. The summary should include: a policy development plan; an immediate action plan; and the EMS project management plan.

◆ Use lots of graphics in the report. Nothing can be as vivid as a series of charts, photographs and maps in demonstrating the environmental setting.

◆ Don't make the IER report too long – anything between 20 and 40 pages is the norm. Anything longer, and it is either too wordy, or you are going into too much detail and covering issues that should be covered when producing the registers of environmental aspects and impacts.

CASE STUDIES

The Rubicon and DuPont

When consultant Tony Lambert of The Rubicon carried out an IER for Du Pont's Kevlar® plant in Maydown, Northern Ireland, he used the requirements of the EMAS Regulation when defining the scope of the Initial Environmental Review. There were two reasons for this. First, they produced a suitably wide framework which would meet the requirements of both ISO 14001 and EMAS, and second, Du Pont is considering registration to EMAS as well as its existing ISO 14001 certification.

This meant that if Du Pont decided to opt for EMAS registration, then the IER would be in the correct format for the assessment, as the IER is an assessable component of EMAS. The report also cross-references another report on the geology and hydrogeology of the site, which was the result of an investigation by consultant Dames and Moore. The consideration of geological issues does not have to be directly included in the report, although it was considered relevant here and enhanced the quality of the report. The scope of the IER in the EMAS Regulations is outlined in *Chapter 4*.

Elmwood College

Early in 1994, the Head of Agriculture produced a Preliminary Environmental Review according to the requirements of BS 7750. This took the form of a comprehensive listing of all processes which either affected or could affect the environment, and all the legislation, regulations and codes of practice which affected the college. The college did not prioritize particular processes for immediate action, but with hindsight, the college felt that a more thorough review would have saved time later on.

The review highlighted energy use, transport, agricultural and horticultural processes, engineering processes, and waste management. Most importantly, the college realized that the single most important area was the influence which the college exerted on the environment through the attitude of its students. The management realized that if they could produce graduates who were more environmentally aware, then the college's environmental benefits could spread well beyond the front gates of the actual establishment. So the college gave a priority status to this area, which was reflected in subsequent developments of the system.

AIG Consultants – use of the pre-survey questionnaire

Appendix 4 shows an example of a pre-survey questionnaire which consultants AIG developed for environmental audits, such as pre-acquisition audits, due-diligence and Initial Environmental Reviews. AIG's team of consultants has found the course extremely effective, with just one *caveat*. 'You have to send out the questionnaires in plenty of time for the auditees to fill them in', says Jonathan Mills of AIG, 'or you won't get much of a response. Ideally you should allow at least 10 days to get a decent response – anything less, and the people you are auditing will not have really enough time to find out all the information they need.'

GUIDING SUMMARY

'Start with the end in mind' – this concept is a useful aid if you are in any doubt about your IER programme. If, for example, you are aimed at conformity with ISO 14001, EMAS or Responsible Care, *work back* from the compliance you desire.

12

THE ENVIRONMENTAL POLICY

(4.2)

Objective

The goal is an established environmental policy for the organization.

ISO 14001 REQUIREMENTS

Your organization's top management must define your environmental policy, and it must include all of the following:

- Be appropriate to the nature, scale and environmental impacts of its activities, products or services.
- Commit to continual improvement.
- Commit to prevention of pollution.
- Commit to comply with relevant environmental legislation and regulations, and with other requirements to which the organization subscribes.
- Provide the framework for setting and reviewing environmental objectives and targets.
- Documented, implemented and maintained and communicated to all employees.
- Available to the public.

SO WHAT EXACTLY IS A POLICY?

The policy is a succinct and open demonstration of public commitment. The policy is not just in place as a public relations exercise; it serves as a basis for developing more specific environmental objectives and targets throughout the different levels of the organization: sites, functions, departments and individual job descriptions. The policy statement has to meet the defined criteria to satisfy the requirements of ISO 14001.

Because the application of the policy will result in changes in the way the organization is managed, from the investment and strategic plans to the day-to-day operations, your organization's top management must own and lead the policy.

PREPARING A DRAFT ENVIRONMENTAL POLICY STATEMENT

Building on the process for obtaining commitment discussed in *Chapter 9*, we now follow the plan agreed in *Chapter 10*. With the project team, review and agree the policy areas that were identified as a result of the IER, and prepare a draft environmental statement for the organization.

Ask each member of the project team to review and obtain comments and approval from their managers. It is a line management issue and line management must have the opportunity to review and approve. After all, you want them to own the solutions they put in place, so it is important they are motivated to own those solutions by owning the problem statement.

Consolidate the feedback you get from the project team. You may be asked to make some changes. Consider them on their merits and discuss them if you are not clear about the concerns. Accept, modify or reject the proposed changes, but acknowledge and inform the commentators what you have done. With that agreement you are now in a position to go to the executive team.

GETTING SENIOR MANAGEMENT TO APPROVE THE POLICY

You will need a 'slot' on the next executive meeting agenda. This will be in the plan so should be no surprise to anyone. Send the project-team approved draft to the executive team members ahead of the meeting. Your presentation then can be crisp and precise. It should:

- position the policy in the overall programme;
- state the requirements that the policy must meet;
- check they have read it;
- present the policy, and expand and explain with examples the possible implications at each level;
- explain how they can measure attainment of the policy.

You must also listen to the responses and document any changes or qualifications. You can use a flip chart to write up any changes in wording to get it agreed at that time. Remember that the policy is the key to the whole system, so although it will be subject to change and fine-tuning, it has to be as 'right' as it can be. When you have consensus, stop. Review both the internal and external communication plans in the light of the current consensus.

Immediately after the meeting, i.e., within 24 hours, send the agreed final wording to the executive for confirmation so that there are no errors or omissions. Confirm you are implementing the agreed communication plan.

Designing the environmental-awareness presentation

The results of the work done to date will provide the material for the awareness-presentation, the purpose of which is to raise the level of understanding in the organization of the activities due to take place.

You should design the presentations as something which can be used as a self-contained package by yourself, members of the project team, departmental environmental co-ordinators or line managers themselves, depending on the type of organization and skills available.

The presentation should be short, taking up to 40 minutes, and be used within a management meeting agenda. It will introduce the audience to the environmental influences and potential pressures on the organization that will result in some form of follow-up action by management to implement change.

The presentation will cover the following:

- **the environmental issue generally:** legislation press reports, other companies' actions;
- **the pressures relevant to the company or business:** industry specific issues, future legislation;
- **the company response:** the project outline, scope, resources and timetable, objectives and measurement;
- **the initial environmental review results:** strengths, weaknesses, opportunities and threats;

- the organization's environmental policy;
- the next steps in the programme.

In identifying the roles and responsibilities of various team members, highlight the need for a nominated environmental co-ordinator at departmental level. Allow the audience to consider how such a role might be filled and who might be most appropriate.

The presentation should conclude with some time for questions and answers, keeping notes of any issues raised that may need resolution after the conclusion of the presentation.

Checklist

? *Does your environmental policy statement meet the criteria?*

? *Is it appropriate?* The policy must relate to the activities of the organization, the things produced and the effects identified in the IER. Check back to the review conclusions.

? *Does everyone understand it?* Check that all the managers are familiar with the policy throughout the organization. Have the team members documented the policy, and then distributed it to all employees?

? *Can it be effective?* Check that the organization can meet the commitments in the policy. Can it be turned into actions and measured? Can the policy (when coupled with the results of the IER and research into environmental aspects) serve as a framework for the objectives and targets?

? *Is it public?* Check that the procedure to publish the policy is effective.

? *Does it commit the organization to continual improvement and prevention of pollution?* Check that the improvement element is understood and is accepted.

? *Is it consistent?* Check that there is no conflict with other policies, such as those on health and safety or quality.

? *Does it cover the key environmental impacts?* The policy must be comprehensive. Make sure it includes all the environmental impacts of your company, e.g., energy use, waste minimization, resource use; pollution risks from plant and processes; upstream and downstream activities; projects and strategic plans.

? *Is there a commitment to comply with legislation and regulations?* Check that the policy includes a commitment to comply with all relevant legislation, Codes of Practice and industry regulations.

COMMUNICATING THE ENVIRONMENTAL POLICY STATEMENT TO THE WORKFORCE

Tell the managers first. Check that they have all they need to advise staff of the new policy. Give them some time to go back to their task force representative and agree any clarifications before releasing the policy more widely. Then tell everyone clearly and precisely. It is awareness and not action you are looking for, so keep it simple, and place it in the context of the overall EMS programme.

Use different media – newsletters, posters, internal mail. Remember that an audience receives information in many different ways so use them all. Measure the impact by a follow-up survey to ensure that the message has been received.

Communication hints

The policy should not be a bland statement, e.g., 'To be environmentally friendly …' It need not be a performance pledge, e.g., 'To reduce VOC emissions by 50% in the next 12 months', or 'Get energy consumption per unit of production down by 10% per year for the next three years.' It should be a broad statement of the intentions of the organization in the area of environmental performance that can be used by all departments to develop their own targets in relation to the policy. The policy should also provide the guiding principles on which the organization can build its EMS, as well as being a public statement of its commitment and values.

You should consider carefully how you will make the policy available to the public. Many organizations have a wide spectrum of stakeholders, and each different sector might need a specific response.

CASE STUDIES

British Telecom

BT is a large organization, divided into several business units. This means that each unit has its own specific objectives and targets – as well as policy issues – but the company has an overall, all-embracing environmental policy for the entire organization. As well as distributing this policy to its staff, and situating the policy in common work areas, BT prints the current policy in its annual environmental report, and places it on the Internet via its own web site. The contents of the policy are as follows:

BT's environmental policy

BT is committed to minimizing the impact of its operations on the environment by means of a programme of continuous improvement. In particular BT will:

- meet and, where appropriate, exceed the requirements of all relevant legislation – where no regulations exist, we shall set our own exacting standards;

- seek to reduce consumption of materials in all operations, re-use rather than dispose whenever possible, and promote recycling and the use of recycled materials;

- design energy efficiency into new services, buildings and products and manage energy wisely in all operations;

- reduce wherever practicable the level of harmful emissions;

- market products that are safe to use, make efficient use of resources, and which can be re-used, recycled or disposed of safely;

- work with our suppliers to minimize the impact of their operations on the environment through a quality purchasing policy;

- site our buildings, structures and operational plant so that we minimize visual, noise and other impacts on the local environment;

- support through our community programme the promotion of environmental protection by relevant external groups and organizations;

- include environmental issues in discussions with the BT unions, the BT training programmes and encourage the implementation by all BT people of sound environmental practices;

- monitor progress and publish an environmental performance report on an annual basis.

BT's environmental policy can be obtained from BT's Environmental Issues Unit, or from their Internet site at: http://www.bt.com/corpinfo/enviro

Source: Janet Quigley, BT Environmental Issues Manager and Steven Mehew, BT, Supply Management, Environment Business Manager.

UK Waste Management

UK Waste's environmental policy is detailed and wide-ranging and, as well as committing them to comply with legal requirements, it takes a proactive, forward-looking approach. Their service takes account not only of all current relevant health and safety and environmental legislation, but also of future Acts. The company's environmental policy is reproduced in full on the next three pages.

The company offers a full waste-management service, rather than the traditional route of waste disposal; as well as landfill sites, they offer alternative routes of waste disposal such as composting, recycling and the conversion of non-recyclable paper, board, packaging material and other fibrous wastes into their Fibre Fuel cubes. Fibre Fuel is suitable for combined heat and power use. It reduces the amount of waste sent to landfill, and burns with lower chlorine and sulphur emissions than coal. This action means that the company complies with clauses 2 and 9 of their environmental policy.

▶

UK Waste Management Environment Policy

The Company is committed to the environmental policy of Waste Management International Plc as presented below.

Waste Management International Plc, as a member of the WMX Technologies Inc. family of companies is committed to protecting and enhancing the environment and to updating its practices in the light of advances in technology and new understandings in health and environmental science.

Prevention of pollution and enhancement of the environment are the fundamental premises of the Company's business. We believe that all corporations have a responsibility to conduct their business as responsible stewards of the environment and to seek profits only though activities that leave the Earth healthy and safe. We believe that the Company has a responsibility not to compromise the ability of future generations to sustain their needs.

The principles of this policy are applicable to the Company throughout the world. The Company will take demonstrable actions on a continuing basis in furtherance of the principles.

Principles

1 Environmental protection and enhancement

The Company is committed to improving the environment through the services that we offer and to providing our services in a manner demonstrably protective of human health and the environment, even if not required by law. We will minimize and strive not to allow any releases to the atmosphere, land or water in amounts that may harm human health and the environment. We will train employees to enhance understanding of environmental policies and to promote excellence in job performance on all environmental matters.

2 Waste reduction, recycling, treatment and disposal

The Company will work to minimize the volume and toxicity of waste generated by us and others. We will operate internal recycling programs. We will vigorously pursue opportunities to recycle waste before other management practices are applied. The Company will use and provide environmentally safe treatment and disposal services for waste that is not eliminated at the source or recycled.

3 Biodiversity

The Company is committed to the conservation of nature. We will implement a policy of "no net loss" of wetlands or other biological diversity on the Company's property.

4 Sustainable use of natural resources

The Company will use renewable natural resources, such as water, soils and forests, in a sustainable manner and will offer services to make degraded resources once again useable. We will conserve non-renewable natural resources through efficient use and careful planning.

5 Wise use of energy

The Company will make every reasonable effort to use environmentally safe and sustainable energy sources to meet our needs. We will seek opportunities to improve energy efficiency and conservation in our operations.

6 Compliance

The Company is committed to comply with all legal requirements and to implement programs and procedures to ensure compliance. These efforts will include training and testing of employees, rewarding employees who excel in compliance, and disciplining employees who violate legal requirements.

7 Risk reduction

The Company will operate in a matter designed to minimize environmental health or safety hazards. We will minimize risk and protect our employees and other in the vicinity of our operations by employing safe technologies and operating procedures and by being prepared for emergencies. The Company will make available to our employees and to the public information related to any of our operations that we believe cause environmental harm or pose health or safety hazards. The Company will encourage employees to report any condition that creates a danger to the environment or poses health or safety hazards, and will provide confidential means for them to do so.

8 Damage compensation

The Company will take responsibility for any harm we cause to the environment and will make every reasonable effort to remedy the damage caused to people or ecosystems.

9 Research and development

The Company will research, develop and implement technologies for integrated waste management.

10 Public policy and public education

The Company will provide information to and will assist the public in understanding the environmental impacts of our activities. We will conduct public tours of facilities, consistent with safety requirements, and will work with communities near our facilities to encourage dialogue and exchange of information on facility activities.
11   The Company will support and participate in development of public policy and in educational initiatives that will protect human health and improve the environment. We will seek cooperation on this work with government, environmental groups, schools, universities, and other public organizations.

12 Participation in environmental organizations

The Company will encourage its employees to participate in and to support the work of environmental organizations, and we will provide support to environmental organizations for the advancement of environmental protection.

13 Environmental policy assessment

The Board of Directors of the Company will evaluate and address the environmental implications of its decisions. The Chief Executive will appoint a member of the Executive Environmental Committee of the WMX Technologies, Inc. family of companies, which will, in turn, report directly to the Chief Executive Officer of WMX Technologies, Inc. and will monitor and report upon implementation of this policy and other environmental matters. The Company will commit the resources needed to implement these principles.

14 Annual Environmental Report

As a member of the WMX Technologies, Inc. family of companies, the Company will participate in preparation and publication of an annual report on the environmental activities of the Company and the group. The report will include a self-evaluation of the implementation of these principles by the group, including an assessment of their performance in complying with all applicable environmental laws and regulations throughout their worldwide operations.

UK Waste is committed to the continual improvement of environmental performance.

Environmental objectives will be established relevant to this policy which will be available from the Company's Quality Manager or the Location Manager.

Signed by the Managing Director, 1st December 1996, Issue No. 2

▶ The detail in the environmental policy translates into concrete action. UK Waste Management's landfill sites are planned and engineered to reduce their environmental effects. Waste is compacted during the process of landfillling. Leachate and landfill gas are contained, monitored, collected and treated. Where possible, energy is recovered from landfill gas. After use, landfilled areas are capped with impermeable material, restored and replanted for uses such as farmland, woodland, wetland or recreational facilities. UK Waste continue to monitor sites after they have been filled and restored.

Clauses 10, 11 and 12 of their environmental policy address public policy and education, and the Company's work with environmental groups. They allow tours of sites, and form community liaison groups to address public concerns over landfill sites. They work with organizations like the Groundwork Trust, Waste Watch and Landwise in Scotland. In conjunction with Norfolk County Council they have produced educational material to teach pupils about the value of waste minimization and recycling.

Clause 12 of the company's policy states that it will participate and support environmental organizations for the advancement of environmental protection; in the 1996/7 Landfill Tax year, UK Waste Management Ltd donated over £3 million to environmental bodies for a range of educational, research and environmental improvement projects.

PART

13

ENVIRONMENTAL ASPECTS
AND IMPACTS
(4.3.1)

Objective

The goal is to determine the environmental aspects of an organization's activities, processes and products, and then assess which of these have significant impacts. You do this by developing procedures for documenting and analyzing these aspects, and then communicating these to all relevant, interested parties.

ISO 14001 REQUIREMENTS

You have to establish and maintain procedures in order to identify the environmental aspects of your activities, products or services which have (or can have) significant impacts on the environment. These activities, products or services are those over which you can reasonably be expected to influence or control. You must create a summary register of these aspects and their impacts, and keep this up to date.

You must also consider the aspects with the most significant impacts when setting immediate objectives and targets.

ENVIRONMENTAL ASPECTS, IMPACTS AND SIGNIFICANCE

Aspects and Impacts

ISO 14001 uses the terms *aspects* and *impacts*. So what are these?

- **Environmental aspect:** This is an element of an organization's activities, products or services that can interact with the environment.

- **Environmental impact:** This is any change to the environment, whether adverse or beneficial, wholly or partly resulting from an organization's activities, products or services.

This approach is flexible, as the terms *aspect* and *impact* cover the positive as well as the negative facets of an organization's environmental performance. Recognizing the positive aspects can be just as beneficial to improving environmental performance as correcting the negative aspects. Companies must document and communicate their effects on the environment, both positive and negative, direct and indirect, not only to be able to set environmental targets and objectives, but also to demonstrate to independent assessors that the organization is meeting the requirements of ISO 14001.

Streamlined approach

EMAS requires a comprehensive evaluation of environmental effects. ISO 14001 adopts a different approach in this area, and also a correspondingly different terminology. It requires the organization to 'establish and maintain a procedure to identify the environmental aspects of its activities, products or services that it can control and over which it can be expected to have an influence' [*i.e., this includes a test of reasonableness*] 'in order to determine those which have or can have significant impacts on the environment'. In effect this approach avoids the need to evaluate environmental effects over which the company has no control or influence.

THE EVALUATION OF ENVIRONMENTAL ASPECTS AND IMPACTS

The role of the environmental aspects evaluation is to ensure that the organization assesses its activities, products and processes so that the EMS is targeted on appropriate standards of performance. An organization has to know what impacts it is having on the environment, determine how significant these are, and then use this analysis to develop its objectives and targets. So in addition to ana-

Table 13.1 Examples of environmental aspects and impacts

Aspect	Local impact	Global impact
Carbon dioxide emissions	—	Global warming
Sulphur dioxide emissions	Acidic deposition to plants, people and objects	Acidification; long-distance transport and forest decline
Oxides of nitrogen emissions	Ground level ozone formation, acidification	Global warming
Volatile Organic Compounds (VOCs) emissions	Ground level ozone formation, toxicity	Some deplete the stratospheric ozone layer, ozone and add to global warming
CFCs and halons	Some are toxic	Deplete the stratospheric ozone layer
Smoke from uncontrolled fire	Visibility; toxicity	Visibility
Discharge of trade effluent into storm sewers	Pollution of rivers via treatment works	Sea pollution
Discharge of trade effluent into sewers	Harmful to health of sewer workers Damage to sewerage system Water pollution on final disposal	Sea pollution Air pollution due to incineration of sewage sludge.
Domestic discharges into sewers	Harmful to health of sewer workers Water pollution on final disposal	Sea pollution Air pollution due to incineration of sewage sludge
Accidental chemical spills or leaks from tanks into storm sewers	Pollution of watercourses	Sea pollution
Water from fire fighting	Pollution of watercourses and sewers	Sea pollution
Storage of waste	Visual impact, odour, degradation of local environment if waste escapes	—
Transport of waste	Local effects of vehicle emissions, degradation of local environment if waste escapes, noise and other disturbance from increase in road use.	Global effects of vehicle emissions
Disposal of waste: landfill	Visual disturbance, odour, noise from site traffic, groundwater pollution, methane production leads to increased fire risk	Methane production adds to global warming.
Land contamination	Damage to animals and plants on site. Water pollution if contaminants reach rivers or groundwater.	—
Noise and vibration	Disturbance to local residents	—
Use of pesticides	Harmful to human, animal and plant health	—
Company vehicles	Air pollution, use of roads contributing to building of new roads (visual impact, noise, damage to habitats)	Air pollution, global warming, depletion of resources
Site development	Damage to ecosystems on site, visual impact	—

lyzing each impact, the organization needs to rank these in some order of significance. A good rule of thumb is that the top 20% of significant aspects will have 80% of the impacts, so an organization will deal with these first and give them most attention. By analogy, scientists in the USA and UK have found that about 50% of traffic pollution from cars is caused by just 10% of the vehicles, so any control strategy would target these first. Table 13.1 shows some examples of aspects and impacts.

The impacts analysis, therefore, is at the heart of the management system. The policy may set the scope and vision of the company's environmental goals; the management organization may identify roles; the objectives, programme, manuals and controls will implement the EMS; audit and review assess performance: but the impacts analysis takes you into new areas. It establishes where the effort should be spent to improve environmental performance and, for some, establishes in detail your environmental performance.

You will need to establish criteria for identifying what is environmentally significant in your business or industry. The results must then be documented in a logical way – such as a matrix – which the organization then uses to measure environmental performance. Remember that the objective of this process is to identify and target every impact from the most significant to the least. Such data then gives you the information to target which ones to control, and in which order. A matrix is a good way of documenting these aspects and impacts, because it provides not only a logical summary, but also the objective evidence you need for certification.

The procedures for environmental evaluations

These procedures can bring together all the information on the environmental evaluation of the organization's activities in a comprehensive reference document. This may be a part of the environmental management manual in a small organization. In a larger organization with a significant amount of data or environmental effects evaluation, it may be a separate document or documents; if so, then the environmental management manual must indicate where these are, and the means by which the data are controlled and kept up to date. Such procedures for identifying effects must include the following conditions:

- normal
- abnormal
- shut-down, start-up
- incidents, accidents and emergencies
- current, future and past activities

The matrix or register should include the following factors with regard to the environmental effects evaluation documentation:

- why the product or activity is deemed significant for evaluation of the environmental impacts;
- who is responsible for the evaluation procedure;
- what is the scope of the evaluation;
- how the evaluation was carried out, and a summary of the results;
- where the procedure and records are available;
- when the evaluation was carried out, and is due to be reviewed.

Environmental aspects and impacts evaluation procedures

The IER (*see Chapter 11*) provided basic information on the activities of the organization, established potential environmental impacts in a qualitative manner, and then recommended areas of further analysis. Now you need to integrate analysis of environmental aspects and impacts in much more detail and quantitatively into the day-to-day business procedures at two levels:

- **At a general level,** the sweep assesses, the current status of environmental performance. This needs to be broad and look beyond the current environmental programmes and pressures to assess new issues, new directions in legislation, and potential pressures from stakeholders, the local community, and market forces. The management review process (*see Chapter 27*) addresses this requirement.
- **At the specific level,** environmental impacts evaluation procedures vary according to the issues and activities under examination. For example:
  - **Products:** life cycle assessment
  - **Projects:** environmental impact assessments
  - **Sites:** site environmental audit
  - **Processes:** process assessment techniques (PAT)
  - **Systems:** system evaluation techniques
  - **Acquisition:** due diligence audits
  - **Waste:** waste stream assessments
  - **Risk:** risk assessment procedures.

All of the procedures for assessing environmental impacts described below can be called an environmental audit. The key factor that differentiates the type of audits is the scope of the activity. An environmental impact assessment or audit is just another form of project, so the scope and terms of reference are essential. Set the scope, schedule and resources, action, reporting and follow-up for each assessment procedure at the **outset**.

Product analysis

The most commonly used form of environmental audit for product assessment is the life-cycle analysis or cradle-to-grave assessment. This is well established with several national product labelling schemes in Canada (Environmental Choice), Germany (Blue Angel), Japan (Eco-mark), Scandinavia (White Swan), and now the EC Eco-Label scheme of which the UK is a participant. Companies can only display eco-labels if products reach certain environmental standards.

Scope: The scope of an assessment must define clearly the product type and range, the key environmental criteria to be considered, and the product's fitness for purpose. For example, a washing machine may be very efficient in water, energy and chemical use. It is also required to wash clothes to certain standards.

The criteria should include comparison with global issues, including the methodology to be used to select criteria of significance.

Schedule and resources: The plan to assess the product should follow a pre-determined programme designed to test the product against the criteria defined in the scope. Adequate resources, from appropriately independent sources must be made available, e.g., by using an independent testing laboratory such as BSI Product Testing or the Consumers' Association.

Each step in the life cycle may require a different assessment approach. For example, raw materials sourcing may require research, whereas the finished product performance can be physically tested.

Action: Assess product performance in all the life cycle areas:

- *raw materials*: where do materials come from, what are the potential impacts, or is there any choice?

- *pre-production processes*: what are the significant impacts? Where does it start and stop? How much influence does your organization have?

- *production processes*: distribution; what are the significant impacts? What can be done to improve? Reduce energy use, pollution, waste, transport? Are we using the best available techniques, not exceeding excessive cost? Are we using the economically viable application of best available techniques (EVABAT) option? Can I reduce my costs impacts?

- *utilization*: and what are the impacts in use? How does it compare with others?

- *disposal*: what are the impacts? Can I reuse or recycle?

As an example, Figure 13.1 shows an EC eco-audit matrix.

Reporting: Focuses on the performance of the product against the pre-set criteria, in the case of eco-labelling schemes. These criteria are usually set for particular issues that are shown to be significant for particular product groups.

Follow-up: Results from the product analysis are fed into the product devel-

Indicative assessment matrix

Product life cycle	Pre-production	Production	Distribution (including packaging)	Utilisation	Disposal
Environmental fields					
Waste relevance					
Soil pollution and degradation					
Water contamination					
Air contamination					
Noise					
Consumption of energy					
Consumption of natural resources					
Impacts on eco-systems					

Fig. 13.1 An EC eco-audit matrix

opment activities to ensure that the environmental performance criteria for the product are incorporated into the design process.

Projects analysis or Environmental Assessments

The prime UK legislative driver for assessing the potential environmental impacts of projects is the EC Directive (85/337/EEC) adopted in 1985, implemented in the Town and Country Planning Act (Assessment of Environmental Effects) Regulations 1988 – Statutory Instrument 1199/88. The result of the assessment is an *Environmental Statement*, while the process of evaluation is called an *Environmental Assessment* (EA). These are specific terms. In an international context, an EA is a form of environmental impact assessment (EIA), which looks at the project's potential impacts on the air, water, land, and society. In other words, the scope is very broad.

Many organizations use this type of assessment procedure to analyze the environmental impacts of site developments, planning applications or project reviews.

Scope: This is determined to establish the extent to which the environmental statement will address the existing environment and the effects of the proposed project. The effectiveness of the completed process in identifying relevant issues is determined at this stage.

Schedule and resources: This will involve detailed discussions with the relevant planning authority, where appropriate. If an internal company process, the plan will help define the issues to be examined and reported (as well as make it clear those areas that will not).

Action: This includes descriptions of the project or proposed activity and the existing environmental situation before the project or proposed change is implemented, an analysis of the effect of the project or change on the existing environment, and an analysis of the possible mitigating measures to reduce the anticipated environmental effect or to enhance any beneficial environment effects.

Reporting: The *Environmental Statement* includes all the information indicated in the action phase, as well as a shorter, *non-technical* summary explaining in simple terms the project intent, the environmental impact and recommended mitigating measures.

Follow-up: Includes the introduction of those mitigating factors, agreed at the report stage, into the project proposals and actions. Monitoring will be needed to ensure that the planned impact levels are accurate, and some form of corrective action may also be needed if the project impact is to be constrained within the predicted targets.

Site assessment

Refer to *Chapter 11, Initial Environmental Review*, for guidance on this process.

Process analysis

This is a systems approach to determining environmental impacts. In simple terms, it uses one holistic model to determine the inputs and outputs of the organization, and then uses another simple model known as the *source-pathway-sink* concept to determine the fate of any outputs. For example, a source could be a chimney emitting nitrogen oxides, the pathway could be the air in which it disperses, and the sink is the environmental receptor which reacts with the dispersed emissions.

Input-output models can include formal process analysis using flow chart methods, through to empirical methods devised to suit the business needs of individual organizations. Any business process from a production activity to an administration activity can be analyzed by understanding the various process steps as activities that have an input, added value and an output.

Scope: This defines the extent of the process being assessed: how far upstream and downstream you plan to go. Map out the process in diagrammatic form using a 'tree' diagram or similar technique.

Schedule and resources: Plan the necessary effort and skill mix to look at all the aspects of the process. Establish the assessment criteria to look at the process against a matrix that relates the activities to global issues. This will allow you to assess the specific environmental loads and possible directions for improvement.

The pro-forma matrix requires consideration of the primary effects of an activity. Does it use energy? Has it got problems of greenhouse gas production or resource use of fossil fuels? Does it use lots of water or chemicals which can deplete resources or risk pollution incidents?

Action: Using the assessment criteria, measure the actual performance. It will involve looking at the steps in the process and seeing the actual impacts on the various media (air, water and land), looking at the use of resources, wastes and energy, and the impacts on special habitats. Record the findings and assess possible actions to improve performance. Use the ratings as a tool to decide which are the more significant.

Reporting: The report to management will provide the data to be built into the EMS skeleton on impacts, measurements and activities to form the action plan.

The summary of the truck wash assessment might result in a report that recommended action in the areas of chemicals management; water recycling and re-use; reduction of energy use from the steam cleaner and improved control of spills in the wash area and 'carry-off' by trucks out of the area.

Follow-up: May include actions to set targets and management responsibilities for water and energy savings, or to establish better control over chemicals use and wastes. The objectives are integrated into those of the line managers and staff as well as into any cross-functional service agreements, like the site services personnel. Key points are held over for the next system audit and review.

DEFINING SIGNIFICANCE

There are a number of ways of classifying significance. For example:

- the process is regulated by legislation
- the process consumes resources which are finite
- the process is not sustainable in the long term
- the process has measurable, negative and unsustainable impacts on the environment
- Codes of Practice exist for the process
- there is scientific evidence indicating risks
- there has been a history of complaints regarding the process.

It is important to note that some assessments which quantify significance will be somewhat subjective. However, many organizations have successfully applied risk analysis to quantifying the significance of environmental impacts. One common approach, for example, is to use a Failure Modes Effects Analysis (FMEA). Risks, in this instance, are defined as factors related to:

- the chance of an environmental incident occurring

    added to
- the chance of detecting the problem in time to prevent it

    multiplied by
- the severity of the environmental consequences.

The formula looks like this:

RISK = (CHANCES OF OCCURRENCE) + (CHANCES OF
DETECTION) × (SEVERITY OF CONSEQUENCE)

This approach assigns a score between zero and 100, and the higher the score, the more significant the effect. As a general rule, anything over 50 merits attention, and the scaling allows an organization to prioritize the management programme. Table 13.2 shows the factors used to assign the risk factors.

Table 13.2 Risk factors

Chances of occurrence		Chances of detection		Severity of consequence	
Criteria	Rank	Criteria	Rank	Criteria	Rank
Very high	5	Certain	0	None	0
High	4	Very high	1	Minor	2
Moderate	3	High	2	Low	4
Low	2	Moderate	3	Moderate	6
Very low	1	Low	4	High	8
None	0	Very low	5	Very high	10

Example 1 – an underground aviation fuel tank

In this first example, there is an underground, aviation-fuel storage tank (Figure 13.2) which has the following features:

- it is very old and past its design life
- it has no detection system for leaks
- it is in a soil which is highly corrosive
- the tank is above a water table, separated by permeable soil.

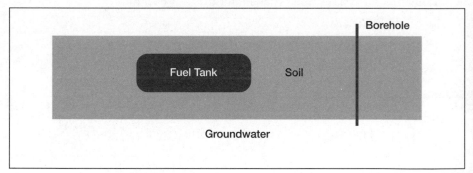

Fig. 13.2 Underground storage tank

When doing the risk assessment, look at the following:

- the environmental setting
- the chances of *occurrence (leaks), detection, and severity of consequence.*

Then provide a score for each criterion.

See tables 13.3, 13.4 and 13.5 for the likelihood of occurrence, chances of detection, and severity of consequences respectively.

130

Table 13.3 Likelihood of occurence

How old is the tank	20 years
Does the tank have two shells?	no
Is the tank provided with a corrosion inhibitor?	no
Do the owners intend to replace it with an above-ground storage tank	no
Is the soil corrosive?	yes
Your score:	

Table 13.4 Chances of detection

Are leak detection systems used?	no
Is a strict material inventory maintained?	no
Any unaccounted losses of aviation fuel?	not known
Any formalized maintenance programme for underground storage?	no
Your score:	

Table 13.5 Severity of consequence

Is the fuel a potentially damaging material?	yes
Is there a local aquifer for industrial/domestic use?	yes
Would the spill be contained by natural geological conditions?	no
Would a leak result in prosecution?	yes
Would a clean-up be expensive?	yes
Your score:	

Summary – Example 1

Likelihood of occurrence

The tank is very old, has no secondary containment, it is past its design life and it is in a corrosive soil. So there is a very high chance of tank failure.
RANK 5   (Very high)

Chances of detection

In table 13.4, there is no detection system, nor any formal material inventories to account for losses.
RANK 5   (Very low)

Consequences

The consequences would be severe.
RANK 10 (Very high)

Score

The final score would be $(5 + 5) \times 10 = 100$.

Example 2 – above-ground fuel tank

Now suppose that the owners of the tank build a new, above-ground storage tank. This tank contains the same fuel, but in a different situation (Figure 13.3). It has the following features:

- it is an above-ground storage tank
- it is above the same, sensitive environment
- the tank has two shells, bunding and a detection system.

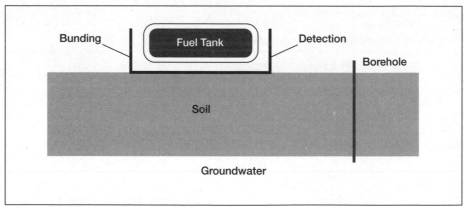

Fig. 13.3 Above-ground storage tank

See tables 13.6, 13.7 and 13.8 for likelihood of occurrence, chances of detection, and severity of consequences respectively.

Table 13.6 Likelihood of occurence

Is there secondary and tertiary containment?	yes
Does the organization operate a spill prevention and control policy?	yes
Have any serious spillages been reported?	no
Are containment walls regularly checked for integrity?	yes
Does the containment provide at least 110% capacity for materials stored?	yes
Are spill containment gullies present?	yes
Your score:	

Table 13.7 Chances of detection

Are the storage vessels inspected daily?	yes
Is there a detection system?	yes
Your score:	

Table 13.8 Severity of consequence

Are the materials considered as potential high pollutants?	yes
Would regulators prosecute?	yes
Would a clean-up be expensive?	yes
Is the river of high amenity value?	yes
Is the type of incident liable to generate poor publicity?	yes
Your score:	

Summary – Example 2

Likelihood of occurrence

The chance of spillages or escape of material is low, based principally on containment procedures.
RANK 1 (Very low)

Chances of detection

The facility is inspected frequently, there is also a detection monitor, and the

operator would quickly detect any spills.
RANK 1 (Very High)

Consequences

The aquifer is environmentally sensitive and the consequences of a spill would be dire.
RANK 10 (Very high)

Score

The tank has a score of $(1 + 1) \times 10 = 20$
The above-ground fuel storage tank presents a significantly lower risk than its below-ground counterpart. However, the weighting of 20 may be considered significant as the severity of consequences would be high, so it is essential for the owners of the tank to minimize the risks of any spillages and escapes of fuel.

ENVIRONMENTAL PERFORMANCE INDICATORS

In 1997, the BSI released a new guidance note in the ISO 14000 series, known as ISO 14031, Guidelines on Environmental Performance Evaluation (EPE). Organizations can use ISO 14031 alongside ISO 14001, or as a stand-alone technique. It provides guidance on verifiable information, as well as helping to identify the most appropriate figures and indicators for environmental performance.

When you use EPE as a part of environmental reviews and audits, the techniques described within it help management to identify environmental aspects, determining which aspects are significant, set criteria for environmental performance, and then evaluate this performance against these criteria.

There are three main elements to EPE, which are:

- **Environmental Condition Indicators (ECI):** These tell you about the state of the environment, and include factors such as air quality, water quality, and significant risks based on the sensitivity of the environment.

- **Operational Performance Indicators (OPI):** These apply to the physical control of environmental aspects. They include quantifiable factors such as emissions, resource use, effluents, recycling, waste minimization and energy conservation.

- **Management Performance Indicators (MPI):** These tell you how well management are handling environmental issues. MPI includes four components; (i) implementation of environmental policies and programmes, (ii) conformity with requirements and expectations, (iii) financial performance, (iv) and community relations.

COMMUNICATION REQUIREMENTS

As well as evaluating environmental aspects and impacts, ISO 14001 also requires organizations to take appropriate notice of the views and opinions of interested parties when formulating the environmental objectives and targets. The interested parties can be anyone with an interest in the environmental effect of your activities, products or services. This can mean *everyone* from the regulators to the staff, from the bank to the neighbours, from the customers to the insurance company, and *everything* from the raw materials sourcing to the disposal of the packaging, from the plant effluent to the distribution system, from the site services to the annual report.

Primarily then, the environmental impacts requirement necessitates (a) a procedure to capture the communications received from people and organizations outside the company, (b) a system to document those communications and (c) a system to respond to those communications.

It is not necessary to respond to every inquiry or complaint about your company's environmental impacts. You only need be concerned with 'relevant' interested parties and these will vary depending on the nature of your business. It may be relevant to manage communications with your local authority or the local Inspector of Pollutants, or to demonstrate to the local fire officer that your company has in place appropriate emergency action plans. It may be relevant to consider the requirements of your site neighbours, or to liaise with local environmental groups, or simply to understand the environmental concerns of your staff, customers or suppliers. What is crucial, however is that you demonstrate that your communications procedures are relevant and effective.

The communications procedure

Within the project you will have identified one person with responsibilities for communications, and this person should be the owner of the environmental communications process. The process should be designed to ensure that all communications are channelled to an appropriate owner for a response. The incoming communications will vary in source and in the interface with the organization. They may be telephone calls, correspondence, meetings or customer complaints, and may be directed toward senior management, middle management or to activities on the shop floor. From whatever source, you need a centralized control point to track the incoming communications, apportion responsibility to the appropriate department and to measure to ensure an adequate response.

The control point will need access to centres of competence throughout the organization, responsible for answers to the issues raised and for reporting back to the control point what action has been taken. The process must also identify who is responsible for receiving, documenting and responding to the issues raised.

Senior management will also want to monitor the progress of communications to ensure that responses and appropriate records are kept. They should be kept informed of the issues raised and the actions taken.

Finally, you will have identified the possible interested parties outside your organization. Does your communications procedure have mechanisms to reach your potential audiences?

Checklist 1

? *Do you have a documented procedure for managing communications?*

? *Does that procedure indicate who is responsible for:*

- *receiving communications from interested parties?*

- *documenting the communications received?*

- *responding to the interested parties?*

? *Have you identified the centres of competence for areas of environmental inquiry?*

? *Do you have a plan for communications in crisis?*

? *Have you identified the areas of risk and assessed possible scenarios of environmental failure?*

? *Have you identified possible audiences for communications, and the mechanisms for communication?*

Communication hints 1

In order to convince others that you are serious about environmental management issues remember the CAT factors:

◆ Commitment to the improvement of your environmental performance will be shown by the things you do, not the things you say. You must have evidence of the actions you are taking.

◆ Accuracy in the message is important. You must be consistent and truthful.

◆ Trust is the objective. The public want to trust you, but there is a fear of the unknown that is real and must be eased effectively. You must explain in language that the recipient can understand, not your jargon.

Checklist 2: Evaluating environmental aspects and impacts

? *Is there a procedure for determining your environmental aspects and impacts?*

? *Have you documented your findings in a matrix?*

Does the matrix describe the status quo?

? *Does the matrix describe the proposed project or activity in a clearly defined scope clause?*

- project: extent and boundaries of the project activity.

- process: extent for the process input to output.

- product: extent of the product life, upstream and downstream.

? *Is the matrix regularly reviewed as part of the management review?*

Communication hints 2

◆ In assessing those areas of activity for inclusion in the aspects and impacts matrix and scoring high in the significance criteria, it is worth considering the 80:20 formula. This will indicate that 80% of the environmental burdens will probably come from 20% of your activities. While all aspects of the organization must be assessed, the 80/20 approach will ensure you are addressing the significant activities.

◆ The matrix should be accessible to all appropriate employees to demonstrate the commitment to the environmental policy for continual improvement. It will, over time, show the improvement in performance.

◆ When reviewing the results of environmental evaluations, include a commentary on the process itself, as well as the results. It will allow you to improve the assessment procedures when it is time for a re-evaluation.

CASE STUDIES

Perfecseal

Perfecseal first produced a matrix of all their environmental aspects, and then used several criteria to assign a degree of significance. In many cases, an FMEA was not appropriate, so the company had a set of criteria based on questions relating to obvious significance. Were any aspects, for example, regulated by legislation? In using this system, Perfecseal were able to rank the impacts of each aspect (see the example in Table 13.9) and thus see at a glance which areas needed their immediate attention when developing their objectives and targets. ▶

Table 13.9 Perfecseal's Register of Significant Environmental Aspects

Code	Issue	Criteria	Source	Medium Affected
A	Controlled waste disposal to landfill via skip	Legal compliance	Warehouse (packaging) Blending area – filter bag – IBCs General and maintenance Coater-cores Returned goods Converting – cores – reels Spills – all areas Canteen and office waste	Land Water
B	Special waste disposal – landfill – incineration	Legal compliance	Waste and redundant inks and solvents from printing Nominally empty containers Paint and nominally empty paint tins Trichloroethylene	Land Air Water
C	Controlled waste to landfill via compactor	Legal compliance	Slitting, converting, set up and operational	Land Water
D	Controlled waste to landfill (other)	Legal compliance	Settlement pit	Land Water
E	Consented water discharge	Legal compliance Consent to Discharge – COD – SS – pH – Temperature – Oil/grease – Volume and rate of discharge	Settlement pit – mixing/blending vessels – coater – spill management – site discharges	Water
F	Water use/discharge	Economic use of resources and legal compliance	Process use of water	Water
G	Air pollution/odour	Statutory nuisance	Ammonia from mixing/blending Emergencies Particulates/ammonia from coating	Air
		EC Regulation on ozone depleting substances	Cooling system	Air
H	Potential threat to water discharge	Legal compliance	Material control/handling/use/spills	Water
I	Resource depletion	Public/staff/economic concern	Use of energy on site – LPG/oil/electricity	Air
K	Potential pollution arising from a major incident – fire/explosion oil or chemical leaks or spills	Public concern Health and Safety	Emergency situations	Land Air Water

▶ Fenland Laundries

Fenland Laundries used a similar approach, as well as a risk analysis to assign significance scores to each aspect. The company found a few surprises in their analyses. Some local residents, for example, pointed out that they perceived the emissions of steam as a significant and damaging pollutant. In fact the steam emissions ranked low on the significance scale if the public perception was excluded from the equation. However, as Fenland Laundries consider public views as important, the company implemented a system to eliminate visible emissions of steam, by designing and building further energy recovery systems to complement those already in place.

Fridays (Cranbrook) Ltd t/a Oasters

When developing its procedures, this egg producer and food manufacturer used a flow-chart (Figure 13.4) to determine environmental aspects and their significance. They found that their most significant impacts were food safety, and effluent production. While the company said that it found the significance issue the hardest part of their EMS, their procedure and flow-chart illustrate an efficient and extremely logical approach. The company's experiences and comments on the difficulties in determining environmental aspects and the significance of their impacts is very common; this is without any doubt the hardest part of any developing EMS.

Du Pont

Du Pont uses a combination of qualitative classifications and a FMEA to assign a level of significance. There are five classification criteria for significance, designated A to E. An environmental aspect is automatically considered as significant if it meets at least one of the criteria in A to D. If an aspect is significant under A to D, then it is considered significant under normal, start-up, shut-down, accidental and emergency conditions. If an aspect is considered insignificant under A to D, then Du Pont uses criteria E – this is based on a numerical method to assign a significance value called SV, which is a function of the probability of occurrence and the severity of the consequences. Briefly, the significance criteria are as follows:

A. Any process which is subject to either national, international or company regulations.

B. Any process emissions (including waste and energy) which contribute to a major portion of the plant emissions, and are addressed within the Du Pont Corporate Environmental Plan. Du Pont uses the Pareto Principle when considering plant emissions, which typically applies the 80:20 rule, i.e., 20% of the emissions cause 80% of the aspects.

C. Any environmental aspect which gives rise to persistent complaints or comments from customers, employees, the public. This includes positive as well as negative comments. Persistent is defined as two or more complaints from different sources in any year, or four or more complaints from the same source.

D. Specific environmental effects or aspects, actual or potential, which are noted within the Corporate Environmental Review Process.

▶

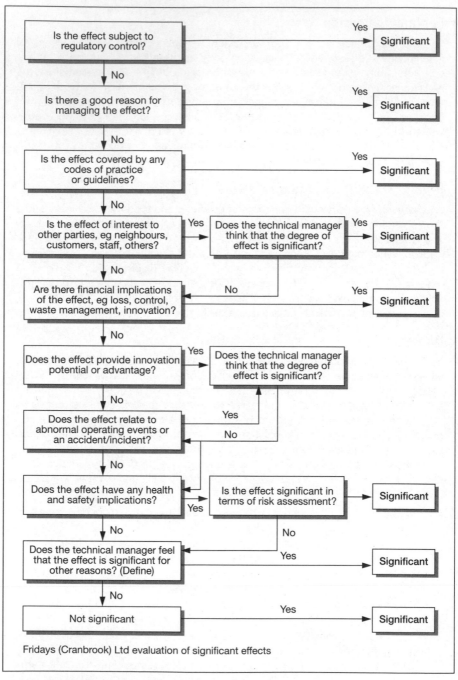

Fig. 13.4 Fridays (Cranbrook) Ltd evaluation effects

Table 13.10 Du Pont's consequence criteria

Consequence, f{X}	Consequence criteria
1×10^7	Irreversible pollution damage resulting in prosecution (and death)
1×10^5	Physical damage to people/property, possibly leading to prosecution
1000	A pollution incident which results in a complaint
100	Off-site release which does not result in a complaint, or on-site release
10	Known minor environmental aspect
0.01	Release with no known environmental consequence

▶ **E.** Any other specific environmental aspects or effects which were designated to be significant are analyzed using FMEA.

When calculating the value SV, Du Pont begins by assigning a value to the severity of the consequences of an event, f{x}. It does this by pooling the knowledge and experience of several people in a team, which also estimates the probability of particular events.

A spectrum of values and their meaning is shown in Table 13.10. The value SV is the product of the probability of an event occurring and its consequences, where the probability is the proportion of years in which the given event happens at least once. If the value for SV is 100 or more, then the environmental aspect is considered as significant.

14

LEGAL AND OTHER

REQUIREMENTS

(4.3.2)

Objective

The goal is to establish and maintain procedures for understanding, analyzing, accessing and documenting the various regulations which apply to your organization, and communicating these effects to relevant interested parties.

ISO 14001 REQUIREMENTS

You must establish and maintain a procedure to identify and have access to legal, and other requirements which apply to the organization and the environmental aspects of your activities, products or services

ACCESS TO LEGISLATIVE, REGULATORY AND OTHER POLICY REQUIREMENTS

Your organization has to comply with the law. Furthermore, many organizations need to meet the requirements of other regulations, codes of practice and industry standards. ISO 14001 requires you to have access to the latest regulations, and to have a procedure which helps you to identify, access and keep up to date with latest developments and requirements. However, while a register is not a requirement, many organizations still use some form of matrix or tabulated summary.

Such a mechanism within the management system ensures that your organization knows, understands, documents and monitors the applicable legislative, regulatory and other policy requirements. This allows you to feel confident about legal compliance and to audit that compliance.

Organizations may use many routes in compiling their documentation. Some use professionals, for example external legal advisers (your company solicitor), internal legal advisers (your company secretary); or technical experts with specific areas of legal knowledge (safety managers). Others use a combination of internal professional skills and support documentation. Publications from *Croner Publications, Barbour Index, Gee Publishing* and the *BSI Electronic Book* all provide comprehensive data that are current and automatically updated with the latest environmental regulations. You may employ professional staff and then encourage or plan a series of continuous professional development (CPD) training courses to keep the knowledge current. The results from different actions gel at this point:

- **The initial review results** which will have provided some basic information about the activities, legal issues and stakeholder issues you face.

- **The output from the implementation workshops** at every functional/departmental level in the organization. Output from the workshops should include a response to a skeleton EMS which requires consideration of the requirements, the key documentation and the 'deliverables' in terms of environmental performance.

Documentation requirements will be different in the various parts of the organization, depending on the criticality of legal and regulatory affairs in relation to the activities and processes involved. For example, the machine shop will have very different issues from the site services department or the transport department. The levels of knowledge required by staff and management will also be significantly different. Procedures will therefore need to be department-specific to be effective. The documentation framework can be consistent across the organization, but must be different on a departmental basis. In addition to listing the legislative, regulatory and other policy requirements relevant to the department, the documents should:

- specify ownership;
- indicate who has access to the information (for updating);
- identify a system of measurement or assessment (for compliance);
- specify when the information is to be reviewed.

What the legislative, regulatory and policy requirements are

Because the procedure must be thorough and comprehensive, you will need to assess existing company records, focusing on areas such as waste management practices and supplies of raw materials; review key business processes and safety requirements; check the local authority's requirements for control of accidents and emergencies; consents for discharges, licences to treat or dispose of waste, Duty of Care procedures, LAAPC and EPA consents, and other requirements of current legislation.

Have you incorporated all the legislative requirements relevant to your industry? For example:

- Planning – requirements or restraints included in planning consents
- Safety – Health and Safety at Work Act, 1974, COSHH, fire precautions and safe working practices
- Consents – discharge and extraction authorizations from the Environment Agency
- IPC and IPPC – scheduled process authorization
- Protocols – Montreal protocol on CFCs
- Asbestos – location registers
- Corporate – energy plans, environmental master plans.

Signpost your documentation where these things can be found.

Ownership

The procedure must specify who in the organization is responsible for keeping the documentation current and in place. The responsibility goes with the position, not the individual, who may move on to another job within the organization. For example, the fire certificate might be the responsibility of the Site Services Manager, or the discharge consents the responsibility of the Process Engineer.

Accessibility

The procedure also has to say who needs to have access to the information for action and information. It may be an individual who holds the data (as with the fire certificate), or it may be that, in order to ensure that the discharge consent is met, many more people on the shop floor need to know about permits and measures of compliance.

Other aspects of the legal requirement may require an 'indirect' knowledge level. For example, health and safety regulations require safe systems of work for the entire workforce. Not everyone needs to know the detailed requirements, but all must have access to the safe systems of work information, whether inside or outside the company, and all contractors coming on to sites need to know about issues such as safety procedures, permits to work and access arrangements to confined spaces.

Measurement systems

The procedure must identify the key documentation that should be present in order to measure your company's compliance to the criteria you have set out. Your audits should regularly assess the extent, currency and accessibility of the legislative and regulatory information. You must also check people's understanding and application of the information.

Dates

The procedure must specify when the data is due for review, updating, reporting, measuring or replacing if out of date. You also need to look forward to planned legislation as well as current requirements. When planning the future performance targets of your organization, it is essential that you consider forthcoming legislative requirements so that new product development, for example, can take into account the possible implications of new legislation and not waste investment. It would be inappropriate to design a process to current legislative requirements, knowing when criteria for compliance are likely to change.

In addition, because requirements change and legislative demands are becoming more stringent, you will find a need to retain some historic data. The environmental effects of past activities can have significant consequences. At some time in the future, it may be essential to be able to demonstrate that, at the time of the discharge or event, you were operating within relevant legislation.

Checklist

[?] *Is there a procedure for recording legislative requirements?*

[?] *Is the information available where it is needed?*

[?] *Is the information regularly updated?*

[?] *Is the procedure comprehensive?*

- Safety requirements.

- Local authorities – requirements for control of accidents and emergencies.

- Consents – Environment Agency consents for discharges.

- Licenses to deposit, treat or dispose of waste.

- Duty of Care – waste management procedures.

- APC – Air discharges and consents.

- EPA (1990) – wastes, processes and discharges.

- Major Accident Hazard Regulations – accidents and consequential limitations.

- Water Resources Act 1991 – use, contamination and control.

- Dangerous Substances (1990) – notification and marking of sites.

- Hazardous Substances (1990) – site plans and substances lists.

- Special Waste Regulations, 1996

- Packaging Regulations, 1997.

? *Do the people at the business understand the procedure and the information? Are they acting on it?*

CASE STUDIES

Du Pont

Du Pont uses a variety of external databases and CD-ROMs for keeping up to date with the latest regulations, and then documents a summary of these. According to Patricia Shaw, Safety, Health and Environmental Supervisor for the Maydown site in Northern Ireland, the summary should provide an interpretation of what legislation requires. 'Much of the language in legislation is complex, and our managers only want to know what they have to do, and when they need to do it. Therefore a plainly worded interpretation is important.'

UK Waste Management Ltd

This is a very large, complex organization which has developed a system for dealing effectively with legislative issues which most companies would rather avoid. UK Waste Management provides a wide spectrum of waste management and recycling services, so a vast number of regulations apply to its many operations.

This can make access and distribution of the regulations something of a problem, so the organization employs a small team of people whose role is to research and disseminate regulations as they evolve.

The UK head office at High Wycombe has an industrial and government affairs manager who keeps up to date with the UK legislation and regulations, and whenever there is something new, he interprets, summarises and distributes the information to the appropriate parts of the organization. He also produces a regular newsletter which keeps people updated on regulatory developments, and provides an advisory service for staff and managers in the field.

The international head office in Hammersmith has a similar manager who researches and monitors international legislation, while the company employs another researcher who is located in Brussels, which is the focal point of developments in EC legislation.

15

ENVIRONMENTAL OBJECTIVES AND TARGETS

(4.3.3)

Objective

The goal is a comprehensive set of objectives and targets, from the board-room to the shop floor, integrated into the day-to-day business activities of the managers and staff. The objectives and targets must be clear and consistent. If staff can see management practising policy application, it can be highly motivating.

ISO 14001 REQUIREMENTS

You have to establish and maintain documented environmental objectives and targets at each relevant function and level within the organization; therefore when establishing and reviewing your objectives, you must look at the following issues:

- legal and other regulatory requirements
- the significant environmental aspects
- the organization's technological options and its financial, operational and business requirements
- the views of interested parties.

The objectives and targets must be consistent with the environmental policy, especially the commitment to prevention of pollution. An environmental target is a detailed performance requirement, which is quantified where practicable, and relevant to the organization. The targets derive from the environmental objectives, and the organization may need to meet several targets in order to achieve those objectives.

AIMS AND ASPIRATIONS

The purpose of this requirement of ISO 14001 is to ensure that there are clear and measurable environmental goals for the organization as a whole and for each departmental management team. These goals can be set to achieve a year-on-year improvement but not necessarily in every area of activity, i.e., they can be strategic and quick wins. The environmental impacts analysis of the organization will indicate areas for improvement so you have a clear and discernible link between policy, impacts evaluation and improvement targets.

The targets should be demanding, so they require special efforts to achieve them. There is little point in setting targets at low levels as they provide little gain, motivation or satisfaction on achievement. However, it is always useful to have some 'quick wins' to report when it will be important to show how well some people are doing. Objectives and targets should be quantified to ensure that real attainment is recorded against the targets.

ESTABLISHING ENVIRONMENTAL OBJECTIVES AND TARGETS

If you look at the characteristics of activity management in organizations, you often find that the business processes (e.g., tank cleaning, environmental measurements) are not designed by the operator, but by the managers or technical experts. Very often, therefore, the results of environmental monitoring go to the expert rather than the operator. The operator may get a report only when an emission exceeds a set alarm level. To be more effective, operators could be given a trend chart which shows when things are deviating from normal standards – before a problem arises.

The use of the interactive implementation workshop to set targets is an effective way to achieve this at all levels of an organization, from the senior executive team down through the various departments to the shop floor. Managers and staff can work together in teams, in a non-threatening way to look at *how* things are done – the technique highlights gaps or overlaps in a management system. The result is a management system review with an environmental focus, which will lead to action plans to improve environmental performance in day-to-day operations – with a 'buy-in' from all levels of staff.

In setting targets and objectives, the workshops should take the following into account:

- compliance with all legislative and regulatory requirements documented in the departmental register;
- other documented objectives and targets elsewhere in the organization;
- the financial, operational and business requirements;
- the views of interested parties; and
- the general environmental policy statement of the company.

The environmental targets must be written down, realistic timescales for completion should be set, and managers and staff should monitor progress together to achieve the targets within the timescale. Remember that objectives and targets should be consistent with environmental policy and quantify the commitment to continual improvement in environmental performance.

QUANTIFYING ENVIRONMENTAL OBJECTIVES AND TARGETS

Because they are drawn from the implementation workshops and the environmental impacts analysis, the objectives and targets will be focused; but to manage improvement in these areas, some form of quantifiable measurement is essential – 'If you can't measure it, you can't manage it.' Phrases like 'minimize effluents and maximize recycling' are too vague to be useful.

These measurements may be set at a strategic level; for example: reduce air emissions by 10% over 1996 levels by the end of 1999. For a specific function, this may be translated into: implement a project to install catalytic converters to clean air emissions from production line A, or an objective to change adhesive material from solvent base to water base in a defined timescale.

The quantification is usually easy in technical areas; chemical oxygen demand (COD) of effluent can be measured and tracked; amounts of effluent sludge can be recorded as well as the percentage of chemical content in waste waters. Electrical consumption and cost of waste can be calculated in providing real benefits in achieving reduction.

Physical actions can also be measured; bunding of effluent filtration systems, oil tanks or hydrogen peroxide tanks are done/not done? Projects to install vapour recovery systems installed and the amount of recycled material in products can be tracked.

Administration improvements are more difficult, but can still be measured: establishing emergency recovery systems; suppliers' and contractors' compliance with your policy, and codes of practice. These can include the contribution of turnover to environmental investment, the beginnings of environmental accounting.

Checklist

? Do the objectives and targets establish realistic and meaningful improvements?

? Do they have realistic timescales?

? Have you used all available documentation in establishing your objectives and targets?

? Have they been properly quantified?

? Does somebody own each objective and target?

? Do you have agreed measurement criteria for each objective and target?

Communication hints

◆ Within the organization, the individual or departmental objectives and targets can be communicated as part of the regular process to update progress towards policy implementation.

◆ External communications can be by means of a booklet or brochure which explains the link between the policy, objectives, targets and the resulting actions that may effect suppliers, contractors, customers and other external interested parties.

◆ Regular reporting is important to ensure that progress is maintained against the policy, tracking the views of interested parties to ensure that the appropriate issues are being addressed.

CASE STUDIES

British Telecom (BT)

BT uses a dynamic, iterative approach when developing its objectives and targets. BT continually reviews progress, and modifies them if they differ from the original plan. The company publishes its objectives and targets in a tabulated form (Table 15.1), and reproduces these in its *Environmental Performance Report*. The company classifies targets under type and status.

▶

Table 15.1 Examples of BT's objectives and targets – fuel and energy

Target	Type	Status	Report
In 1996/97 BT's energy managers will survey 200 buildings to establish opportunities for further energy reductions.	1996 Improvement	Completed	During 1996/97 the BT energy management team undertook 201 building energy surveys. These surveys identified a number of opportunities to reduce energy consumption. Reports have been completed and recommendations made to obtain the savings identified.
To reduce energy consumption in the BT network and estate by 15% over the five-year period April 1992 to March 1997.	1994 Strategic	Superseded	Over the five year period BT reduced its energy consumption by 13.8% against a background of increasing new services. This did not quite meet our original target of 15% but still represents major annual savings of 465 GWh of energy and over 90,000 tonnes of CO_2
BT will reduce energy consumption across its network and estate by 11% over the five-year period from April 1997 to March 2002.	1997 Strategic	**New**	
As a trial, BT will fit 60 diesel vans with catalytic converters and assess their effect on emissions and fuel use by March 1997.	1996 Process	Delayed	Initial findings on fuel consumption are satisfactory and reliability has been good. The effect of the catalytic converters on emissions has not yet been assessed. This will take place during 1997/98.

Full details can be obtained from *A Matter of Fact: A Report on BT's Environmental Performance 1996/7*, available via BT's Environmental Issues Unit or from their Internet site at: http://www.bt.com/corpinfo/enviro

▶ *Target type*

BT has classified each target into one of three categories, so that people can know something about its level of development. These are:

- **strategic targets** which describe a long-term objective or goal;
- **improvement targets** which BT often quantifies, and describe incremental progress;
- **process targets**, which cover preliminary work such as developing monitoring systems or a review of current practice.

Target status

BT classifies targets published for the first time in any given year as 'new' and the company reports back on progress the following year. Each of BT's previously published targets carries a status that depends on its progress as of 31 March 1997. The status types are:

- **Completed:** BT reached the target, and successfully completed its aims;
- **Ongoing:** the target has a completion date after 1 April 1997 and BT is continuing to work towards it;
- **Delayed:** the target has a completion date before 1 April 1997 which BT failed to meet – the company will continue to work on it;
- **Superseded:** the target was not completed, but has been superseded by a new target published alongside;
- **Abandoned:** BT abandoned the target.

BT's experience of what makes a good target

Over the last five years BT has learned which factors contribute to a good environmental target, and the results show that the process of developing and aiming for targets is a dynamic and iterative process. BT has found that a good target needs the following factors:

- **A specified completion date:** vagueness with the target date can make a target appear meaningless;
- **A well-defined measure of success:** it is very difficult to tell if a target is completed or not if there is no measure of success agreed with the target owner at the very start;
- **Evidence and audit trail:** a clear definition of what is required to prove target status is agreed with the target owner prior to publication. This enables the verifiers to easily ascertain the target status at the end of the reporting year;
- **Clear ownership:** essential for co-ordination of the target within the relevant division and for tracking progress.

Source: Janet Quigley, BT Environmental Issues Manager and Steven Mehew, BT, Supply Management, Environment Business Manager ▶

Table 15.2 Part of Fenland Laundries' spreadsheet of impacts

Item	Description	Impact	Score
1	Washing #1 (Senking)	Water	58
2	Washing #2 (CT Levers)	Visual Water	58
3	Steam raising	Visual	44
4	Land use	Visual	40
5	Steam raising	Resource air	37
6	Steam raising	Air	32
7	Materials storage	Visual	30
8	Transport	Air	29
9	Transport	Vibration	29
10	Finishing/repair	Visual	28
11	Washing #2 (CT Levers)	Resource use	28
12	Transport	Resource use	25
13	Washing #1 (Senking)	Air	24
14	Packaging	Resource use	24
15	Washing #3 (Ideal)	Water	22
16	Finishing/repair	Dust	19
17	Staff welfare	Visual	19
18	Air handling	Visual	18
19	Transport	Noise	18
20	Air handling	Vibration	18
21	Waste disposal	Air	17
22	Washing #2 (CT Levers)	Air	16
23	Transport	Odour	14
24	Waste disposal	Dust	14
25	Maintenance	Resource use	14
26	Garment use	Resource use	14
27	Washing #3 (Ideal)	Air	13
28	Steam raising	Vibration	12
29	Waste disposal	Vibration	12
30	Waste disposal	Resource use	12
31	Transport	Dust	11

▶ ## Prioritizing objectives and targets – Fenland Laundries and Fridays Foods

Deciding on which objectives and targets to set is one of the biggest challenges. 'There is always a limit to what you can do in any year, so we target the most significant effects first. Then having drawn up a shortlist each year, we look at those where we can make the greatest improvements with the most efficient use of resources', says Simon Fry, Managing Director of Fenland Laundries.

Fenland Laundries' objectives are designed to match their environmental policy. The Board review the ranked list of the site's significant environmental effects; an example of this is shown in Table 15.2. The company then uses this to set or amend targets to support the environmental policy. Their environmental procedures manual states that each target shall address one or more significant effects, be quantifiable where possible, be achievable, have a time scale for completion, be capable of compliance assessment, and have an identified staff member responsible for its completion. All targets reflect:

- the significance of the effect
- financial considerations
- operational impacts
- the requirements of the business.

For example: water use, resource use in transport and resource use in raising steam are some of Fenland Laundries' highest-ranked significant environmental effects. Fenland Laundries' company environmental objectives for 1997–8 include:

- reduction in process water use, per garment by 3%;
- reduction in gas fuel use for steam-raising, per garment by 3%;
- transport fuel use reduction, per garment by 3%;
- greater recycling of waste skip material of 10%;
- improvement of environmental awareness amongst staff.

The company quantifies the latter during the regular assessments for each member of staff.

Oasters

Oasters (Friday's Foods) use a similar approach, and the company follows a similar, logical method in determining its targets as it does when working out the significance of environmental aspects. The method for deciding on targets is shown in the flow chart in Figure 15.1. ▶

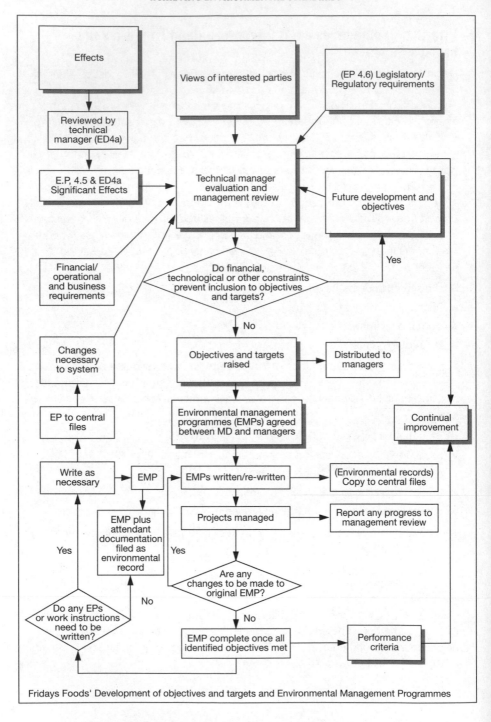

Fig. 15.1 Oasters (Fridays Foods) flowchart for objectives and targets

PART

4

16

THE ENVIRONMENTAL
MANAGEMENT PROGRAMME
(4.3.4)

Objective

The establishment of a co-ordinated implementation programme throughout the organization to achieve the company's environmental objectives
and targets.

ISO 14001 REQUIREMENTS

You have to establish and maintain a programme for achieving its objectives and
targets. This programme must include the following elements:

- the designation of responsibility for achieving objectives and targets at each
  relevant function and level of the organisation
- the resources and time-frame by which the organization is to meet its objectives and targets
- if a project deals with new developments and new or modified activities, products or services, then the organization is to amend the programme to ensure
  that environmental management applies to such projects.

EFFECTIVE PROJECT MANAGEMENT

The purpose of this requirement of ISO 14001 is to ensure that within the organization the policy goals, objectives and targets are supported by a realistic pro-

gramme for implementation. The programme will exist at every level where objectives and targets have been set. In large organizations, therefore, there will be several 'layers' of programmes and these should be related. For example, an organization may, at a national level, set a target of reducing the waste that goes to landfill by 20% over a 12-month period. But at a site level one might expect to find different programmes for the same objective. These would relate to the type and amount of waste generated, the maturity of site management in improving waste streams and the capacity of local suppliers/removers to respond to a change to more recycling.

IMPLEMENTATION PROGRAMMES

Each workshop group that developed the objectives and targets must have an implementation programme to go with it. The plan should include milestones to be achieved against key dates and the activities necessary to make it happen. Programmes will vary according to the products, processes and activities involved.

For example, environmental programmes to improve a continuous process (e.g., a paper mill) have a different type of programme from a construction project. In the paper process, the objective might be to achieve a higher standard of waste water purity, which is dependent on a particular change in the process involving the installation of new equipment. The programme will show a 'step' performance improvement to occur when particular plant or equipment is installed. In the construction industry the programme might include waste reduction targets, transport savings or noise containment targets that are heavily dependent on changes in the behaviour of operatives. This programme will show a planned 'graded' improvement in performance, linked to education, training and the application of new operating procedures.

The role of the environmental programme manager is to ensure that the key milestones of each 'sub-programme' are linked to a realistic overview that demonstrates a movement towards meeting the targets. It is important that the programme identifies not just the things to be done; it will also state who is responsible, how plans will be achieved and how the owner (and everyone else) will know they have been achieved.

A lot of your time could be spent chasing information to ensure that you know that the overview programme is correct, and that the sub-programmes are maintaining momentum. In addition to owning the achievement of the sub-programmes, you should ensure that the departmental co-ordinators own the maintenance of their parts of the overview programme. For example, in your regular management progress review meetings, ask each functional or departmental head to make a report of his or her own progress, while you report on the overall achievements only.

A structured approach to implementation programmes

The implementation workshop and the departmental EMS skeleton will identify the key activities, ownership, dates and criteria that form the environmental programme. The way to integrate these into a common programme is to use a structured approach which ensures some consistency in the presentation of the material. If all implementation programmes or projects follow the same sequence of steps, you will find it easier to monitor progress and fit all the activities into your general overview. All projects go through phases, and these can be set-up as 'gates' against which reports are made. For example, a problem-solving methodology from IBM uses the following steps:

Step 1: Identification

State the problem or opportunity to be solved, i.e., the symptoms. Understand the complexity, resource requirement, availability, impacts and potential benefits. The 'output' at this stage is a formal 'problem statement' – a simple and succinct statement which captures the essence of what will be changed as a result of the activity. It is an equivalent to a scope statement for a project.

Step 2: Cause analysis

Determine the root cause of the problems. This may involve the further gathering of data, specific analysis techniques and some testing to ensure that the causes of the problem are properly understood. The 'output' at this stage is an expanded problem statement that is specifically focused on the *root causes* – the real issues to be solved.

Step 3: Solution analysis

Determine the changes necessary to resolve the root cause of the problem. Define the solution criteria to be met if the problem is to be successfully eliminated. Carry out pilot activities to test the proposed solutions. The 'output' at this stage is a proposal which meets the solution criteria. Obtain the necessary approvals and establish a project plan for implementation to be communicated straightaway.

Step 4: Implementation

Plan and manage the solution so that you achieve the improvement you seek. The 'output' at this stage will be the implementation of changes in the practices, processes and procedures necessary to achieve the improvement.

Step 5: Review

Check that the solution which has been put in place has solved the problem. This means going back to the original measurements to check that the new procedure has resulted in the right kind of changes. The 'output' at this stage will be a report demonstrating the achievement against the original criteria.

So, establish a protocol for the development of sub-programmes and use it as the mechanism for measuring progress against the plans. If you want the model programme to be effective, it must combine a sensible, structured approach that people will use because it helps them, and the correct elements to ensure that you can track what is happening. Each sub-project is, at any one time, somewhere along the path.

Remember the 'off-target' approach to problem-solving. Do not make each step such an onerous activity that progress and enthusiasm are inhibited. It is better to run through quickly and improve the programme on a new level than to revisit the systems already put in place to finetune the improvement.

BS 6079 – A FRAMEWORK FOR PROJECT MANAGEMENT

BS 6079 provides a generic framework for project management; again, a useful tool to help you develop effective programmes, enabling managers to be *proactive* rather than *reactive*. There are two important definitions here, which are:

- **Project:** a unique set of co-ordinated activities, with definite starting and finishing points, undertaken by an individual or organization to meet specific objectives within defined schedule, cost and performance parameters.

- **Project management:** this is defined as the planning, monitoring and control of all aspects of a project and the motivation of all those involved in it to achieve the project objectives on time and to the specified cost, quality and performance.

BS 6079 identifies five phases in a project (*see* Figure 16.1), which are:

- **Conception:** The project idea is born, either to solve a problem or to realize an opportunity.

- **Feasibility:** The idea is assessed for benefits, risks and practicality.

- **Implementation:** The project is implemented and completed.

- **Operation:** The results are fed into day-to-day operation and the benefits accrue.

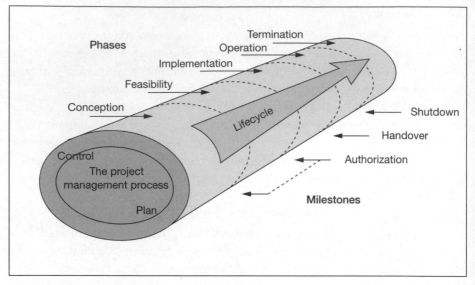

Fig. 16.1 A project lifecycle according to BS 6079

- **Termination:** The project is closed.

The boundaries between these phases are defined by four intermediate milestones. The first two indicate where the project team needs authority to progress to the next stage, the third is where the project teams hand over the product or service to the client, while the last milestone initiates the closure of the project, before termination or decommissioning.

Within this framework, BS 6079 splits the project management process into two parts, which are *project planning* and *project control*. Planning is the development of an operative, feasible plan which defines responsibilities, schedules, timing, costs and specifications at each phase. Project control then uses the plan to track, control and co-ordinate the progress of the project.

The project plan not only represents a schedule of tasks, but also describes 28 separate elements which the project manager can include in the project plan, such as the project brief, procurement methods, configuration management, risk management, financial control and earned-value performance measurement – all as relevant to the project complexity.

A programme such as an EMS can be very large, so it makes sense to divide it into manageable parts (*see* Figure 16.2). These parts are known as *tranches*. Each tranche comprises a number of mini-projects, and the tranches are demarcated by *islands of stability*. These are simply breathing spaces between major sections of the programme, allowing the project team to review the progress to date, and to take an objective view of the work to date.

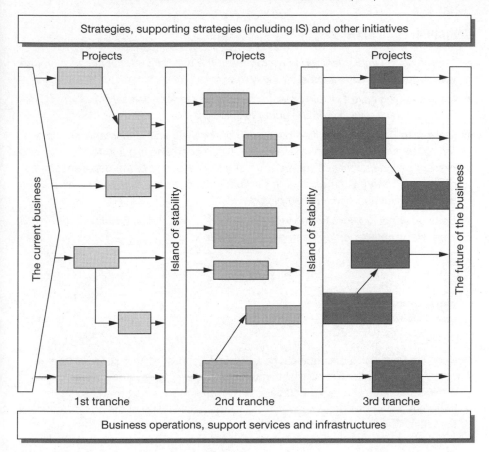

Fig. 16.2 Islands of stability

Checklist

? Does the environmental programme show how the objectives and targets will be met?

? Can you see the relationship and the links between the programme and the goals?

? Does each activity of the programme state who is responsible?

? Does the programme show how the targets will be achieved?

? Have you established a structured approach to ensure consistency of the implementation programmes across the company?

? Are the priorities clearly identified and relevant to the whole organization's goals?

Communication hints

◆ *Publishing the implementation programme in the company newsletter and through your regular reports is a important way to ensure that staff commitment remains.*

◆ *Make sure you have a visible programme with memorable dates from which it is difficult to default, even when the going gets tough!*

◆ *Make sure you have specified ownership of the programme elements so that you are not bearing other people's messages. If someone else is going to stand up and present progress, it leads to lazy reporting. Make sure it is the departmental co-ordinator's report. After all, it is the co-ordinator's programme and he or she will want the plaudits when it is completed.*

◆ *Be open about changes or delays in progress; your reputation is built on trust in this area. Inaccurate reporting damages your credibility.*

CASE STUDY

Du Pont

When Du Pont defined its objectives and targets, it divided them into immediate, medium and long-term aims. As it would be progressing towards several targets at the same time, in effect it had several mini-projects running at the same time. Therefore it used the project management approach similar to the good practice described in BS 6079, where individuals would take ownership for a particular project.

Du Pont would then have periodic reviews of each set of projects, and make any changes either to its plans or resource allocation depending on the progress and success of a project. By allowing individuals to take ownership of a particular mini-project within a tranche, the project managers could keep everything on track without disintegrating into chaos.

17

THE
IMPLEMENTATION
WORKSHOP

Objective
The goal is to achieve a draft environmental management system for each department of your company.

In setting up the original plan we identified two types of cascade. We have already seen how the *awareness presentation* can be used in communicating the environmental issue generally, introducing the policy, the environment project team, the commitment to achieving compliance to ISO 14001 and EMAS. The *implementation workshop* is the main tool used in integrating the environmental management system into the business systems.

In large organizations the workshop will be one of many cascaded from the top of the organization to the operations departments. In a small organization there may be just one workshop. Workshops usually work best on a departmental level, with managers and their direct reporting staff.

SETTING UP THE AGENDA

The workshop is a form of meeting, so like all meetings it must have a specific purpose. An agenda (*see* Example 17.1) should be designed to include the following aspects.

Example 17.1

Environmental management system programme: implementation workshop agenda

- Introduction
- Objective
- Knowledge base
- Drivers for change
- The organization's current status
- Environmental management standards
- Applied standards
- Action plan
- Knowledge review
- Workshop assessment

Introduction

As the programme manager you are responsible for introducing the workshop. You are there as the facilitator to enable the team to make progress.

Objectives

The programme manager establishes the objectives for the workshop, so that the participants will know what the goal is and when you have succeeded. A suggested set of objectives is shown in Example 17.2. These can be varied but should not exceed three if the workshop is to be successful.

Example 17.2

Environmental management system programme: implementation workshop objectives

At the end of this workshop you should have:

- An understanding of environmental aspects and impacts in [name of company/department]
- An understanding of an environmental management system (EMS)
- An understanding of the process for implementing an EMS in [name of company/department]

Knowledge base

This is a simple element that has two functions: (a) to get your audience thinking and interested (it is important in interactive workshops that you facilitate knowledge assimilation by the participants – do not try to force information into unwilling participants); and (b) to demonstrate that some knowledge has been gained after the workshop (an important reward for you and the participants). This part of the agenda should be fun. Example 17.3 demonstrates a 'quiz' technique for acquiring knowledge on ISO 14001 and EMAS.

Example 17.3

Environmental management system programme: implementation workshop knowledge base

Answer *true*, *false* or *don't know* to the following statements.
1. ISO 14001 is a mandatory British standard.
2. Compliance with the EMAS Regulation is mandatory for some industries.
3. Parts of [name of company] are certified to ISO 14001 by an accredited assessor.
4. It is a requirement of some of our customers that we comply with ISO 14001.
5. Non-compliance with ISO 14001 can be a breach of contract.
6. In order to comply with ISO 14001 and the eco-management and audit regulation you must achieve zero emissions.
7. In order to comply with ISO 14001, you must continuously improve your environmental performance.
8. In order to comply with the eco-management and audit regulation, you must continuously improve your environmental performance.
9. Compliance with ISO 14001 confirms your legal compliance.
10. Assessment to ISO 14001 is just an extension of ISO 9000.

Drivers for change

This takes the form of a guided discussion. Using one or two OHPs as a stimulus, ask questions of your audience to stimulate discussion and views from them. For example, 'What recent incidents or accidents have been reported in the news?' 'How might they affect us?'; 'What recent environmental legislation are you aware of?' 'What particular legal issues are relevant to us?'; 'What is meant by a duty of care?', etc.

Try to let the discussion move around the room by prompting for answers and providing information where needed. What you are looking for is the recognized desire to learn about this topic from the participants. A guideline for the discussion can be found in Example 17.4.

Example 17.4

Environmental management system programme: implementation workshop drivers for change

- Legal issues   UK   – EPA (Environmental Protection Act)
                             – Duty of Care
                   Europe – EIA (environmental impact assessments)
                             – CFCs
- Customers   Expectations and procurement policies
- Competitors   Actions, market growth and share
- Stakeholders   Banks, insurance, community, employees, suppliers, etc.
- Corporate   Programmes and policies
- Benefits   Energy and waste savings, cohesion and motivation
- Marketing   New products and services

Ask them to put the questionnaire to one side for now.

The organization's current status

With information from the initial review it should be possible to share with the workshop team as much as possible about the **actual** environmental performance of the organization. Be factual and accurate. If you work in generalizations, you will lose the audience.

Put the information across in a fun way. Get the audience to present parts of the data or provide some raw data and ask for an interpretation. Try always to relate the issues back to the responsibilities of the participants. If they are in building or site services, focus on energy use, insulation and space efficiency. If they are in marketing, focus on product performance, if in manufacturing, look at the use of resources and waste management factors.

Environmental management standards

This section is best done as a working exercise. Can you imagine being lectured to on the contents of an international standard? Although a bestseller and designed for easy comprehension, ISO 14001 still contains much 'standardese'. Anyway, do you think your learners will learn if you just tell them?

So, ask the workshop participants to tell each other what they think the requirements mean. You can arbitrate any gross misunderstandings. Exercise 1 (*see* Example 17.5) is designed to challenge the participants to read, think about and tell others in the room how they understand the requirements and the implications for their current practices.

Example 17.5

> **_Environmental management system programme: implementation workshop –_**
> **_Exercise 1_**
>
> Review a specification clause of ISO 14001 and prepare a three-minute presentation to explain your understanding of the content.

Applied standards

This section provides an opportunity to explore with the workshop group how the standards might be applied in each participant's area of responsibility. Again, the best way to explore this is through an exercise (*see* Exercise 2 in Example 17.6), not through your own or the manager's interpretation. This example uses eight headings to establish a 'skeleton' departmental EMS document.

- purpose
- dependencies
- procedures
- change management
- strategy
- deliverables
- measurements
- improvement

Example 17.6

> **_Environmental management system programme: implementation workshop –_**
> **_Exercise 2_**
>
> Review the following questions. Write down some notes under each heading. The results will be collated on flip charts for the group.
>
> *Note*: The elements of your business process have been divided into eight parts for simplicity of analysis.
>
> **1(a)** *What is your main business purpose?*
> Mission/objectives/goal.
>
> **1(b)** *What is your environmental policy relative to the mission?*

Example 17.6 contd.

2(a) *What is your strategy to achieve the main business purpose?*
Input/major activities/outputs/roles and responsibilities/flow chart.

2(b) *Within this strategy what are the activities for implementing the environmental policy?*

3(a) *What are you dependent on if you are to achieve your mission?*
CSFs/customers/suppliers/staff/skills/job descriptions.

3(b) *Within those dependencies what are the significant environmental criteria?*

4(a) *What must you deliver to meet the requirements of your mission?*
Outputs/contracts/documents of understanding/service level agreements/performance plans.

4(b) *Within those deliverables what are the potential objectives and targets for environmental performance?*

5(a) *What are the main procedures in implementing the strategy?*
Operating instructions/process guides/schedules/checkpoints/detailed flow charts.

5(b) *What changes will be made to achieve the environmental performance objectives and targets?*

6(a) *What do you measure to ensure the process is working effectively?*
Process measurements/key indicators/statistical quality control/self-assessments/reports/meetings.

6(b) *Within these management controls how should environmental objectives and targets be measured?*

7(a) *How do you manage change in the process?*
Requirements change control/error correction procedures/corrective action/document control/communications/preventive action.

7(b) *Within these procedures how would you manage environmental performance change requirements?*

8(a) *How do you manage process improvement?*
Customer satisfaction/best-of-breed comparisons/process simplification/work elimination/cycle time reduction/productivity improvements.

8(b) *Within these improvement procedures how would you manage environmental improvement?*

Example 17.6 contd.

> Each of the participants should have some notes on the questions. Draw up a flip chart and under each question go to a participant and capture his or her thoughts. Then check with the rest of the group that you have covered all the points. Hopefully the variety of thinking will result in additional contributions from all the participants.
>
> The flip chart is now a valuable document! On it is captured the main business activities of the department or function, and the views of the manager and staff of the main environmental elements to be added to the management system. This chart provides data for:
>
> (a) the departmental environmental management manual; and
> (b) the action plan of environmental performance improvement.

Action plan

This part of the workshop is your opportunity to obtain the agreements of those present to proceed towards a programme of improvement in their area. They now know:

- that the problem or challenge exists; they even know they don't know all the answers
- the standards to be attained
- where they will start to look at implementing change, within their own activities.

Now you need to ascertain the key activities. Do not forget that for each action you must ascribe ownership, set a date by which the action is to be complete, and establish a measurement by which you will all know it has been completed.

Knowledge review

Having agreed the action plan, now is the time to review the knowledge questionnaire – some notes may help you with anything not already clear.

1. Compliance with ISO 14001 is voluntary.

2. Participation in EMAS is voluntary. It is aimed at certain industry sectors defined in the Regulation.

3. Accredited certification is available worldwide, so ensure you have checked if you are a multinational organization.

4. Compliance with ISO 14001 may be required by some purchasers in the future.

5. If compliance with ISO 14001 was a contract condition, not complying would be a breach of contract.

6. There is no requirement for zero-emissions.

7. ISO 14001 requires *continual* improvement in performance.

8. EMAS requires continuous improvement.

9. ISO 14001 does not confirm legal compliance. Even though it requires commitment to compliance, breaches of the law may still occur.

10. The requirements for ISO 14001 include activities not addressed in ISO 9000, although the two are designed to be complementary.

Some of these points will encourage further discussion and clarification of the meaning and intent: it is not a competition!

Workshop assessment

The workshop is key to implementing the programme. Therefore you need to know if it has been successful. If you have a number to run, it provides feedback on any improvements that can be made.

A simple assessment sheet (*see* Table 17.1) will provide you with feedback on the success of the workshop, assessing the audience satisfaction in three areas; met objectives; presentation content; presentation style.

Table 17.1 EMS implementation workshop – assessment

1. How satisfied are you that the workshop met its objectives?				
Very satisfied	satisfied	neutral	dissatisfied	v. dissatisfied
2. How satisfied are you with the presentation materials?				
Very satisfied	satisfied	neutral	dissatisfied	v. dissatisfied
3. How satisfied are you with the presentation style?				
Very satisfied	satisfied	neutral	dissatisfied	v. dissatisfied

Have you any suggestions for improving the workshop?

Ascribing a score to each response will allow you to evaluate the workshop's success in achieving the objectives.

Checklist for action

[?] *Do the actions establish realistic and meaningful improvements?*

[?] *Can the actions be quantified?*

[?] *Are there areas where more information is needed to establish objectives and targets?*

[?] *Check with the superior department or function to see if they are properly aligned.*

[?] *Check with preliminary review considerations.*

WHAT NEXT?

Having completed the workshop, document the discussion and outcome, the action plan and dates for future reviews. Ensure that this information is shared both up and down the management line, and to all related departments, suppliers and customers. Remember this will result in some changes in those relationships. The best way to ensure that the change is accepted, is to share the thought process behind them. Emphasize that this is not revolution but evolution. It does not supersede or replace the core business needs and demands. It is not another management system.

Communication hints: facilitation

Facilitation is not training under another name; it is a conscious attempt to focus the learning experience on the learner. To do this you need to think from the learner's perspective.

◆ *What does the learner need to know and why?*
◆ *What are the benefits from learning?*
◆ *How can the learner be stimulated to learn?*
◆ *What fun can be had in learning?*

The last point is essential. The learning experience is one divorced from the day-to-day issues of the workplace where to take a risk and fail is bad, so people do not do it. In a workshop, however, you can encourage risk taking and making mistakes because it doesn't really matter.

In designing workshops like these, remember the intention is to help the participants 'grow' their knowledge, not give you an opportunity to demonstrate yours. The acronym GROW is useful in this context.

G – goals
R – reality
O – options
W – wrap-up

- *Goals – establish what you want to achieve and provide a test to know when you will have succeeded. Prioritize the goals to a limited number that are achievable.*

- *Reality – identify the perceived problem, what the symptoms are, what the inhibitors or constraints to resolving the problem are, and what the potential enablers to achieve success are. Do you need more information? What should the solution look like? Establish your criteria.*

- *Options – open up solutions, choices and directions. Test them against the criteria, and model the possibilities or instigate a trial.*

- *Wrap-up – implement the agreed direction, follow-up the action plan, and track and measure against the agreed action plan.*

CASE STUDY

Formosa Plastics Corporation

When Formosa Plastics Corporation (FPC) went ahead with its implementation programme, the company's environmental managers decided to use the evaluation of environmental aspects and impacts as a framework. They did this by holding a series of two-day workshops and brainstorming sessions, asking everyone to describe how they saw environmental management, and then list what they perceived as the most significant impacts. The company reports that there was an incredible difference in the perceptions of significant effects and at times the workshops became quite heated, but at the end of each session, the company not only had a consensus on their environmental impacts, but a clear idea on how to plan a system to manage them effectively.

18

ESTABLISHING
MANAGEMENT RESPONSIBILITIES
AND RESOURCES
(4.4.1)

Objective

The goal is to establish a set of management responsibilities and resources sufficient to implement and control the environmental management system.

ISO 14001 REQUIREMENTS

The organization has to define roles, responsibilities and authorities to make the EMS work effectively. Management must provide the necessary resources to implement and control the environmental management system. This means giving the right people the resources they need to do the work necessary to achieve environmental policy.

- The organization's top management also have to appoint a specific management representative who has a defined role, responsibility and authority for the following:

  (1) ensuring that EMS meets the requirements of the standard

  (2) reporting on the performance of the EMS to top management for review and as a basis for continual improvement.

MAKING PEOPLE MAKE THINGS HAPPEN

This chapter is about establishing the necessary management authority, organization, skills and resources to deliver the environmental policy. The requirements of the plan will commit you to the involvement of all the managers and staff throughout the organization. You must define the roles and responsibilities for *all* those who manage or perform work that affects the environment. That is just about everyone!

To ensure that you have all the roles, responsibilities, authority and interrelationships defined you must have a *documentation mechanism*. You will already have some form of organization chart from the highest level down to the job descriptions and performance plans at the individual level. The intention is not to re-invent the wheel, just to make effective use of the processes you have in place. If you are going to take your managers and staff with you, it is much easier to build on an existing foundation than to start from scratch when your peers are not sure what kind of new structure you have in mind. The end result should be an extension to the management system that ensures that all managers and staff have an environmental objective in their individual job descriptions and performance measurements. If your organization pays on performance, then such an integrated approach will ensure that the environmental performance issue has the correct balance in the organization's activities.

Each manager must be able to act in a way appropriate to the environmental responsibilities that are relevant. The integration of each functional and departmental manager's activities within the overall policy is the role of the management representative. Together the network of integrated responsibilities must be adequate to implement the system. Finally, a management representative should be appointed, whose responsibility is to ensure that the requirements of the standard are met, and that performance of the EMS is maintained.

In order to know if the system is designed and operating effectively you will need to verify compliance. There is hence a need to provide adequate audit resources. Verification is the process of checking or testing to ensure that a process, practice or procedure complies with the requirements. In the EMS, this includes the activities to assure compliance with the Standard, through self-assessment, audit and review.

ROLES AND RESPONSIBILITIES

The key to establishing the network of management responsibilities is the elements of the implementation workshop that identify the roles and responsibilities ('strategy'), set job descriptions ('dependencies') and performance plans ('deliverables'). Integrating the environmental policy and performance standards into these categories will provide the matrix of authority necessary. A departmental organization should be established to ensure that each key activity is clearly identified as belonging to a specific job holder. The allocation of activities to job holders should be outlined in a *job description*, which will define the outputs for which the job holder is responsible. This is important, because, given the organizational changes that frequently occur, a continuity of processes is essential if environmental performance to ISO 14001 standards is to be maintained. When jobs are changed and the organization expands or slims down, it is important to know all the responsibilities that are being affected. It is often easy to overlook infrequent activities in a time of change – an oversight which can have significant repercussions.

Job descriptions

These define roles in the company in such a way that you and others with whom you interact, have a clear understanding of the responsibilities and authority which enables you to act. It puts structure around the job. The job description should specify the performance criteria deemed necessary to complete the task, e.g., a performance criterion for a secretary might be the ability to type 60 words per minute.

The most important factor in the job description is the balance between responsibility and authority: responsibility for certain tasks must be supported with the resources to complete the task and the authority to act if the task is to be completed. For example, if you are responsible for providing an emergency response service to tanker drivers, you need to know the performance criteria, e.g., 'respond within a specified time'. You then need the resources – and the authority to use those resources – to achieve the call-out time.

Job descriptions, therefore, usually have two elements: (1) a general description of the role and responsibilities and (2), elements of performance management. The performance part of the job description will expand on the responsibilities part. It should set out the achievements that are required if the job holder is to meet his or her key responsibilities and major goals. For example, within a departmental function, say 'site facilities management', the role of energy management may be delegated to one member of staff. The job description should provide the boundaries of the individual's activities. If the description requires that bills are to be *paid* on time, then that is what the individual should do. If, however, the intention is to *manage* energy use, then the job description will be different. The description may therefore include an analysis of energy use; tariffs, equipment, installations, practices and procedures in order to achieve better energy use and efficiency. Job descriptions can form a major element of the EMS documentation.

Within the job description and responsibilities must lie clarification of authority to act in emergency situations. Detailed descriptions of emergency procedures will be documented in the emergency plan; it is ownership of any documentation and emergency response that must be ascribed in the job descriptions. This includes the authority to act and commit resources in emergency situations.

Performance planning

Performance planning translates general roles and responsibilities into specific and observable end results or 'outputs'. Most job descriptions list a range of responsibilities which result in between six and nine outputs – any more and it becomes difficult to prioritize. For every output there will need to be some measurement or indicator to determine the quality of the output. Does it meet the specified requirements? Only then can the individual be appropriately assessed. The performance plan should indicate the outputs and the performance criteria against which the assessment will be made (*see* Table 18.1). Sometimes the performance plan may include reference to some of the activities to be undertaken in achieving the objectives.

Table 18.1 Performance plan

Objectives	Performance criteria	Assessment
Output: To reduce energy demand and costs on the Saltmarsh site by 5% over 1992 (assumes constant demand)	*Indicators* ● Achievement against budget ● Impact on business ● Investment payback criteria met ● Quarterly control reports ● Supplier relationships	

ESTABLISHING RESOURCES

From the implementation workshop you have gained an understanding of the dependencies to achieve the desired environmental performance. These resources include

● people with dedicated responsibilities to support the programme of work, e.g., environmental programme managers, departmental co-ordinators and EMS auditors;

● some equipment and systems support will be needed to establish the integrated EMS network in a co-ordinated manner across the business;

- some financial resources to support specific areas of technical expertise, e.g., consultants and/or technical training;

- some financial resources to provide equipment or tests to support the operational control activities at technical level.

Resources will need to be identified in every function, department and level, balanced to meet the needs of that particular area in achieving its environmental performance goals. You will need to ensure that each departmental co-ordinator reviews the need for resources in a timely way, through regular reviews in the project team meetings.

ESTABLISHING VERIFICATION METHODS

The requirements for verification include the necessary protocols and procedures for auditing the environmental management system, together with appropriately trained personnel.

You will need to have a programme and procedures for any proposed EMS audit plans and protocols (*see Chapter 26*).

The audit staff, as well as being impartial and objective, will need to have a range of skills:

- *Leading audit programmes*: the lead auditor will require experience in audit practice and procedure, project management and interpersonal skills. A thorough knowledge of ISO 14010/11/12 (Environmental Auditing Standards) and ISO 14001 is required.

- *Auditors*: In support of the lead auditor, the team will need familiarity with systems auditing and good interpersonal skills, a thorough knowledge of ISO 14001. Specialist auditor skills may be needed:

  - Industry specific: where the organization faces specific issues it may be necessary to ensure the resources include relevant expertise e.g. steel, oil or chemical production process knowledge.

  - Environmental specific: where the organization faces particular environmental performance problems, it may be necessary to ensure the resources include relevant expertise: e.g., environmental pollution monitoring, waste minimization techniques or emission control.

THE MANAGEMENT REPRESENTATIVE

The management representative is a senior manager appointed by the top tier of the organization's management.

The role involves working with peer executives to ensure the commitment to the goal is consistently applied, overseeing the progress to plan and representing the organization externally. They will also report back to the top on the achievement and maintenance of the system so that review and improvement can take place.

·INTEGRATION OF ROLES AND RESPONSIBILITIES

It is important to review the roles and responsibilities of personnel with defined authority to ensure that there are no gaps, which might lead to errors or omissions, or overlaps, which might lead to duplication of effort and resources.

In order to achieve this integration, there are a number of actions you can encourage:

- *service level agreements*: mini-contracts between departments to ensure co-operation in areas of mutual dependency;

- *co-ordination meetings*: regular cross-functional or departmental meetings to review areas of common concern or changes in practices and procedures;

- *central directory*: maintain a directory of process ownership, roles and responsibilities in the environmental management manual to ensure a complete matrix of responsibilities is available;

- *publishing departmental representatives*: in any appropriate EMS documentation, house magazine or quality system, publicize the key contacts for activities and processes related to environmental performance issues.

Checklist

? *Do all the departmental staff have documented job descriptions?*

? *Does the job description cover:*

- *staff and resources adequate to achieve the objectives?*

- *clear descriptions of authority to act?*

- *clear responsibility for investigation and documentation?*

- *clear authority to take action to solve problems?*

? *Have you identified the requirements for verification activities?*

? *Have you identified the verification resources?*

? *Have you assigned trained personnel?*

? *Has the management representative been appointed by the top tier of management?*

Communication hints

◆ Establish an award for managers, as well as staff, to win for significant contributions to the promotion of environmental performance improvement in any of the key functions.

◆ Establish a voluntary programme of workshops or committees to work on aspects of environmental improvement in the community around the organization's sites.

◆ Contribute to local education and training establishments with presentation material and staff resources.

◆ Build environmental aspects of individual jobs into the appropriate reward and appraisal schemes that already exist in the organization.

CASE STUDY

Vauxhall Motors

Vauxhall has two manufacturing plants in the UK at Ellesmere Port in Cheshire and Luton in Befordshire, with its Corporate Headquarters in Luton. Its factory in Ellesmere Port was the first to gain ISO 14001 and EMAS registration, and the first vehicle manufacturer in the UK to achieve either standard. (Vauxhall Motors is part of General Motors' worldwide operations.)

The company has a Board Director with overall responsibility for the environment, and this person is assisted by an Environmental Affairs Manager at each manufacturing plant. Each business area has a senior manager with direct responsibility for the development of environmental programmes, and continuous improvement targets in their areas. These managers convene at least every three months, as the Plant Environmental Steering Group, where they decide on matters of policy and strategy.

At Ellesmere Port, the ISO 14001 team is led by a senior management representative at executive level, while the EMS implementation and continuing activities are managed by a Manufacturing Engineer who is now the Site Environmental Co-ordinator.

Ten Business Unit and Departmental staff were recruited as part-time environmental auditors, while a further six managers became responsible for implementing action plans for covering the main environmental issues at the plant. These issues comprise air pollution control, water pollution control, waste and hazardous materials, energy management, external noise management, radiation control and communications.

19

COMMUNICATIONS
AND TRAINING

(4.4.2/4.4.3)

Objective

Your objective is to implement an effective training and communications programme within your organization.

ISO 14001 REQUIREMENTS

An organization must identify training needs and ensure that all the people whose work could have a significant environmental impact receive appropriate training. The organization shall establish and maintain procedures to make its relevant personnel aware of the following:

- the importance of conforming with the EMS
- the potential or actual significant environmental impacts of their work, and the environmental benefits of improved personal performance
- their roles and responsibilities in relation to the EMS
- the potential consequences of departure from the operating procedures.
- personnel performing tasks which can cause significant environmental impacts have to be competent upon the grounds of education, training and/or experience.

The organization must establish and maintain procedures for

- internal communications about performance and management
- receiving, documenting and responding to relevant communication from external interested parties with regard to its environmental aspects and EMS.

The organization must consider what processes to use for external communication about its significant environmental aspects and needs to record what it decided.

ESTABLISHING COMMUNICATIONS

Unless your organization has good communications, the EMS is unlikely to be effective. This chapter is about establishing the necessary communications, training plans, training records and people's involvement to enable the environmental programme to be sufficiently understood and integrated into the business. The training and communication programme must therefore be designed to ensure that the managers and staff have access to the necessary information to enable them to fulfil their duties.

Communications such as environmental bulletins and updates maintain interest in the EMS, and communications are vital for formal and informal feedback on the EMS and its effectiveness. Staff will need training to enable them to understand the relevance and content of environmentally orientated communications. Details of the training available need to be communicated, and training for internal and external communications relating to environmental matters need to be dealt with.

During the assessments, the assessor does not expect you to have completed all your training programmes, but they will expect you to have identified your training needs, and the training programme must be underway – particularly for auditors and key responsible people – and, of course, you must hold records of training which has been undertaken.

GETTING THE MESSAGE ACROSS

Motivating the workforce and maintaining interest is an important issue for any training initiative. Therefore the training programme must not be a one-off event, but should start the process of ownership and commitment on the part of the management and the workforce which good communications will support.

EFFECTIVE TRAINING AND COMMUNICATIONS

As well the formal and informal components within an EMS training programme, there are three key components to effective training and communication:

- Know the desired response;
- Know the level of leadership interaction required; and
- Know the complexity of the information.

Figure 19.1 illustrates the interaction of the components. Leadership interaction is the extent to which managers involve themselves in supportive or directive behaviour with their staff. There is no 'best' leadership style. The balance depends on the maturity of the individual in the new role and the challenges being faced (*see* Figure 19.2). Complexity of information is the extent to which the content of the message is readily understood.

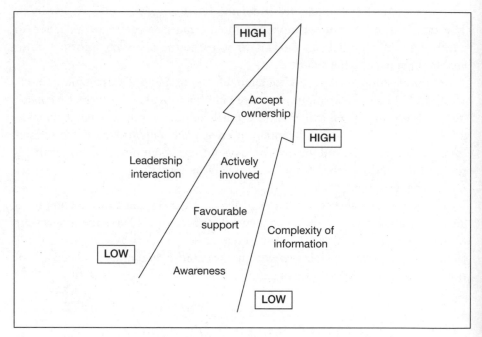

Fig. 19.1 Communications components

Leadership interaction in Figure 19.2 suggests:

- *Directing* – low supportive behaviour with high directive behaviour – 'Please do it this way'
- *Coaching* – high supportive behaviour with high directive behaviour – 'Please do it this way, but before you do, let us discuss any points you have!'
- *Supporting* – low directive behaviour with high supporting behaviour – 'How do you think we should do this?'
- *Delegating* – low directive behaviour and low supportive behaviour – 'Please deal with this!'

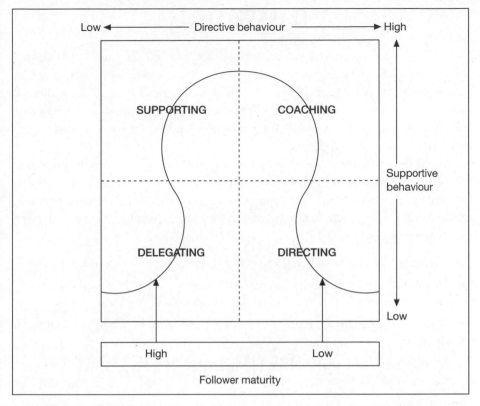

Fig. 19.2 Leadership style

If the objective of the message is merely to make staff aware of something, the level of leadership interaction will be small, and the content simple. However, if your message requires action the level of leadership interaction will increase, as can the message's complexity. The same is true in reverse. If you are not prepared to put the appropriate management time into a complex communication, you will not get the response you desire. Your training and communications plan, therefore, must be designed to balance the desired response with the necessary leadership interaction and complexity of information.

A further consideration in both training and day-to-day communications, of course, is the capacity of the recipient to understand and implement the new information. To communicate effectively, you must take into account the learning styles of the communication's recipients.

LEARNING STYLES

We all learn. However, as we move through life, we find the process of learning changes. At school we are taught by others who know things we do not. Whether through discovery or by rote, we have information pushed at us. As adults we tend to learn what we want to learn or that which is presented in such a way that learning is easy and pleasurable. If we are not interested we have the capacity to 'switch off' and cease to learn.

An important factor in developing training and communications programmes, therefore, is the learning styles of their intended recipients. In the same way that we are biased towards different aspects of activity – thinking (theorist), planning (pragmatist), doing (activist) or measuring (reflector), people have a bias to learn in different ways:

- *Theorists* learn better when there is a conceptual approach to the subject.
- *Pragmatists* understand that theory is all very well, but how can it be translated into reality? How would we plan to implement the idea?
- *Activists* like to know what has to be done, and learn best by participating in the process.
- *Reflectors* like to understand the anticipated results of the actions and measure the responses that are achieved.

We all possess a variety of these traits. Therefore, if trainers and communicators want their messages to be absorbed and acted upon, they must present the message in a combination of ways to cover the range of learning styles of the audience. In designing the training support necessary to the EMS implementation programme, trainers must make the learning pleasurable and stimulating, and combine the different learning styles. You are more likely to achieve buy-in to the EMS if the people being trained feel involved, and are learning in a style which suits them.

OBSTACLES TO EFFECTIVE TRAINING AND COMMUNICATION

The success of your communications effectiveness can be measured in the ability of the workforce to implement the organizational changes required to improve environmental standards. In order to encourage an active and participatory approach, managers must give staff members the capacity to effect change. There is nothing more frustrating than to be encouraged to change the way we carry out our day-to-day activities, only to find that the changes we propose are inhibited by others in the organization who do not appear to have the same message about the need for change. Those at the top of the organization hold the key to making changes. Organization hierarchies mean that often those who 'own' the business processes (i.e., senior managers) have less awareness of the impact and effectiveness of these processes than do the staff whose function is to make them work. If the management approach is *not* to encourage change, because to do so challenges the authority of the process owner, then ineffective processes often continue to operate even though the operators know they can be improved. The fear factor is at work. Table 19.1 shows how the management tiers usually operate within organizations. The understanding of managers as inhibitors to change has led to the movement of 'empowerment' in training today. Empowerment encourages staff to make change happen and to accept their individual roles in making the processes work by contributing to the system design and taking ownership of the quality of work they see in front of them. Empowerment requires you to remove the 'fear factor' of failure.

Table 19.1 Management tiers with respect to process ownership and practice

	Process ownership	Process practice
Senior management	HIGH	LOW
Middle management	MIXED	MIXED
Operations staff	LOW	HIGH

BUSINESS PROCESSES

Precisely what it is that is being changed is not always clear to those involved in a change programme. A common definition of what constitutes a business process must therefore be shared by all.

Business processes are a series of linked activities that have a defined start point, from an input, and proceed through a series of actions which add 'value' to a defined end-point, i.e., the output.

For example, paying a supplier invoice starts with the receipt of an invoice (the input) and goes through various checks to ensure validity of work done, validity of the value against an order and a check to ensure authority to pay is appropriate. Payment (the output) to the supplier follows (*see* Figure 19.3).

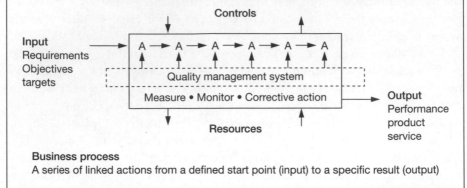

Fig. 19.3 Business process

The 'fear factor'

The root of the 'fear factor' in process change is the fear of the unknown and it can seriously affect your ability to change the management system. It is essential to eradicate the 'fear factor' if you are going to succeed in implementing your EMS programme. You want to encourage good performance from staff in areas which are unfamiliar to them. Your staff must gain confidence and knowledge in those areas. Reduce the fear of the unknown and the fear of failure at the outset and you are more likely to succeed in your objective. The fear of failure is the key – do away with this and people will respond to change enthusiastically.

You can reduce the 'fear factor' in many small ways at the lowest level in the process, but to allow that to happen you have to start at the top and displace the current paradigm of 'management knows best'. Managers have to start to see themselves as enablers, supporting the staff in implementing the goals and objectives set by managers. Managers remove inhibitors to progress, they do not create or support them. An education programme will go through a number of phases to achieve this: from awareness and consciousness, through understanding and agreement to implementation.

Implementing a training programme

Establishing a training programme, therefore, is essential not only for educating your organization's workforce about environmental issues, environmental management and environmental management standards, but also for removing fears and easing through the change necessary for improving environmental performance. You will need to identify training groups and their needs at all levels of

188

your organization. Training needs will not be identical; what is appropriate on the shop floor will not be right for directors. While workshops are an excellent way of educating staff at various levels of the organization, they may not be universally appropriate.

IDENTIFYING YOUR TRAINING NEEDS

A training programme must enable personnel to meet the requirements of ISO 14001 without bureaucracy. Like your approach to the rest of the EMS, your approach to training should consider the risks and the opportunities for business benefit.

A SWOT analysis in the IER can reveal areas of weakness, and the training programme should therefore address such gaps. Such a programme should also develop with your implementation of the EMS rather than isolate it as a discrete task which you deal after setting up the system. In other words, training is a core element of implementation.

Skills analysis

The *skills gap-analysis technique* is a useful tool in identifying training needs. It establishes what kind of training is needed on an individual basis. In the development of your departmental EMS documentation you have incorporated detailed job descriptions of the key personnel. Each job description can now be analyzed to establish the range of skills required to implement the role satisfactorily. Ask your staff to indicate their individual levels of skills against the skills requirements of their specific job descriptions. Where the level of skills fails to match the skills requirement, you have identified the training needs.

It is important to consider the different skills that are involved. These can be divided into two categories.

1. **Technical** – the knowledge required to do the jobs; vocational or industry-specific knowledge, e.g. environmental effects analysis, technical knowledge of processes.
2. **Personal** – the interactive and personal skills that enhance ability to do the job, e.g., auditing requires interviewing and good communications skills.

New skills are required for implementing the EMS standards programme. For example, quality management techniques; process assessment analysis; audit and assessment activities; legislative knowledge; or environmental effects analysis procedures.

Having identified your training needs you now know what components your training programme must include. From here, identify similar groups of people – such as managers, workforce, and specific individuals – and then produce a matrix for each group. Develop a training module with both general training and specific EMS needs. Identify each group's objectives in training. Objectives must be very specific and result driven; for example, directors must be able to identify key legislation.

KEEPING TRAINING RECORDS

ISO 14001 (4.5.3, *Records*) specifies that 'the organization shall establish and maintain procedures for the identification, maintenance and disposition of environmental records'; this includes training records. Records need to be kept in a way that is appropriate to the system and to the organization, to demonstrate conformance to the requirements of the Standard.

You need to keep training records

- to ensure that you know the extent of the trained resources available to you
- to help identify training needs
- to ensure you have an appropriate audit trail.

To avoid an unwieldy system, training records can be kept in a single place, owned by the environmental programme manager, or training department. You can keep individual records maintained by managers, but you will still want a co-ordinating register to demonstrate that the full range of skills required is available.

GOOD COMMUNICATIONS

We have indicated that to communicate effectively, you must know what you want to achieve as a result. You must also establish at the outset who the audience is and how best to interest them. If it is simply to tell people about an event, e.g., the opening of a new location, which may not require any action or response, it can be done by newsletter, management announcement or notice-board message. However, if you wish your audience to *do* something about the information they receive, then you have to design the message and use the right medium to provoke the response you need. As with training, you need to plan the style, method of distribution and level of any communication with respect to its intended audience and how you want them to respond to it.

A MODEL OF THE RESULTS OF A SUCCESSFUL TRAINING AND COMMUNICATIONS PROGRAMME

You will know when you have succeeded in implementing an effective training and communications programme because your company will be well on its way to reducing its environmental impacts and achieving the requirements of ISO 14001. The goal of your integrated communications programme, as part of your EMS, is to move the company along from unconscious incompetence to unconscious competence.

Unconscious incompetence

Staff are unaware of the environmental issues and the present management system's shortcomings. New issues are being introduced, although staff are unaware that anything is wrong or that there are other, better, ways of doing things – either to achieve the same standards more effectively and with less resources, or to achieve higher standards with similar effort through continual improvement.

Communications at this stage start at a low interaction/complexity level to raise awareness of the environmental issues. 'I understand that there are global environmental problems. Other organizations understand and are changing their responses. We will be considering our position and responding to these issues.'

The initial review has highlighted areas of performance which fall short of the best practice or desired direction. The initial communications programme and awareness presentation will have started communications at the 'unconscious incompetence' level using the information received from the initial review. A review of the draft organizational environmental policy and its potential impact on the organization, together with a look at the anticipated schedule for the next steps in the communication programme will indicate where communications should be focused.

It is important to measure where information has got to and whether it has been understood. It is difficult to move on to the next stage unless you have agreement at this one. Repeat the awareness programme if you are less than 50% satisfied that people have understood the issues.

You are likely to be at this stage when you are considering an EMS.

Conscious incompetence

Staff are aware of the issues and some of the system's failures, strengths, weaknesses, opportunities and threats. There is a consciousness of the issues at a

191

global and a local level and some immediate changes may be proposed by action-orientated staff.

Communications at this stage are high in interaction/complexity and aim to achieve commitment to the issues and make changes to achieve the new goals. 'My function/department has a role to play in support of the organization's over-all business goals. In doing so we have these environmental effects, can manage them better, and this is what we are going to do ...'

The follow-up implementation workshop(s) will do this with a detailed study of the department or organization's operations and existing management systems, identification of the environmental effects, objectives and targets, and programmes for implementation. A number of actions will arise which will initiate the gathering of more information, the commencement of initiatives or projects and the building of teams to address the issues. At this stage, if it is well done, there will be a demand for more information on process analysis, effects analysis, statistics and improvements in project management. You must ensure that there is an appropriate level of expertise to respond and maintain momentum.

You are likely to be at this stage during the early stages of implementing an EMS.

Conscious competence

Having made changes to processes and systems to achieve higher standards of performance, staff are now aware of the benefits and improvements in performance standards. At this stage they are sustained because they *know* that they are doing things in a better way.

Communications at this stage focus on the inward recording and reinforcing of achievements and support to the changes. 'I understand the environmental policy and targets and the role I and my department can play in contributing to the organization and global environmental issues. We are doing things differently now and I can show you what and how.' Communications activities are focused on recognition, reward and highlighting the changes.

You will probably be at this stage when your EMS has all its systems running, but it is all still new and not fully effective.

Unconscious competence

This is the state of an organization with a fully implemented, functioning, habitual and trouble-free EMS.

Staff are now unaware of the automatic management processes now in place to establish and maintain performance to high environmental standards in all existing or new activities.

Communications should focus on business-as-usual reporting and measurement but include all the new and evolving environmental criteria. Staff are now more proactive and outward-facing, ensuring that full benefits are obtained from the investment. The organization is involving and developing partnerships with customers, suppliers and the community. 'I include environmental standard issues in my day-to-day business management systems. I can help you improve your environmental standards performance, so let's discuss the mutual benefits and how to do it.' However, although communications are business-as-usual, they are monitored to ensure that the correct balance is retained in reporting the successes and benefits flowing from the programme implementation. Staff and managers, as a matter of course, take ownership and responsibility for implementing change in the organization at every level.

Checklist

? *Have you established a training programme that:*

- *analyzes the knowledge, awareness and skills needs relevant to the new requirements?*

- *assesses the knowledge, awareness and skill mix currently available?*

- *identifies the knowledge, awareness and skill gaps for training?*

? *Have you established an effective training records system? Is it:*

- *available at a central point?*

- *owned and maintained by a specified jobholder?*

? *Does the training content ensure awareness of:*

- *importance of compliance with environmental policy and objectives?*

- *potential environmental effects of work activities?*

- *roles and responsibilities in relation to environmental performance management?*

- *risks of non-compliance with environmental performance standards?*

? *Have you established a communication programme that:*

- *is relevant to the message – information or involvement?*

- *is supported by the right amount of leadership interaction?*

- *is designed to appeal to all the learning styles in the audience?*

CASE STUDIES

Cascade Training – Formosa Plastics Corporation, USA and Perfecseal

In order to reach the wide spectrum of people who would ultimately be involved in implementing the EMS programme, FPC USA used a cascading training approach. After some workshops on ISO 14001, the Corporate EH&S people then trained other people. In all, the Corporate Group trained nearly 120 people, including up to 50 people at each of the first three plants in the company aiming for certification. Perfecseal used a similar approach, when their QA manager attended a standard, five-day Lead Assessor course in EMS auditing, and then propagated his new skills to his internal auditors at the factory. Both organizations used BSi Training Services to deliver their initial training programmes in EMS and auditing.

Environmental Auditors Registration Association (EARA)

EARA is a professional organization for those involved with environmental auditing, EMS and related subjects. The organization has identified the basic generic training needs for such professionals, and developed syllabuses of courses which include:

- A five-day foundation course for environmental auditing and initial reviews
- A five-day Lead Assessor Course for EMS auditing
- A three-day Internal Auditors' EMS course
- A three-day EMS implementation course
- A two-day course in understanding EMS.

Attendance at an EARA approved course gives assurance that the course content is both relevant and professionally delivered – BSi provides EARA approved training. EARA also has a scale of qualifications for professional auditors, and coupled with the training courses, the EARA's schemes and courses have become the *de facto* standards.

Brake Linings Ltd

During a visit to Brake Linings Ltd's factory in Derbyshire, it is easy to notice the way in which the company generates a high degree of environmental awareness. The walls and noticeboards display an abundance of simple reference cards and posters which both provide clear instructions for the grassroots activities of environmental management, and update all staff on the company's environmental performance. The company uses the same approach for communicating the important issues of quality, health and safety.

This is especially apparent in the area of waste management. In addition to the logically ordered system of skips, containers and areas for managing waste, there is also just the right amount of weather-proof posters which tell the workforce what to do with certain types of waste. The company has even labelled every single drain – indicating whether they are part of the storm-water or foul-sewerage systems – which means that it is very unlikely that any workers would accidentally pour a substance down the wrong drains.

The Body Shop plc

Table 19.2 sets out The Body Shop's advice on reporting and disclosure, from The Body Shop's 'The Body Shop approach to ethical auditing', in their *Values Report 1995*.

Table 19.2 Seven dos and don'ts of public reporting

Do put internal monitoring systems in place and ensure that senior management and staff are committed to regular monitoring, auditing and reporting.	**Don't** attempt to publish an ethical statement without having the infrastructure in place and support of management and employees for systematic auditing.
Do consider who your key stakeholders and design your communications appropriately.	**Don't** attempt to meet the needs of all stakeholders in one communication vehicle: a report designed to meet everybody's needs could end up serving nobody's.
Do agree what your objectives are – not only for ethical management but also for reporting. Ensure that these relate to overall company goals.	**Don't** decide to report without a clear direction on your ethical management being defined. Reporting is easier to start than it is to stop.
Do concentrate on priority issues and report on them in depth whilst keeping it simple, clear and user-friendly.	**Don't** be tempted to report on every aspect of ethical issues in exhaustive detail.
Do represent raw data clearly in diagram format to allow reader interpretation.	**Don't** detract from the information by over-use of graphics or photographs.
Do be honest. Report on the problems as well as progress. Your performance should be transparent and accountable.	**Don't** attempt to over-hype information. PR will be seen for what it is and judged accordingly.
Do ask for feedback. You need to understand whether you are meeting the needs of your stakeholders by offering questionnaires or discussion forums for completion.	**Don't** underestimate the importance of stakeholder feedback. You are not just reporting on what you say but also on what you think your stakeholders want to know.

Source: The Body Shop's 'The Body Shop approach to ethical auditing' in their Values Report 1995

Some ETAC Advice

Training company ETAC offers the following advice for EMS programmes.

Before you start

- Conduct a training needs analysis
- Use your environmental review to identify skills and awareness needs – if there is a problem is it because someone is lacking a skill, knowledge or motivation?
- Draw up a matrix of training groups (e.g., managers, staff) versus training-module content
- Write training objectives for each training group – this will help to focus people's minds on what they want the training to achieve
- Develop key messages which need to be delivered to the whole workforce
- Write training procedures

Cascading the programme

- Keep the messages and the information consistent
- Change the emphasis according to your audience

Directors' briefing

- The emphasis should be on the strategic issues. Directors want the overview, not the detail.
- Time – keep the training short and to the point. Handouts should be in bullet-point format.
- Work with selected staff to develop case study material from the site to provide practical illustrations of the environmental issues faced by the company.
- Take photographs to make the training practical.
- Look at potential cost savings and environmental risks, not bugs and bunnies.
- Look at waste minimization and materials management as two key areas because they could yield tangible savings and benefit the bottom line.
- Look at the environmental risks for the business, and the strengths and weaknesses in management controls, as seen by the directors.
- Look at directors' liability – always an issue to get them to take notice.
- Get the directors to make recommendations to the managers – control and report what they want to see. By cascading the EMS implementation, you will achieve greater buy-in.

Managers' training

- Build on the course materials developed for the directors' briefing and add further detail for the managers' training – this will help to build a consistent picture as you go further down the organization.

- Tailor course manuals and the course programme to focus on the issues for their industry – this is vital as it ensures that you gain their interest and support during the delivery.

- Start the managers' training with an introduction from a director – the commitment message!

- During the training, task the managers with identifying the issues for their area of the business – this gets them to think about issues which are relevant to them.

- Get the managers to work with a risk assessment methodology or significance assessment to identify the most significant environmental effects for their area of the business.

- Involve the managers in the embryonic stages of the EMS development – this is less likely to lead to the duplication of effort and the development of bureaucratic systems that management and staff will not follow.

- Give the managers the opportunity to shape the company's environmental management programme during the process of the training initiative – you will achieve greater buy-in and the programme will be focused on the company's environmental liabilities and business issues.

- Ask the managers for their guidance on the EMS and the tools they need to manage the risks, i.e., checklists – this helps them to identify and manage the priority issues when they are out in the workplace.

- Train the managers during the EMS development and not as a last thought just before the assessors arrive.

- Use a benchmark company that is ahead to show what can be done.

- Encourage the managers to identify reporting mechanisms and management controls that are successful, already in place and could be developed to integrate environmental issues – health and safety or quality management systems.

- Get the managers to feedback to a director at the end of the training. This will reinforce the commitment message.

- Develop an induction module which can be used to train new starters or those who have missed the programme.

Environmental awareness for other staff

- Start with global, day-to-day issues and move towards 'what can I do?'

- Make sure they understand the part they play in the EMS – procedures and roles.

197

- Be careful about too much emphasis on business benefits – you are trying to appeal to their hearts and minds.
- Use data and information to show that every little bit counts.

Training for auditors

- Internal quality auditors are familiar with audit techniques but their skills and knowledge gap can be in the assessment of environmental significance.
- Use any QMS experience and the lessons they have learnt to avoid creating an over-bureaucratic system and duplicating management time and effort.
- Auditors often need knowledge of environmental effects in order to judge whether a particular issue is significant.
- Make the programme highly interactive and cover the specific site activities and impacts.
- Give a foundation knowledge on the relevant legal and business drivers, environmental risk, screening criteria for identifying significance, emissions to air, land water and waste.
- Remember pollution prevention, emergency preparedness and response and continual improvement – how can auditors judge these unless they understand significance, source-pathway-sink, receptor and the basics of how pollution guidelines are developed (toxicity, bio-accumulation and persistence).
- Auditors need sufficient knowledge to enable them to effectively challenge information they are given during the audit.
- Build in a site visit and get the participants to look at the adequacy of management controls, monitoring, feedback and reporting mechanisms on their own site.
- Task the auditors with identifying the main issues for the area of the business that they have visited during the site audit.
- Encourage the auditors to identify reporting mechanisms and methodologies already in place as part of the quality system which could be developed to integrate environmental issues.
- Collate this feedback and present it to the client's senior manager at the end of the training.

Give the auditors the opportunity to shape the company's environmental management programme, particularly the reporting mechanisms for non-conformance and concern and corrective action reports.

Source: Jane Laffan and *Environment Business Magazine*.

20

ENVIRONMENTAL MANAGEMENT DOCUMENTATION

(4.4.4/4.4.5)

Objective

The goal is to compile a set of documents that:

- is integrated into the existing management system;
- meet the requirements of the Standard;
- is effective in implementing environmental performance improvement;
- includes a co-ordinating document, the environmental management manual.

ISO 14001 REQUIREMENTS

The standard requires you to establish and maintain procedures for controlling all necessary documents so that:

- Current versions of all documents are accessible to anyone who needs to know what is in them, and act upon them.
- The organization reviews them whenever necessary, revises them as needed, and ensure that 'authorized personnel' approve their adequacy.
- Obsolete documents are promptly removed from all points of issue and points of use, or otherwise treated in a way which prevents accidental use.
- Any obsolete documents retained for legal or other reasons are marked in such a way that they are obviously not the current, valid versions.

199

- Any documentation must be legible, dated (with dates of revision) and readily identifiable, maintained in an orderly manner and retained for a specified period.
- The organization must create procedures and assign responsibilities for the creation and modification of the various types of document.

ENVIRONMENTAL MANAGEMENT MANUAL AND DOCUMENTATION CONTROL

So why have documentation?

The purpose of these requirements of ISO 14001 is to ensure that there is adequate documentation to support the EMS. In addition to the specified environmental management manual, the organization must control all documentation relating to the EMS. In simple terms, the EMS documentation does three important things:

- It provides the means of control for all the relevant data and information which forms the core of the EMS.
- It gives instructions to the relevant personnel, so that they know what they need to do to meet the objectives and targets of the EMS.
- It provides a framework for the assessors, which they can then use to assess the level of compliance with the standard.

In these respects, the EMS documentation is very similar in principle to any other types of controlled documentation which supports the management of systems, so the principles of data and document control in the ISO 9000 series, for example, apply in the same way.

The meaning of control

Controlled documentation is managed documentation. In simple terms, *controlled* means two things. First, the people who need to know something have access to it; and second, they will always have the most current versions of any piece of documentation.

THE IMPORTANCE OF DOCUMENTATION

Bureaucracy is one of the most overused words in the business world. We complain about it, yet we know documents are essential. We would not buy, for example, a digital camera or some computer software without a user manual. We use contracts, invoices, letters, files and records every day to keep the business running. We create new ways of doing things every day, ask people to provide new measurements or different reports. Yet when we are asked to document *how* we get things done, up goes the cry 'bureaucracy'!

So, we accept that documents need to exist. They are essential to the operation of the business. What is important, however, is to know what amount of documentation is necessary: that which is essential *must* exist; only what you need *should* exist. The essential documentation must be managed so that it is kept up to date. It must be owned so that a specific job holder has responsibility to keep it up to date, change it, or withdraw it. In other words, *document control*.

It is helpful if each document is unique, has a specific purpose, is designed to meet that purpose, and does not duplicate another document or any part of another document. In the case of the environmental management manual this is particularly important. The manual will almost certainly refer to other documents in the organization – reporting structures, operating instructions, protocols and procedures. If they are all repeated in the environmental management manual, it will be prohibitively expansive, expensive and impossible to keep up to date. The manual should be a very slim document – ideally in electronic form. Documentation must also be accessible and 'user friendly'. A consultant from ERM once spoke of *dog-eared manuals* being the real test of usable and appropriate documentation system. Documents should be written in plain English with short words, short sentences and the minimum of jargon. It must also be designed and written to suit its audience.

The three levels of documentation

Like Quality Management Systems, there are three levels of key documentation. These are:

● **Level 1 – The Environmental Management Manual.** This is the core of the EMS. A good manual should be succinct, self-contained, and relate to the structure of the standard. It should, for example, describe in simple terms the means for evaluating environmental aspects and their impacts. The manual should also act as a signpost for any other relevant documentation, data and information. If, for example, an organization's system for dealing with emergencies dovetails with the requirements of the EMS, then there is little point in duplicating this, but simply to indicate where a reader can find the appropriate information.

- **Level 2 – Procedures.** These go into more detail for particular areas of the manual, and specify what the organization must do. A procedure could typically cover areas such as waste management, nature protection, energy auditing and defining the significance of environmental impacts. As a minimum, you must have procedures for (i) environmental aspects and impacts, (ii) legal and regulatory requirements, (iii) roles and responsibilities, (iv) monitoring and measurement, (v) corrective and preventive action, (vi) records, (vii) EMS audits, (ix) training and awareness, (x) document control, (xi) emergency preparedness and (xii) communications.

- **Level 3 – Working Instructions.** Also known as *working practices* or *Standard Operating Procedures* (SOPs). These are sets of specific instructions which relate to particular operations. For example, an SOP could tell an employee how to calibrate a specific instrument and how to measure for a particular pollutant.

Types of documentation

Traditionally, documentation has been in paper-based formats. More recently, many organizations have exploited the power of computing and developed on-line documentation. There are considerable advantages in this. It is very easy to control on-line documentation. If the documentation is on a server, then users all read one source document, so you only have to maintain one document. The growing power of the Internet, intranets and workgroup computing means that it is very easy for large organizations to distribute documentation very quickly and effectively. On-line tools such as hypertext, multimedia and search engines give users a lot more power to work with documents.

Computers, however, are not always appropriate, so there will always be a role for so-called hard copies. In a factory, for example, users often require SOPs, so these are best produced in rugged formats such as laminated, quick-reference cards.

Standards for documentation

There are some simple rules when creating any documentation. Let the needs of the user guide the content and its format, and keep to what the reader *needs* to know. Use language that the user will understand and keep all documentation as simple as possible – use diagrams, keep it short and lively, then a user is more likely to read and use it. Don't fall into the trap encountered by a well-known engineering consultancy, which thought that controlled documentation had to be complicated to work. Its procedure for internal and external communications ran to 27 pages!

There is some guidance for documentation. The computer giant ICL is a pioneer in effective documentation, and through the BSI, has created guidance notes:

- BS 4899: User's requirements for manuals. This provides guidance for users on how to write manuals and similar documents – such as procedures and SOPs – using the needs of the end-user to drive the content and style.

- BS 7830: This is a new guide for on-line documentation. While there is plenty of software to convert printed documentation into on-line formats, the conversion does not work on a like-for-like basis.

THE ENVIRONMENTAL MANAGEMENT DOCUMENTATION

For an EMS assessor, the assessment process will begin with a request to see the environmental management documentation. He/she then evaluates whether the system you have in place is sufficiently comprehensive and mature to warrant a site visit. Assessors require *documents* to show what should be done, and *records* to demonstrate that it is being done. For example, if you have a particular process to monitor and record the handling and disposal of hazardous waste to meet the requirements of national legislation. The necessary documentation will be reviewed, and the activities and records assessed for conformance. In addition, the appropriateness of the environmental control practices and procedures will be considered, to ensure that the right test method is being used in the right place and is providing the appropriate management control.

You must establish and maintain documentation which brings together the environmental policy, the objectives, targets and the implementation programme. It must specify *who* is responsible *for which* areas of activity, how the system is designed to work, and should contain 'signposts' to other related documentation.

The documentation must cover the day-to-day activities, abnormal operating conditions, and incident, accident and emergency situations. It must ensure that emergency plans contain information and instructions that address environmental risks and pollution problems.

COMPILING THE ENVIRONMENTAL MANAGEMENT DOCUMENTATION

The implementation workshop, *Chapter 17*, will generate the information you need to document the EMS at every key level. Each department, function or branch will have a local EMS for the operational elements particularly relevant to them. At a higher level there will be a co-ordinating document that brings all the constituent parts together. Figure 20.1 shows a typical distribution of documentation within an organizational framework.

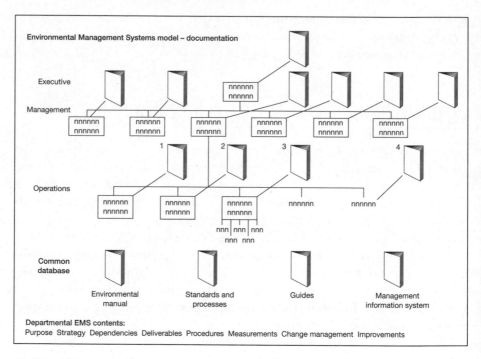

Fig 20.1 The distribution of documentation within a structured framework

At departmental level, there is a local document designed around the common framework or 'skeleton'. Each should be a crisp, concise document, directing you towards other common documentation, except where there are specific points relevant to the areas of responsibility of the department. At the higher level, the documentation comprises common practices and procedures, standards, emergency plans, and management information systems which provide the necessary co-ordination of the operational elements. One of these will be the environmental management manual.

Each department aligns its mission, plans, dependencies, deliverables, procedures, measurements and improvement programmes to the company's wider programme.

The environmental management manual must include documentation on all the relevant practices, procedures and activities to fulfil the ISO 14001 requirements and be a fully integrated element of the management system. It, and the other necessary documentation, must record effective activities in implementing, monitoring, reviewing and improving your company's environmental performance.

Checklist: environmental management manual

? *Is there an appropriate level of documentation?*

? *Does the manual exist?*

? *Does the manual contain: environmental policy; environmental objectives and targets; environmental programme; roles and responsibilities; and a description of the system?*

? *Does the information cover abnormal operations?*

? *Does the information cover incidents, accidents and potential emergency operations?*

? *Do the emergency plans contain relevant environmental information?*

PROCEDURES FOR CONTROLLING DOCUMENTATION

Part of the common database will be the document control procedures, a brief summary of the actions essential to control documents. Staff support functions may own a document like this. Smaller organizations often find that sharing out the ownership of common processes between line managers provides a balance between tactical and strategic views. This has the added benefit of encouraging mutual support and co-operation. It also avoids the creation of large staff departments as an unproductive, but expensive burden, and usually ensures that the documentation you have is only the essential information – busy line managers do not create paperwork for the sake of it.

When preparing the documentation control procedures, you should consider the following factors:

- Every document must have a purpose, whether to advise, guide, describe a process or report a requirement. The beginning of the document should define *the scope*, what it covers and what it does not.

- Every document must have an owner. The owner is not an individual but *a job-holder*. For example the owner of the internal EMS audit may be the environmental programmes manager, not 'Bill Bloggs'.

- Every document must have some method of indicating its currency – when it was *last updated* and when it will next be updated.

- Every document must be *available* to those who need to refer to it in their day-to-day activities in support of the environmental objectives and targets.

Checklist: documentation

? *Is there an established and maintained documentation control procedure?*

? *Does the procedure cover*

- *identification of documentation by division or function?*

- *the scope of each document?*

- *the current edition and next revision information?*

- *change approval procedures?*

- *name of the owner.*

? *Does the procedure indicate how access will be controlled?*

? *Does the procedure cover the withdrawal of obsolete documents?*

? *Does the procedure include a specified period of retention?*

Communication hints

◆ One of the problems that busy staff face is the 'help' they get from staff documents. Document owners must ensure that the users of documents have the opportunity to comment on what they will have to work with. Listen to what the users say and reflect their views.

◆ Ensure 'readability' is implicit in the documents. Aim at a comprehension level appropriate to the recipients.

◆ Measure the use of documents regularly and set yardsticks for maintaining documents in circulation.

◆ Withdraw documents that do not meet your criteria for usage.

◆ Update and change documents immediately they are out of date. Your users will appreciate your commitment to accuracy.

◆ Aim at 'well thumbed' documentation.

CASE STUDIES

Schlumberger

Schlumberger breaks the mould which says that documentation has to be unexciting and boring. The company has several innovative mechanisms which enhance the documents and make sure that they fulfil their purpose. For a start, the company uses lots of colour, graphics and photographs in its manual and procedures. An SOP, for example, can contain a sequence of photographs and diagrams, rather than lengthy text. Each procedure is assigned to a member of staff, whose role is to manage it. This wide-ranging ownership has increased the motivation of staff by giving them a hands-on role with the EMS.

The company has also made full use of the intranet and the Internet both in distributing the documentation and in managing the EMS. A member of staff, for example, can use a search engine to find a particular procedure or SOP for their own tasks, thus eliminating the need to plough through information which is not relevant to them at that time.

Shotton Paper plc

This paper manufacturer has several sites throughout Europe, all of which have standardized systems which can be tweaked and tailored to the needs of each country or region. The company has a very proactive approach to exploiting IT as a tool for business management, and in recent years, the company has installed an enterprise-wide network-computing environment.

The company uses a well-known workgroup computing programme on top of this network, which enables people at different sites to communicate as 'virtual' teams, and share information. The company has documented its EMS using this system. It has also ensured that the EMS documentation dovetails with the company's existing systems and documentation for health and safety and operations.

Elmwood College

This college of horticulture and agriculture was one of the pioneers in the BS 7750 programme. It says that its first attempt to produce an environmental management manual was singularly unsuccessful and not accepted by the external assessor. It was produced by an environmental scientist who wrote it without due regard for the standard. The second version of the manual was produced by the environmental manager who consulted with a quality co-ordinator. The new manual took each clause of the standard, and then stated how the college would deal with each clause, retaining the system of numbering in the standard, which simplified matters enormously. ▶

▶ John Salter, the Environmental Manager and a lecturer in horticulture, has plenty of useful advice. 'In compiling the manual, some matters require fleshing out in terms of how they are to be achieved in practice. It is these items which are placed in the environmental management procedures. These were again numbered in accordance with the clauses of the standard and were kept as simple as possible. It is essential to say what you actually do, rather than to make a statement about what you would wish to do in the best of all possible worlds. All our attempts to "gild the lily" in this regard have been mercilessly punished by the external verifiers.'

Formosa Plastics Corporation, USA

FPC USA's EMS manual was prepared by its Corporate EH&S staff. The manual contained a significant level of detail, such as a description of the implementation steps, an assignment of responsibilities, and information about the procedures. The manual built on three important lessons which FPC USA learnt from its experience with ISO 9000. These were:

- Do not create another management system. FPC USA's manual made it very clear that the EMS was to be integrated within the QMS.

- Do not develop a tome. People do not like to read long documents. If a relevant procedure already exists in another system, then the EMS manual should cross-reference the existing procedure.

- Make sure that the documentation contains lots of practical guidance. Facility personnel will appreciate this, and will actually use it.

21

OPERATIONAL CONTROL

(4.4.6)

Objective

The goal is a set of documented practices, procedures and systems to ensure that the activities of the organization which have an impact on the environmental policy, objectives and targets are carried out under specified conditions.

ISO 14001 REQUIREMENTS

The organization must identify its key operations and activities through analysis of its significant environmental aspects, policy, objectives and targets, and then manage these activities to ensure that they are performed within specified or controlled conditions through:

- establishing and maintaining procedures to cover situations where the absence of such procedures could lead to deviations from the environmental policy and the objectives and targets;

- stipulating operating criteria in the procedures. This includes establishing and maintaining procedures related to the identifiable significant environmental aspects of goods and services used by the organization and communicating relevant procedures and requirements to suppliers and contractors.

MANAGEMENT IS THE ESSENCE OF
CONTROLLING IMPACTS

The purpose of this section of ISO 14001 is to ensure that the environmental policy, objectives, targets and programme are translated into action on a day-to-day basis throughout the organization. The standard has three closely related sub-clauses which cover:

- control procedures to ensure activities take place within appropriate parameters (4.4.6);
- verification, measurement and testing to ensure that the control procedures are effective (4.5.1);
- non-compliance and corrective action to change the control procedures when they fail (4.5.2).

All three are an integrated part of an effective operational control programme, but it is easier to understand the elements if we look at them separately.

CONTROL

The expression *specified conditions* is used to define a designed state whereby production processes take place in predictable patterns, under the control of the operating staff. The expression is used for all operational activities, whether manufacturing or administrative. The controlled state provides confidence to management and staff that, provided the operating instructions are followed, the process will operate within the design parameters. The product or service that forms the outcome of the process will then meet the requirements of the organization. The confidence in system performance then allows management to concentrate on improving the processes and products to higher standards.

ISO 14001 does not ask for instructions for everything, everywhere, but it does ask for documented work instructions where the lack of them could result in a deviation from the environmental policy, objectives and targets. For example, if it is a part of your policy to ensure that your suppliers meet your environmental performance standards, you may need to tell your staff responsible for procurement that this is required. Your procurement process will reflect this and terms and conditions of your contracts will include references to your criteria. This is not just a case of adding ISO 14001 alongside the place in the contract where ISO 9000 is documented. You need to clarify the implications of the environmental performance you are looking for and the impact on the product and services you wish to receive.

Whereas ISO 9000 compliance ensures a quality system to get you the products or services you specify, ISO 14001 may result in more wide-ranging changes in the supplier organization which may have an impact on the specification you provide. In a pilot programme, a UK car manufacturer worked with a number of small suppliers to understand the implications of asking for ISO 14001 compliance as a contract term. The results showed that while the specification is achievable, both parties must work together to understand the implications.

If your policy includes a commitment to comply with the requirements of EMAS, then you will need to publish a regular environmental statement. Your staff will need to know who is responsible for what, when and how. If your targets include specific reductions in waste streams, you will need to instruct staff in how this will be measured and what is required of them. If your targets include reducing energy demands to reduce the CO_2 burden, then your instructions on the procurement of plant and equipment, building design standards, transport and product design will need to make that clear.

IDENTIFICATION OF THE CRITICAL ACTIVITIES

The key to the development of operational control procedures is the output from the implementation workshop and the functional/departmental EMS. These provide the identification of the critical activities, i.e., those which, if they went wrong, would most compromise your ability to deliver the environmental performance standards specified. To establish these critical activities, you must look at the environmental Critical Success Factors (CSFs) for the department/function. Follow the steps in *Chapter 10* to identify CSFs in a departmental/functional working group meeting. Let us imagine you end up with the following list of CSFs:

1. We must know our current environmental performance levels as a baseline for improvement.
2. We need to understand the corporate environmental policy to ensure that we set relevant objectives and targets.
3. We need to have well-motivated staff to achieve the new environmental goals.
4. We must provide appropriate training to ensure that the correct skills are in place.
5. We need to have a programme to make effective use of resources.
6. We must communicate our environmental objectives and targets to our suppliers and customers.

7. We need to integrate environmental performance criteria into our day-to-day operational systems.

8. We must have clearly defined roles and responsibilities to achieve the environmental targets.

Now, list the major activities of the department/function and analyze them against the environmental CSFs. Each activity is described using an appropriately paired verb and noun, e.g., measure emissions; educate staff; audit systems; review processes; monitor complaints; practise emergency response; recognize achievement. Each activity should have an identified owner in the department whose job it is to ensure that it gets done. The activity should have measurement criteria attached so that you know how well it is being done.

Draw up a chart, similar to the one in Figure 21.1, to show the interaction of the activities with the environmental CSFs. Then ask the group to identify which of the activities needs to be performed particularly well to achieve the CSFs. Some of the activities will score heavily against more than one CSF. For example, 'measure emissions' will need to be done well to achieve CSFs 1, 5, 6, 7 and 8. The number of crosses against each activity in the chart will give you an indication of its priority. From this analysis you can see that measuring emissions, monitoring legislation and staff training are a high priority. Your list of departmental activities will be longer than the example in Figure 21.1, so try to focus on the major activities rather than the minutiae.

CSFs	1	2	3	4	5	6	7	8
Activities								
Measure emissions	x				x	x	x	x
Train staff			x	x		x	x	x
Monitor complaints	x					x	x	
Control plant	x		x			x		
Process products	x							
Monitor legislation	x			x		x	x	x

Fig. 21.1 Environmental CSF/activity matrix

You then should ask the question in reverse: 'Have we got in place all the activities necessary to achieve the CSF?' In the example there are no activities supporting the need to understand the corporate goals and policy. So, if it did not exist, the activity of 'monitor corporate direction' would need to be created, given an owner and some measurement criteria.

One further thought: you know what critical factors are necessary to achieve the environmental mission for the department and you know which activities are crucial to ensure that the factors are met. Now check with the group how well they think the activities are being done. If you have no formal measurement, ask them to rate the activity against:

A   Excellent
B   Good
C   Fair
D   Poor
E   Not done at all

This rating allows you to check where resources should be focused. If a critical activity is rated as E, it should receive a higher resource priority.

PLANNING AND DOCUMENTATION

For each of the critical activities identified, you must establish the standards of management control you require and document how they are to be achieved in a documented procedure. It helps to map out the process steps in graphic format, as this allows you to see where instructions may be needed to assure compliance.

Each work instruction should, wherever possible, use the standards already within the management system. The goal of integration with existing systems will not be attained if special environmental instructions have to be considered at every step in the process.

Getting down to specifics – minimizing air and water pollution

When dealing with specifics, a good starting point is the list of significant environmental impacts whose control has been included in your objectives and targets. For each significant impact, analyze the parameters in your operations which control these impacts. An effluent treatment plant's capability to prevent the discharge of ammonia could depend upon the pH of the effluent, so the success of operational control could mean the combination of a real-time pH monitoring system and an acid-alkaline buffer mechanism to keep the pH at a level which will minimize ammonia discharges.

The specifics of operational control will vary from one organization to another, and even in similar organizations, the perceived needs for operational control will differ. Two companies in the same industry were heavy users of water for washing processes, which resulted in large amounts of effluent. Both companies decided to reduce their volumes of effluent; the first company recycled most of its effluent, while the second company increased the efficiency of its washing processes, which in turn reduced the need for water and detergents. In both cases, the outcome was a reduction in effluent, yet through different mechanisms of operational control. Table 21.1 shows some significant environmental impacts and examples of operational control measures to minimise them.

MANAGING THE SUPPLY CHAIN

During the early days of formal EMS, many organizations were surprised by the importance of the supply chain, and the profound effect on the environmental performance of individual companies. Every organization has a supply chain both upstream and downstream, determined by its inputs and outputs. These in turn have environmental impacts. A company which manufactures things can influence the design of its products in such a way as to minimize their environmental effects – from cradle to grave.

Many consumer goods are now designed to use less energy and be readily recycled. This area of design is becoming so important that many software houses have produced programs which help manufacturers develop new products, or modify existing ones to have lowered environmental impacts. These software packages are known as Design for Environment (DfE) tools, and are hybrids of the programs for LCA and process optimization tools commonly used in fields such as chemical engineering.

Products, services and procurements

An organization can *influence* what happens to its products once they have left the site boundary, but it can have a far greater *control* over its inputs. While ISO 14001 expects an organization to attempt to control the environmental aspects over which it can have an influence or control, this facet of the standard is open to a wide interpretation and in many cases, organizations have underestimated both the significance of the supply chain, and their ability to control.

This is especially true in service companies, especially those whose environmental performance depends on their supply chain. When BT, for example, conducted a review in 1990 of its environmental impacts, the company recognized that procurement was an opportunity to influence the environmental performance of the supply chain by exerting its policy on its suppliers. BT recognized that it is important to get the environmental issues and associated risks addressed within the procurement process, rather than downstream when they are more difficult to control. This approach also encourages greater supplier responsibility, not only for their products and services, but also in the way they operate.

Table 21.1 Operational control measures

Process	Environmental risks	Operational control
Aircraft de-icing	Water pollution through stormwater drainage	Contained de-icing areas; manual de-icing, as opposed to automatic gantries, to minimize the amounts of de-icer used; recycling systems for de-icers.
Paint-stripping using dichloromethane	Effluent from wash-water; hazardous waste	Use of alternative paint-strippers, such as plastic beads or baking soda; containment and recycling of paint strippers.
Combustion in a boiler	Emissions of nitrogen oxides, particulates, carbon dioxide	Use of gas instead of oil; optimization of temperature and oxygen regimes to maximize efficiency whilst reducing emissions of key pollutants.
Effluent discharges of ammonia	Water pollution	Real-time monitoring of pH and acid/alkaline buffer systems.
Producing packaging	Solid waste; resource consumption	Optimizing production from raw materials; recycling of waste materials.
Transport of goods	Emissions to air; resource consumption	Aerodynamic vehicles; optimizing routes to maximize amounts of goods transported per kilometre per kilogramme of fuel used; use of alternative fuels; training in better driving techniques.
Paint-spraying	Emissions of solvents and paint-particulates; hazardous waste	Use of high-efficiency spray guns; computer control of spraying; use of alternative paints; containment and recycling/recovery of solvents.
Incineration of chlorinated waste products	Formation of dioxins	Fine control of temperature and other combustion parameters; continuous emissions monitoring linked to computerised control systems to optimize combustion.

▶

Table 21.1 (continued)

Process	Environmental risks	Operational control
Energy use for heating	Resource consumption; carbon dioxide emissions leading to global warming	Computerized monitoring and targeting systems to measure resource consumption, external temperature; to optimize energy use for user requirements.
Vehicle washing	Water pollution	Automated, contained washing rigs to maximize water-use efficiency, coupled to recycling systems to minimize water use and effluent discharges.
Weed-killing	Water pollution; unintentional destruction of plants; soil pollution	Operative training; use of alternative techniques or chemicals to remove the weeds; weeding in still conditions only, i.e. not when it is windy.

In terms of procurement, a purchaser's influence on its suppliers means two things. First, an organization can specify minimum criteria for the environmental performance of its supplies such as paper and consumables, and second, a purchaser has the power to improve the overall environmental performance *per se* of its suppliers.

BT adopts a partnership approach with its suppliers – using its policy and standards as a framework – and has an award scheme to encourage environmental innovation, as well as getting suppliers to recognize that environmental factors can give a competitive advantage. This award considers the environmental credentials of a supplier, and so encourages good environmental performance. On the other hand, in areas where the environmental significance of a product or a service is critical, environmental factors can have a strong influence on the purchasing decision.

Dealing with services on site

In many countries, environmental laws state that the owner or occupier of a site is responsible for compliance with the law of all operations on that site, regardless of who performs the activities. This means that if a company employs a contractor to perform a supporting task on the site, and the contractor does something which results in a breach of an environmental law, then the company can find itself liable.

It is important therefore that your contracts require sub-contractors to identify activities, relevant laws and the controlled conditions they will provide to minimize your liability, should things go wrong. This is especially important in the case of waste management. In the UK, for example, the Duty of Care Regulations state that the originator of any waste is responsible for ensuring that the waste is managed correctly all the way to its end-point.

Checklist

? *Have you identified the relevant functions, activities and processes which affect the environment?*

? *Have you put in place control procedures for those relevant activities?*

- *operating instructions where the absence of such instructions could result in failure to meet the requirement*

- *procurement policies, practices and procedures for contracted activities*

- *monitoring and control of waste streams, effluent and discharges*

- *approval processes for plans and equipment investment*

- *performance criteria documented for the key activities.*

? *Have you considered all aspects of the supply chain?*

? *Are any of your suppliers critical to achieving your environmental objectives and targets? More importantly, are your suppliers' activities critical to your compliance with legislation?*

? *Do not worry if the improvements are not huge, because even seemingly small improvements can represent huge environmental gains. A telecommunications company, for example, found that a measurement of a waste-management practice showed a small gain, when in fact the company had closed a loop and eliminated a waste product in a cycle.*

? *Are you using standards as a framework for communicating your requirements to suppliers, encouraging them to go beyond simple compliance, and be innovative? You can do this by having a scheme of awards for the suppliers who have really achieved something special and demonstrated a combination of business and environmental benefits by innovation. The combined use of standards and awards is a carrot and stick approach.*

Communication hints

◆ The presentation of operating instructions and performance criteria must be clear and readily understandable. The graphic mapping of a process may help to explain the process steps more clearly than a written text form.

◆ Operating instructions do not have to be dull – an upper and lower emissions limit may be translated to a red/amber/green visual scoring criteria.

◆ You can find out if the managers and staff understand the operating instructions and procedures by listening to their complaints and comments.

◆ Look for examples of errors or omissions to track weak points in the operating instructions. When you hear people say 'Oh yes! That always goes wrong, always has', you know it's time to act.

CASE STUDIES

Hewlett-Packard

Hewlett-Packard's Queensferry site houses three major manufacturing operations. Each of these has worldwide charters for designing and producing equipment for electronic telecommunications, microwave testing and measurement equipment, and network management systems. In 1995, the site received BS 7750 certification for its environmental management system, making it one of the first UK operations to achieve the standard.

HP had been working with the British Standards Institution since 1991 to help develop the new environmental management standard, and was one of three Scottish electronics firms involved in the pilot programme. Environmental standards are not new to Hewlett Packard: the company has had its own rigorous set of environmental management standards and audit processes in place since 1982. HP's South Queensferry operation has been a leader in adopting these standards and achieving continual improvement in the areas of Environment, Health and Safety.

The South Queensferry site has made tremendous strides in environmental management over the past years. In 1993, it was one of HP's first operations to eliminate completely the use of ODCs (Ozone Depleting Chemicals) in its manufacturing process. Since then, it has removed all halon fire extinguishers and is replacing its refrigeration plant with a with a CFC-free system. Upgrading the building cooling system will also result in a 50% reduction in water usage. Energy savings of 25% have accrued since 1990, with a further 3% savings expected from the cooling system upgrade.

Amongst the Significant Environmental Effects identified and documented at the Queensferry operation was the potential impact of the site's printed circuit board manufacturing operation. This operation requires strict attention to the handling and disposal of hazardous chemicals, of which over 25 tonnes were stored on site. Close co-operation with the Lothian Regional Council ensured that HP continually met and exceeded the Council's standards for trade effluent.

Site recycling programmes now include most recyclables, such as cardboard, paper, plastic cups, etc. In particular, HP was one of the founder members of both EMERG (Electronic Manufacturers' Equipment Recycling Group) and ICER (Industry Council for Electronic Equipment Recycling) to develop a viable recycling infrastructure for scrap electrical/electronic equipment.

BT plc

BT plc spends nearly £5 billion per year on supplies. Recognizing the scale of its operations and its potential influence, in the early 1990s BT established an environmental panel which comprised six main stakeholder groups. These included BT managers, professional environmentalists, community representatives, research and academic organizations, young people and business and local authority managers. The panel helped to develop openness and trust, and brought insights about wider issues and outside initiatives. It acted as a spur for environmental change in other companies throughout Europe.

Since 1992, the company has built environmental considerations into its purchasing decisions. Having so many suppliers and recognising the importance of including environmental factors in the supply chain, BT developed its own generic standard – known as GS 13 – for purchasing, which specifies environmental requirements. Potential suppliers had to take its requirements on board when tendering to supply products and services. As well as giving minimum specifications for its supplies, BT also sponsors annual Environmental Supplier Awards. This scheme rewards innovative and successful suppliers who make substantial efforts to improve their environmental performance.

To give suppliers further guidance, BT got together with Nortel and co-arranged a workshop on environmental purchasing, with presentations by British Steel and B&Q. The workshop's purpose was to raise suppliers' awareness of environmental issues, and to encourage innovation.

In 1995, BT reviewed the effectiveness of GS 13 with suppliers and purchasing managers. What they found was that suppliers needed more guidance on using the standard and more environmental awareness, while purchasers needed clearer environmental objectives. The company found that GS 13 had been a major influence on some suppliers to consider their environmental performance. Others indicated that environmental factors should be given greater weighting in the evaluation process and that there was a need for greater awareness of environmental issues.

At BT, the key to improving the environmental performance of the supply is a combination of control through the environmental management system, and encouraging supplier involvement, responsibility and innovation.

BT's current procurement objectives and targets are shown in Table 21.2. ▶

Table 21.2 Examples of BT's current procurement objectives and targets

Target	Type	Status	Report
Dependent on there being no significant changes to the relative production figures for Phone Books and Yellow Pages, BT will achieve an average of 40% recycled fibre content across its range of telephone directories by the year 2000.	1994 Strategic	Ongoing	An average recycled fibre content of 30% was achieved acrros the range of BT directory products this year. This should show a substantial increase next year as BT's white page Phone Books are now printed on paper with 100% recycled fibre content.
BT will request all its centrally contracted printers to complete the questionnaire concerning their performance by December 1996.	1996 Improvement	Completed	Responses have been received from all of BT's centrally contracted printers. Consequently discussions are now on-going regarding the next steps and a possible action plan.
By January 1996 BT will compare the properties of lower weight virgin paper versus recycled paper in terms of cost, performance, and environmental impact, focusing on copier and computer paper.	1995 Process	Delayed	Based on an analysis of these issues our main paper buyer, who has become an expert on the environmental impact of paper consumption, has concluded that the better environmental option is to reduce the amount of paper used. Buying lower weight papers will contribute to a reduction in BT's overall paper consumption and is in line with the waste hierarchy – reduce, reuse, recycle. We also plan a number of other paper reduction initiatives.
To implement a programme to extend and improve the application of Environmental Standard GS13.	1997 Improvement	New	
BT has changed its procurement specifications for wooden pallets used in warehouses. Using the new specification, BT will reduce the total annual amount of wood purchased as pallets from 2,850m^2 to 2,500m^2 by 31st March 1998.	1997 Improvement	New	
By April 1998, the company will establish an action plan designed to reduce paper wastage at its printing contractors with respect to all work done for BT.	1997 Process	New	

Full details of BT's Objectives and Targets may be obtained from 'A Matter of Fact: A Report on BT's Environmental Performance 1996/7', available via BT's Environmental Issues Unit or from their Internet site at: http//www.bt.com/corpinfo/enviro.

BT's Top Tips for environmental management in procurement

- Do not be complacent about your environmental impacts just because you are not a manufacturer, you work in a services business, or your sector is perceived as environmentally benign. Every organization has environmental impacts and there is always the opportunity for continuous improvement.

- Identify significant environmental impacts in the supply chain using simple Life Cycle Analysis and Whole Life Cost of Ownership tools. These tools will enable you to understand both the environmental benefits and the business benefits. Using this combined approach not only reveals the initial costs of an EMS, but also demonstrates the long-term savings and real business benefits.

- Develop an environmental policy and get top-level commitment for it. The business needs to include environmental factors as an important consideration, and top management needs to be committed to the key drivers for change and improvement.

- Set supply chain and operational improvement targets linked to business benefits, and integrate these with the business planning process.

- Ensure that there is clear ownership of targets and their schedules' timescales. Measure the achievements in the supply-chain and communicate these regularly.

- Win people's hearts and minds to encourage innovation and individual responsibility.

  Source: Janet Quigley, BT Environmental Issues Manager, and Steve Mehew, BT, Supply Management, Environment Business Manager.

22

EMERGENCY
PREPAREDNESS

(4.4.7)

Objective

The goal is to ensure that your organization can respond effectively to emergencies and minimize the environmental impacts when they do occur.

ISO 14001 REQUIREMENTS

You must create and maintain procedures to:

- identify the potential for accidents and emergencies;
- respond to accidents and emergencies effectively;
- prevent and mitigate the environmental impacts that may be associated with them.

Where necessary, your organization has to review and revise its emergency preparedness and response procedures, especially after accidents and emergencies occur. You also have to periodically test such procedures where practicable.

THINGS CAN GO WRONG

Accidents do happen. However well-prepared your organization might be, there will always be some events which are beyond your control – such as natural disasters and even sabotage. Therefore your organization needs to systematically assess the risk of all the potential emergencies which can occur, and then develop emergency plans and procedures to ensure that you respond appropriately to unexpected or accidental incidents.

SO WHAT IS AN EMERGENCY?

In an environmental context, an emergency is defined as any abnormal event which leads to a breach of environmental regulations and potentially significant harm to the environment. From your determination of your environmental aspects and impacts, you may have found that processes have two operating conditions; the normal and abnormal. If the potential environmental impacts of any abnormal conditions are severe, then an abnormal condition turns into an emergency.

In the case of an airport runway-apron, for example, the servicing and taxiing of aircraft would be considered as normal, repairs to the apron would be considered as abnormal, while spills of fuels are emergencies because of the potential risks. Or in the case of a boiler, shut-down for unscheduled repairs is abnormal, while the failure of pollution control technology is classed as an emergency.

DEALING WITH EMERGENCIES

The best approach is to avoid emergencies in the first place by minimizing the chances of an abnormal event with extreme consequences, while having the resources to cope with them should they occur. The following sections describe a methodology which is based on those developed by several registered organizations.

Define the potential problem

Any abnormal event can be potentially hazardous, so you need to list and describe the consequences for every process on site. This activity is an extension of the evaluation of environmental aspects, except that you are looking for the extreme events – a form of risk assessment. So for every process, ask yourself what could go wrong? When things do fail, determine all their potential environmental impacts. For example, an operative spills some aircraft fuel. This spillage poses three immediate hazards:

- it is a fire risk;
- aviation fuel is slippery;
- the fuel can contaminate land and water resources.

Brainstorming is especially useful here, particularly with the people involved with the processes on a day-to-day basis, because they will have a strong appreciation of the finer details of any activity. Work through each possibility systematically, examining the inputs and outputs and determine the worst-case scenarios. The results from this first step will then tell you about the hazards.

Determine the risks associated with any hazard

An event or activity can be hazardous if any abnormal conditions associated with it are severe. Flying in an aircraft, for example, is hazardous. On the other hand, the probability of an accident while flying is extremely small, so there is a low *risk* associated with this hazard. Walking beside a road is also hazardous, but as statisticians like to say, you are more likely to have a road accident than you are to be hurt in an aeroplane crash. In other words, the risks of an accident associated with roads are much higher than those for flying.

Similar principles apply to environmental hazards. So having determined the abnormal and potentially deleterious aspects of any processes, you need to assign a risk factor to them. There are standard and proven risk analysis methods such as Failure Modes Effects Analysis (*see Chapter 13*).

Rank each potential emergency in order of significance

Once you have determined the risk of an emergency happening, you can then rank the emergencies in an order of significance. This will allow you to prioritize the allocation of resources to deal with each case. While there is always a degree of subjectivity to risk analysis, the objective here is simply to determine which potential emergencies you should prepare for the most (*see* Table 22.1).

Take steps to minimize the risks of an occurrence

Pollution prevention is better than end-of-pipe solutions, whether the pollution is caused by normal or abnormal events. This is the rationale behind the UK Environment Agency's approach, and why the organization attaches so much importance to environmental risk analysis. It also explains why this regulator wants the organizations it regulates to take steps to minimize the chances of abnormal events and to minimize pollution. So having determined which potential emergencies you should be addressing, now ask yourself what you can do to minimize the chances of them occurring.

Table 22.1 Example of environmental hazards and risks at an airport

Activity	Abornmal	Hazards	Risks of occurrence	Environmental	Mitigation
Refuelling	Spills	Fire River pollution Groundwater pollution	Low High Medium	Medium High High	Training, containment, spill absorbent materials
Fuel transfer through pipelines	Leakage	Groundwater pollution	Low	High	Double-shelled pipes, warning sentinels, containment
Aircraft washing	Wash water effluent getting into stormwater drainage systems	River pollution	Medium	Medium to high	Warning sentinels and containment sumps
Aircraft de-icing	Excessive de-ciers getting into stormwater drainage systems	River pollution	Medium	High	Warning sentinels and containment sumps

Develop emergency plans and procedures for each emergency

Having minimized the risks as far as possible, the next stage is to develop a strategy to cope with emergencies (an emergency plan) and the specific tactics for each particular emergency (the procedures and working instructions). There should be sequential steps within the emergency procedures.

- Deal with the emergency effectively to minimize the potential damage.
- Take steps to remedy any damage which has occurred.
- Carry-out a root-cause analysis to determine why the emergency happened, and see if you can prevent it happening again, or at least minimize the chances of it happening.

The emergency plans themselves should include the following elements:

- the services and personnel responsible for emergency services, e.g., spill clean-up services;
- actions for different types of emergencies;
- data and information on hazardous materials, such as each material's potential impact on the environment;

- steps taken in the event of accidental releases;
- training plans and drills.

Train your staff in rapid response

Timing is critical in the event of emergencies; the quicker you react to an event, then the greater your chances of mitigating any potential damage. There are three crucial components to a rapid response. First, you must allocate the necessary resources, so that they are available in the right places at the required time. While this sounds obvious, a company once had an effective procedure for dealing with spillages and a generous cache of equipment for mopping up spills and neutralizing the spilt chemicals. The staff were also well-trained in what to do. The only problem was that when the company had a spill, the equipment was kept in a part of the factory where the spills were least likely to occur, and by the time the spill-response team reached the site of the accident, most of the chemicals had disappeared down the drain.

Second, an organization needs an effective monitoring system to warn it that there is an emergency in the making. In the UK, there have been several examples of well-managed companies which have had accidental leaks of chemicals which have gone undetected until, for example, the chemicals leak into a river and a member of the public has noticed lots of dead fish. In most cases, the cost of extra monitoring equipment is dwarfed by the costs of clean-up operations and fines following prosecution.

Third, realistic drills are essential for effective responses. Some companies interviewed for this book reported that their first drills were often disasters bordering on comedy, until the staff appreciated exactly what was needed during an emergency. It is better to make mistakes in a drill rather than during an emergency.

Capitalize on experience and other systems

Many organizations, especially those in the chemical, oil and manufacturing industries, already have an emergency response system for health and safety issues. Such systems are invaluable for environmental protection, so long as there is not a conflict of interests between safety and environment. Many airports once dealt with fuel spills by washing them down the surface-water drains. Now that they know the environmental risks posed by this practice, airports have tackled the problem in two ways. First, they have reduced the chances of spills taking place by using automatic shut-off valves on filling hoses, installing drip-trays to catch any small spillages, and carrying out additional staff training to decrease the human errors which often cause spills. Second, airports now typically use absorbent materials to mop up any spilled fuels, rather than washing them down the drain.

Checklist

? *Have you expanded your process analysis from the evaluation of environmental aspects and impacts to determine all the abnormal events which can lead to emergencies?*

? *Have you performed a risk analysis to determine the probability of each emergency?*

? *Have you carried out a brain-storming session to figure out all the worst-case scenarios?*

? *Do you have a system in place already to deal with emergencies for health and safety issues, or disasters such as fires? Are these applicable, or do you need to enhance or modify them?*

? *Have you developed an emergency plan and procedures?*

? *Have you consulted the relevant regulators?*

? *Does everybody in your organization know what to do and if necessary, whom to contact when there is an emergency?*

? *Have all the necessary staff been through rigorous and realistic drills?*

CASE STUDIES

Mobil

Mobil invests a great deal in emergency avoidance and preparedness because of the potential severity of an event in the oil industry. The company's objectives for emergency response, for example, emphasise the avoidance of major oil spills, but at the same time, the company is well-prepared for them should they occur. In 1996, Mobil increased the scope of their emergency preparedness plans.

Mobil first assessed the different types of emergencies, their root causes and the risks associated with them. However much a company takes precautions, there are many things which will always be beyond anyone's control. Emergencies, for example, not only occur through equipment failures or human error, but can also be the results of natural disasters or even malice. They can occur on land, in the water or in the air, and include fires, bombings, accidental releases of oil or chemicals, or the results of natural disasters.

At Mobil, there is a corporate plan and support centres for emergencies while each facility has an on-site emergency response team which plans its own specific responses depending on its needs. If there is a minor incident, then each facility is resourced to respond to these and cope with them. ▶

▶ For severe incidents, the Mobil headquarters in Fairfax, Virginia has a Crisis Centre the resources of which are available all the time. If a facility needs its support, then the Crisis Centre is activated and supplies support 24 hours a day until the situation is under control. In an emergency, the on-site response team would communicate with the Crisis Centre and give its staff updated information on how they are managing the situation, while the Centre would provide whatever resources and expertise were needed.

A crucial part of Mobil's emergency preparedness is its drills procedure. Mobil's emergency preparedness drills are designed to bring a sense of reality to their crisis preparation. They range from local-level desk exercises to field exercises, which can involve hundreds of people and the use of equipment.

The scope of field exercises extends beyond the boundaries of Mobil's facilities. Organizations often involved can be local companies, environmental and mutual aid groups, industry and government agencies. If or when a real emergency arises, the relationships that these exercises build will be vital to a successful response.

Source: Mobil www site.

Brake Linings Ltd – the importance of effective labelling

Brake Linings Ltd is a model for effective communications and this is especially apparent when looking at the firms emergency responsiveness. Throughout the company's factory in Derbyshire, UK, there are succinct and effective notices, warnings and working practices which inform the staff about every issue relevant to them, including accident avoidance and what to do if an accident occurs. All the drains, for example, are labelled as stormwater or foul-sewerage drains, while there is a clear, bold notice above the drain which the local water authority has authorized the company to use for discharges.

The company has identified spills as a significant risk, so it has implemented spill response kits at strategic sites around the factory. Each kit is clearly labelled with essential information – such as the purpose of the spill kits, how to use them, and whom to contact when there is a spillage – while all the staff have been through a rigorous training programme to ensure that they react accordingly.

Brake Lining's procedures for emergency incidents is extremely comprehensive. The company also has a weekly EMS meeting, where the staff review any incidents that have been reported. According to Bob Payne, 'We also check usage of spill kit materials to see if there might have been an accident that has not been reported.'

Whenever there is an incident, Brake Linings Ltd has an effective procedure which ensures a prompt reaction, identifies the root causes, and sets in motion the preventive actions to minimize the chances of a re-occurrence (Figures 22.1 and 22.2).

Brake Linings Ltd

Environmental Procedure: EP8/10-01, issue: 6

Title: Emergency incident plan

1.0   Scope

1.1   This procedure defines the responsibilities for and the action to be taken in the event of an emergency incident.

2.0   Responsibilities

2.1   The Senior Team Leader *is* responsible and has the authority for controlling and co-ordinating all emergency incidents.

2.2   All employees are responsible for informing the above upon discovery of an emergency situation.

2.3   The Health, Safety and Environmental Manager is responsible for the post incident report which includes sending a copy to the Environment Agency.

2.4   The Management Representative is responsible for the periodic testing of this emergency procedure.

2.5   The Engineering Stores Manager is responsible for checking spill kit contents.

3.0   Procedure

3.1   General emergency procedure

3.1.1.   In the event of an emergency incident, the Senior Team Leader must co-ordinate proceedings *from* the incident control point (fire alarm board).

3.1.2   The Senior Team Leader must nominate 'incident investigators' to deal *with* matters arising from the scene of the incident. The Senior Team Leader must also nominate someone to record the chain. of events.

3.1.3   In the event of an emergency incident, the following must be notified immediately:
   ● Senior Team Leader
   ● the relevant emergency services
   ● Environment Agency (stating 'PC site for fast response')
   ● neighbouring sites (if directly affected)
   ● BSI.

3.1.4   A post-incident report must be written and filed under EM8/10-01, the ▶

Fig 22.1 Brake Linings Ltd: procedure for emergency incidents

aim of which should be to record the exact detail of the incident. The report should include:

- a synopsis of the incident;
- the chain of events;
- interview statements; and
- conclusions and recommendations.

The report must be brought up for discussion in the next Executive Committee and an action plan agreed.

3.1.5   The Management Representative should arrange for the periodic testing of this emergency procedure (at least annually) if practicable to ensure its continuing effectiveness and that employees will be suitably prepared for such an occurrence.

3.2   Specific requirements regarding fire incidents

3.2.1   Refer to 11523/3-01 Fire and Evacuation.

3.2.2   Depending on the nature and location of the fire, and particularly any hazardous materials that may be involved, susceptible drains may require blocking to prevent fire water run-off polluting the watercourse. Advice should be sought from the emergency services.

3.2.3   In the event of a fire the Senior Team Leader must ensure the fire is extinguished before returning any plant to service. If in doubt leave it off and call the fire brigade.

3.3   Specific requirements regarding chemical and liquid spills

3.3.1   In the event of routine and minor spillages, the chemical or liquid should be prevented from entering the drainage system using the appropriate spill control equipment. This shall involve covering susceptible drains and containing the spill.

3.3.2   Spills involving hazardous substances under COSHH Regulations require more careful consideration. Evacuation procedures may be required and the emergency services called. On no account should there be an attempt to deal with the spill unless personnel are trained to do so and are under supervision.

3.3.3   After dealing with the incident, all waste must be disposed of in accordance with EP8/3-01.

3.4   Specific requirements regarding dust escape

3.4.1   Dust unit doors should be closed at all times.

3.4.2   In the event of an emergency dust escape, the relevant dust unit must be switched off and all operations connected to the unit stopped.

3.4.3   An assessment must be made of the amount of dust released and the

Fig 22.1 (continued)

approximate wind speed and direction. If the incident is deemed serious enough, the emergency services must be called, who may instigate an evacuation.

3.5   Spill kits

3.5.1   Spill kits must have their contents checked weekly by the Engineers Store Keeper.

3.5.2   The Engineers Store Keeper must submit a weekly report to the USE Manager detailing spill kit usage for the previous week.

4.   General

4.1   Definitions

4.1.1   Emergency incidents are defined as involving a high risk to the health and safety of personnel and public and a significant threat to the environment.

4.1.2   Routine incidents that do not involve actual pollution or a significant threat to personnel should be deal with using internal resources. Examples include spillages on the shop floor of release agent or leaks from machinery. The Senior Team Leader or Health, Safety and Environment Manager should be informed.

4.1.3   Minor incidents may involve environmental pollution and threaten the health and safety of personnel. The Senior Team Leader or Health, Safety and Environmental Manager must be informed. Depending on the nature and outcome of the incident, and to prevent an escalation of the problem, the emergency services and Environment Agency may also need to be informed. Otherwise, internal resources should be used.

4.2   Chemical and liquid spillages

BLUE (storm drain)
RED (foul drain)

NO POLLUTING MATERIAL SHOULD BE ALLOWED TO ENTER THE DRAINAGE SYSTEM OR SOIL. If in doubt, seek advice from the Shift Manager or Health, Safety and Environmental Manager.

4.3   Spill risks

4.3.1   Spills may occur due to a number of situations:
- during bulk deliveries and collections;
- during deliveries and flo-packs;
- through accidental spillages due to handling, through incorrect
- handling, storage and decanting of oils and chemicals;
- by not tightening caps on outlet pipes;

Fig 22.1 (continued)

- by not using lids on containers, through leaks or bursts from drums and tanks and through deliberate acts of vandalism.

4.3.2 During period of factory shut-down when all personnel are off site (e.g., weekends), the police may wish to contact key holders. This information should be updated as required. During shutdown, dust plants do not operate and there will be no transport of liquid. Only fire would be a real concern.

4.4 Minor incidents and potential emergency incidents (those that are dealt with before they become of major concern) should also be logged by the Health and Safety department. Any incidents should therefore be reported to the Health and Safety Manager. A major spillage involves five litres or more of oil.

4.5 Spill kits must be checked once per week to ensure they are adequately stocked. A record of these checks must be kept in the Engineering Stores and of existing spill kits and their locations. Approximate quantities of spill equipment must be attached to each kit.

Fig 22.1 (continued)

BRAKE LININGS LTD
EMERGENCY INCIDENT REPORT
DATE: *8/1/97*   SIGNATURE:

DETAILED CHAIN OF EVENTS

3.30 am	*Oil spillage identified*
3.25 am	*Shift Manager notified*
3.37 am	*Assessment of situation made*
3.40 am	*Spill Sorb applied*
3.41 am	*Bag moved to another area*
3.45 am	*Bag covered in polythene and put into fresh IBC bag*
4.15 am	*Checked area — all okay — no further spread*
5.45 am	*Assessed situation, left spill sorb to soak up oil*

(Interview statements may be attached)

CONCLUSIONS AND RECOMMENDATIONS

See "Measures taken to prevent recurrence of incident"

INCIDENT SYNOPSIS

Oil spill from IBC bag left outside stores door for weighing — slow seeping from bag onto concrete

REPORTED TIME: *3.30 am*

DATE: *8/7/97*

LOCATION: *Roller door RIN-stores*

WERE SUBSTANCES RELEASED TO:	AIR?		LAND?	✓	WATER?	
IF SO, THEN WHAT?						
ESTIMATED QUALITY (L OR Kg) *1.5 LTRS*						

MEASURES TAKEN TO STOP OR PREVENT THE RELEASE?
Spill Sorb applied — drains covered — bag covered in polythene and put into another bag (IBC).

MEASURES TAKEN TO RECTIFY ENVIRONMENTAL DAMAGE?
Spill Sorb left to soak up oil spill and drain area covered with Spill Sorb to ensure oil is contained.

MEASURES TAKEN TO PREVENT RECURRENCE OF INCIDENT?
Department Heads need to notify personnel who handle oil (or similar) of correct disposal procedure.

ENVIRONMENT AGENCY INFORMED?	YES		NO	✓
WHEN AND BY WHOM?				
COLLECT ENVIRONMENTAL PROCEDURES FOLLOWED?	YES	✓	NO	
SPILL MATERIALS AVAILABLE?	YES	✓	NO	
RISK ASSESSMENT OR HS&E AUDIT PREVIOUSLY CARRIED OUT?	YES		NO	✓

Fig 22.2 Brake Linings Ltd procedure for emergency incidents

23

ENVIRONMENTAL MONITORING AND CONTROL

(4.5.1)

Objective

The goal is an established and maintained procedure that will (a) confirm the effectiveness of the operating control procedures and identify areas of non-compliance; (b) ensure that reliable data are generated as a part of operational control.

ISO 14001 REQUIREMENTS

To establish and maintain documented procedures so that you regularly monitor and measure the key characteristics of your operations and activities that can have a significant impact on the environment, and to evaluate compliance with the relevant environmental legislation and regulations.

In line with this, you have to record the right information to track performance, relevant operational controls and conformance with your organization's environmental objectives and targets.

If your organization uses any monitoring equipment, then it must be able to produce objective, verifiable evidence that it has maintained and calibrated the equipment.

MEASUREMENT AND CONTROL

The relationship between measurement and control is quite simple. Unless you measure something, then you cannot control it. Therefore an effective EMS requires measurement and control systems to determine if the operational control procedures are working. Your organization needs to design the system to ensure that it can identify the level of compliance achieved and indicate areas for improvement. Measurements are often designed to advise or inform management of the 'state of play' without regard to the use to which they may be put. They are designed for protection rather than process improvement. Yet operating controls can be complex and the processes subject to fluctuation, so we need a measurement approach that is consistent and comprehensive.

Monitoring and measuring

Many people confuse the terms *monitoring* and *measuring*. Strictly speaking, *monitoring* is defined as *the regular surveillance of the state of a process or condition*. Monitoring can tell us a lot about the state and extent of the emissions from a particular process, such as effluent discharges from an outfall. Monitoring may not necessarily deliver accurate, quantitative data about an emission, but often it does not need to do this; an inference about a particular process can suffice. This process is also called *indicative monitoring* as it tells someone if, for example, a type of control technology is working properly, and whether a process is emitting pollutants within its discharge consents.

Measuring produces accurate and precise quantitative data on the physical or chemical components in a process. However, in most cases, it is acceptable to use the term *monitoring* to include *measuring* as well.

The simplest type of monitoring is known as *grab sampling* or *spot sampling*. Someone takes a representative sample of the air emission, soil or effluent and then transports it elsewhere for analysis, such as a laboratory. Grab sampling is often the starting point of any monitoring programme because this analysis usually delivers a lot of important information for selecting the appropriate system for continuous monitoring. The technique is also used extensively for calibrating continuous monitors or for compliance monitoring. There are drawbacks, however. For example, if the grab sample is taken over a short period of time, then the analysis can miss peaks and troughs in the concentrations of pollutants emitted from a process or occurring in the environment. On the other hand, taking samples over a longer period of time will iron out any variations because the sample is an average.

There can also be several steps between the initial sampling and analysis, which introduces scope for errors, changes to the sample and contamination. Another drawback with grab sampling is that plant operators often need to know the state of play immediately. In this case, the solution is continuous monitoring.

Continuous monitoring provides real-time measurements or indicative readings of the state of the environment or a process. The main benefit is that it reveals the peaks and troughs in a process, as well as providing data for averages. These factors are very valuable both for controlling processes and regulatory compliance. On the other hand, continuous monitoring can be expensive and demands a lot in terms of maintenance and certainly requires firm management if monitoring is to produce good data.

Calibration is another critical area because the data will not be of use unless the readings from instruments and monitoring systems can be verified using traceable standards. Bear in mind that assessors are likely to explore this in detail if your organization's compliance with the law or an EMS depends on effective and accurate monitoring and measuring.

The requirements of a measurement procedure

You need to establish which operations require measuring to show they are under control. Ask yourself what the purpose of measuring is before you begin to design a measuring system. This will help you to focus on the key elements. It is important to know the parameters of the measurement if it is to have any use. Set the acceptable highs and lows of the measurement scale. Set a benchmark or control measurement against which you will gauge performance. Are the measurements likely to be accurate or consistent? Once you know the parameters, you can design the most suitable measurement procedure for each operation.

The nature of the measurement will determine the complexity of the system. For example, if the operation requires the recycling of so many items per week or per month, a simple counting procedure will suffice. However, if it is levels of water purity that must be measured, then the procedure is likely to be more complicated. Whatever type of procedure you design, it must incorporate a recording and reporting system. Be sure you can trust the measurement records – are they accurately recorded? Establish proper documented procedures where necessary and ensure that the records are maintained and regularly reviewed.

Finally, you will need to check that the testing procedure is accurate. The frequency of checks will depend on the importance of the activity being measured. If the testing method is faulty, you will need to validate previous results. Do you have a system in place that can do this? Do you also have a procedure in place to act if the control measurement is not reached or is exceeded? It is pointless to measure, record and report if the data is inaccurate or if the results are not acted upon when necessary. Therefore make sure you have a reporting procedure that generates results that can be used to improve environmental performance effectively.

Measurements techniques

Various techniques can be used to establish the performance measurements. BS7850: Part 2: 1992: *Total quality management guide to methods* provides some practical techniques that have statistical credibility.

● *Control charts* can monitor the performance process within standard deviation control limits (Figure 23.1).

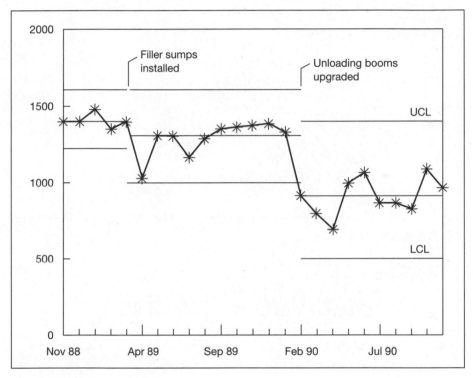

Fig. 23.1 A sample control chart

● *Histograms* provide a visual presentation of data related to a particular attribute you want to measure.

● *Pareto diagrams* are used to identify the significance of problems that contribute to a non-compliance situation, allowing you to focus on the few issues that cause the majority of the problems (Figure 23.2).

● *Scatter diagrams* are a simple, graphic technique to illustrate a relationship between two sets of data. The degree of correlation between the data can be understood from the shape of the 'cloud' of dots that results. It can help to identify areas where, because a strong correlation is shown, it is worth developing further measurements.

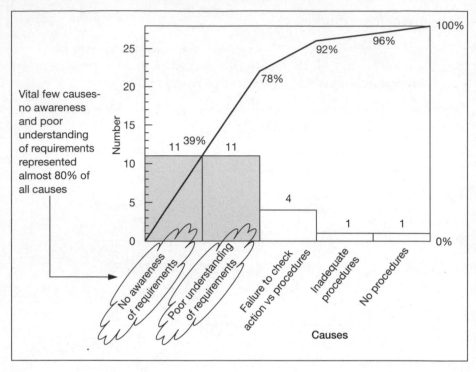

Fig. 23.2 A histogram

STANDARD METHODS OF MEASUREMENT

Tests for process or emission control are essential for adequate control, and standard methods are essential. These provide high levels of confidence and the results can be compared with similar results elsewhere for 'best of breed' comparisons. Bear in mind that verification is an important factor to consider for any measurement or monitoring process; both the equipment and the methods or protocols employed must be verified as providing fitness for purpose. A procedure for sampling and analyzing volatile organic compounds (VOCs) in the paint-spray industry, for example, could be totally inappropriate for analysing emissions from an incinerator.

There are many standard methods of measurement in various industries. The BSI catalogue contains a range of environmental measurements (Table 23.1), while elsewhere, the United States Environmental Protection Agency publishes its methods in books, on CD-ROM and via the Internet.

Table 23.1 Examples of environmental measuring techniques, from the BSI catalogue

Domain	Examples of methods
Water	• BS6068: various parts: Water quality guidelines on the design of sampling systems and field tests. • BS2690: various parts: Methods of testing water used in industry.
Air	• BS1747: various parts: Methods of measurement of air pollution. • BS1756: various parts: Methods of sampling and analysing flue gasses. • BS3405: 1983: Methods of measurement of particulate emissions including grit and dust. • BS6069: various parts: Characterisation of air quality.
Noise	• BS4142: 1990: Methods for rating industrial noise affecting mixed residential and industrial areas. • BS7445: various parts: Description and measurement of environmental noise.

CASE STUDY

March Consulting Group

Salford-based UK consultancy March Consulting Group (MCG) specializes in waste minimization, providing organizations with the technical solutions to maximize the efficiency of resource use. Monitoring is a crucial part of this process, and MCG uses a system known as Monitoring & Targeting (M&T) to track the progress of any minimization programme. According to Niall Enright from MCG, 'Monitoring is an essential part of any management system, whether you are dealing with resource use, waste minimization or an EMS. In M&T, monitoring and measurements provide you with a baseline, for example, of energy usage. Then you set targets, and the M&T system tracks your progress towards meeting these targets'. The process is cyclic and typifies the integrated systems approach. Therefore many organizations use M&T programmes as a central component for programmes in energy efficiency, waste minimization and energy management. M&T programmes reduce utility costs as follows:

- Regularly measuring the utility consumption of key items of plant or areas on a site. Utilities include electricity, gas, compressed air, water and even consumable items.

- Regularly monitoring important items such as production and weather which affect the utility consumption on the site.

- Setting targets for utility consumption, based on best-practice performance of the key items of plant and areas monitored. These targets are simple equations which are used to calculate the best practice utility consumption from the relevant information on production and weather.

▶

▶ • Comparing actual consumption and targets to determine the relative performance of the key utility consumers monitored.

- Determining the reasons for differences between the actual and target performances.

- Using this knowledge to take actions to minimize utility costs in the future.

- Increasing the general awareness of the importance of utility costs. This leads to actions by individuals to improve general housekeeping.

- Continually aiming to improve performance until the best performance possible has been achieved, then ensuring that this efficiency is maintained.

Waste minimization systems achieve savings through a similar methodology.

Checklist

[?] *Have you identified the measurements to be made, their accuracy and control limits?*

[?] *Have you identified what you want measured and when?*

[?] *Have you checked these are consistent with the objectives and targets?*

[?] *Have you identified the measurement procedures, reporting and recording methods?*

[?] *Have you identified what will happen when control limits are exceeded?*

[?] *Is the testing equipment kept calibrated and records kept?*

[?] *Have you a system to re-examine the validity of earlier tests if control limits are exceeded or you find equipment is out of calibration?*

[?] *Would your organization benefit from an M&T programme?*

Communication hints

◆ Measurements need to be simple and understandable. That is why graphical methods succeed so well – a picture says a thousand words.

◆ Always try to understand the learning style of the recipient of the information and present in a style that suits them: statistical data for the reflector, trend analysis for the theorist, predictive information for the pragmatist, and graphical illustrations for the activist.

◆ Keep it simple. A plethora of measurements can be confusing and sometimes contradictory. It is better to aim at a small number of key measurements that all agree.

◆ Track movement rigorously and show progress and achievement honestly. Be prepared to live with the wrong results if they are an accurate reflection of the reality. Don't change the measurement; change the process, the systems, the product. That is what you are measuring for – to tell you when and where you should be improving.

◆ Be prepared to show your stakeholders the progress:

  Internal audiences – how well you are doing and their part in it.

  External audiences – what the targets are and what progress you are making.

  All audiences – new opportunities for improvement and higher environmental performance standards.

CASE STUDY

March Consulting Group: monitoring and targeting at a cheese plant

A cheese plant in Ireland produces about 24 000 tonnes of cheese per year in three separate production units: Cheddar cheese, continental cheese and a whey unit. The factory's annual electricity costs were £400 000 per year, with refrigeration accounting for 30% of these costs.

The plant is highly automated and the company had always used an informal method of energy management. So when the plant's management wanted to reduce its electricity costs even further, they decided to implement Monitoring & Targeting (M&T). March Consulting Group provided the technical expertise and their own software solution *Montage* when setting up the M&T programme. This project was co-funded by the Irish Electricity Board, which uses this site as a case study.

Montage is an M&T program which monitors and tracks the use of utilities such as electricity, water and compressed air. The program can be connected to monitoring instruments to provide real time data, and then provide the mission-critical information which an organization needs to monitor and control the consumption of utilities. In short, *Montage* shows organizations where they are using and losing resources.

After a site audit, approximately 20 meters were installed on site, covering all the services equipment and clearly defining electricity consumption within each department. The services account for almost 50% of the site's electricity usage and so the factory initially concentrated its efforts in this area.

As well as installing *Montage* and setting up the M&T programme, MCG provided an on-site training programme and recommended several ways of improving energy efficiency.

The M&T programme has led to substantial reductions in energy usage. The company achieved its largest savings on two refrigeration plants. *Montage* can also reveal where a piece of equipment is not operating as efficiently as it might. The program showed, for example, that the chilled-water plant for whey was consuming much more electricity than expected when compared to the cooling demand of the plant.

▶

241

▶ The site then improved the refrigeration plant in a way which boosted its efficiency so that it could meet the demands of increased production demands, without the need for major capital expenditure. These improvements to the refrigeration plant's efficiency led to savings of nearly £6 000 (Figure 23.3).

Montage also indicated when a filter was becoming blocked, because the program detected when a compressor had to work harder to drive coolant through it. The M&T system also keeps a check on the number of water pumps that are used on the evaporator cooling tower water, ensuring that the site can run these optimally.

The cost of implementing *Montage*, the M&T and supporting measures was £22k. However, the improvements in energy efficiency saved the cheese plant £24k in its first year, or approximately 6% of the annual electricity bill. The site is now extending the M&T system to the other site utilities where it can achieve further savings.

Source: Dirk Dürster, MCG

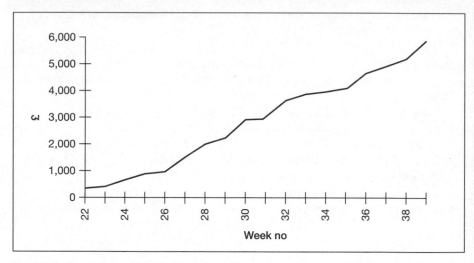

Fig. 23.3 March Consulting Group: cumulative cost savings for chilled-water whey

CASE STUDY

GM Vauxhall motors

Vauxhall's Ellesmere Port plant installed extra measuring equipment with a dramatic effect, reducing its consumption of electrical energy and water. The plant spends about £4 million per year on electricity, so Vauxhall adopted a means of sub-metering to encourage individual sections of the plant to take responsibility for their own fuel use.

The factory installed 33 meters and linked to a centralized, computerized database for energy consumption, which is updated and reviewed every 24 hours. As a result, the electricity consumption in the vehicle assembly area of the plant was reduced by 6% in just six months.

The plant applied a similar strategy to water and gas, producing enormous savings in both areas. In the case of gas, Vauxhall installed meters for each piece of gas-burning equipment. Although this cost a relatively large amount for the meters, the savings of 5% which they generated – through a better control of gas consumption – meant a payback for the investment in well under a year, after which the extra metering meant large, net savings.

24

CORRECTIVE AND
PREVENTIVE ACTION

(4.5.2)

> ### Objective
> The goal is a procedure that will confirm the effectiveness of the operating control procedures and identify areas of non-compliance.

ISO 14001 REQUIREMENTS

Your organization needs to establish and maintain procedures for defining responsibility and authority for handling and investigating non-conformance, taking action to mitigate any impacts caused and for initiating and completing corrective and preventive action. Any corrective or preventive action taken to eliminate the causes of actual and potential non-conformances shall be appropriate to the magnitude of problems and commensurate with the environmental impact encountered.

You also need to implement and record any changes in the documented procedures resulting from corrective and preventive action.

NON-CONFORMANCE AND CORRECTIVE ACTION

The expression *non-conformance* refers to occurrences where environmental performance falls outside the specified requirements. This will be identified by the measurement or verification procedures, with the follow-up action to correct the problem which is essential for continued confidence in the management system.

Root cause analysis

Non-conformance items must be analyzed in a systematic and structured way to establish the cause of the problem to demonstrate a link between the proposed corrective action and the problem. This structured problem solving methodology is sometimes called *root cause analysis*.

The methodology identifies five stages:

Diagnoses

1. Identification of the symptoms and problem definition.

2. Cause analysis.

3. Solution analysis and solution criteria

Remedy

4. Solution proposal.

5. Implementation and review.

Note that the solution implementation follows a great deal of analysis to ensure that it accurately fits the underlying problem.

Each of the stages looks at specific aspects of problem solving and there are useful quality tools and techniques that can be used to assist problem analysis.

Problem definition and analysis looks at the symptoms to understand what happened: where, when, how and who is involved. It sets ownership on problem solving and can hypothesize likely causes for further investigation. The output is a more precise problem definition. Useful techniques include *data collection, measurements, process analysis, pareto charts, statistical quality control* and *brainstorming*.

Cause analysis develops a set of cause and effect hypotheses and tests the probable ones to identify the root causes to be addressed. Useful techniques include *fishbone charts* (an example of which is shown in Figure 24.1) and *data analysis* – an analysis technique that allows a brainstorm to focus on various elements that may cause the problem.

Solution analysis and **solution criteria development** look at the results to be achieved by the solution, as a result of the cause analysis, in order to develop a checklist against which to measure possible solutions.

Solution proposal generates a number of ideas for assessment against the solution criteria. Useful techniques include *brainstorming, solution impact analysis (reverse fishbone)* and *cost benefit analysis*.

Implementation and review develops a detailed action plan and puts in place the solution that best meets the solution criteria, measuring the impact on the problem. Useful techniques include *statistical quality control* to assess effectiveness.

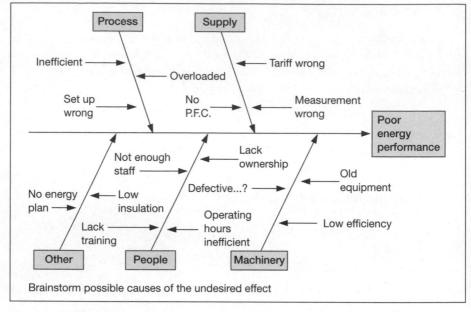

Fig. 24.1 A sample fishbone chart

Example

The structured approach. A director perceived a communications problem in his department. Messages were not getting through and staff were demotivated.

Step 1 analyzed what exactly was wrong with the communications. In this company communications up and down the management line were measured every two years in an opinion survey. By studying the data, the project team were able to go back to the director with a revised problem statement: 'There is a communications problem in the department, but at the level between management and staff. The communications between managers is satisfactory. The target should be to raise manager/staff communications to satisfaction levels equal to those between managers, 80% from a current 56%'.

Step 2 involved a detailed local survey to understand why staff rated their communications with management so poorly. A study of the responses showed that whereas messages were getting out to the staff, the timing and attention managers gave to disseminating information was very patchy, and little was done to respond to issues raised by staff. The expanded problem statement then focused on the need to improve the consistency of communication and so that managers responded to the issues raised and passed them up the line.

Step 3 involved looking at what changes in the management communications system might lead to a resolution of the problems. This involved considering all sorts of ideas from using videos, audio-tapes and newsletters, to special 'communication' meetings. The solution that best met the criteria was to improve the frequency and structure of the monthly departmental meetings as a means of communication. Improved agendas and the formal elevation of issues for management review were agreed, together with a more formal senior management review of the frequency of departmental meetings and issues raised up the line.

Step 4 involved implementing the proposed changes in the departmental meetings at every level in the organization.

Step 5 was a supplementary survey to measure the impact of the changes. Later, the two-yearly full survey showed a sustained improvement in manager/staff communications.

Checklist

? Have you a procedure for identifying non-conformance through the operational control procedures?

? Is there a structural approach to solving problems identified by the operational control procedures?

? Does each phase of the problem-solving approach have clearly defined start and stop points to enable progress to be tracked?

? Have you a training programme in place to train people in problem solving?

CASE STUDY

Brake Linings Ltd

Brake Linings Ltd is a user of asbestos and regulated in the top tier of industries under the UK's *Environmental Protection Act 1990*. In July 1997, a small item in the company's Health, Safety and Environmental newsletter included a small, prominent article which crystallizes ISO 14001's requirements for communications, operational control, environmental monitoring and corrective action.

First, the article states that during one of the quarterly inspection visits from the Environment Agency, the company reported a reduction in the amount of waste it produced, despite an increased growth in output. Furthermore, the levels of dust emissions were below projected levels. This illustrates the importance of communicating the benefits of an EMS, showing the workforce that their actions have resulted in tangible achievements which benefit everyone.

▶

247

Second, the company also reported that it recently discovered that the method it used for monitoring ammonia emissions from its oven was giving erroneous readings, and so it researched and revised its test method to yield greater accuracy. Only by implementing an effective system for monitoring and corrective action, could the company both effectively measure and control its environmental aspects. While the emissions were also low – even when considering the errors – the erroneous readings prompted the company to investigate suitable abatement equipment.

More noteworthy, the company notified the environmental regulators as soon as it identified the non-conformance, describing in detail the root causes and the proposed remedial action. According to Bob Payne, Engineering Manager at the company, 'It is important to establish a good relationship with the regulators and keep them informed about everything potentially significant to them.'

PART

5

25

RECORDS AND
RECORD MANAGEMENT
(4.5.3)

Objective

The goal is a set of records to demonstrate compliance with the ISO 14001 requirements. The records should also show the extent to which the programme to achieve the environmental objectives and targets has been successful.

ISO 14001 REQUIREMENTS

You have to establish and maintain procedures for the identification, maintenance and disposition of environmental records, such as training records, the results of audits, management reviews and monitoring. The records have to be:

- legible;
- identifiable and traceable to the activity, product or service involved;
- stored and maintained in such a way that they are readily retrievable and protected against damage, deterioration or loss;
- retained for however long they are needed, and the organization has to record this retention time.

SIMPLY GOOD DATA MANAGEMENT

Organizations which have a quality system which complies with the requirements of ISO 9000 will find the requirements of this part of the standard extremely straightforward. The purpose of the requirement is to provide an audit trail to demonstrate to you and any assessor the status of the environmental management system and the environmental performance of the organization. Records are evidence of what has been achieved. The assessor will ask you to show him or her the documented evidence – it is all he or she will believe.

It does not mean that you record everything the organization does. Keeping records costs money and you should not design your system to keep more than you need, but you must maintain all that is necessary. It should be focused on those areas that are significant and relevant to the main activities and environmental issues of the organization.

The system of records will cover a wide range of topics to provide the necessary evidence of compliance, i.e., the records required by:

- management;
- legislation;
- the Standard; and
- EMAS.

THE REQUIREMENTS OF A RECORDS MANAGEMENT SYSTEM

There needs to be an established and maintained procedure for the management of records, from identification to storage and disposal. The records will include information on procurement, audits, reviews and training. They must be legible and identifiable so that they can be related to the activity, product or service to which they refer. Retention times must be established and recorded, and they must be both protected and retrievable during the storage period. The policies on access within the organization and to outside interested parties must also be established and followed.

The records need to cover all aspects of the system and the environmental performance. Together they must paint an accurate picture of the whole organization, i.e. no gaps or overlaps. They need to be integrated, but also kept where they are likely to be needed so they maybe dispersed throughout the organization, with local managers having responsibility for maintenance.

ESTABLISHING A RECORDS MANAGEMENT SYSTEM

The departmental environmental management system, together with the co-ordinating environmental management manual, will provide the elements of the records system. At the department level, you have the identified key measurements to be noted. The environmental management manual provides the overview of key activities and the interrelationships of records, and signposts the assessor along the audit trail to the other documentation required to demonstrate compliance. What is also required is a co-ordinating set of management procedures that will guide managers on what should be kept and for how long – in other words, a record management system (RMS). This is useful as many managers keep records far longer than is necessary and yet may not have access to a key piece of information when it is really needed.

The RMS is a documented procedure that identifies the main activities of business and the types of records that are likely to be generated. It should allocate the responsibility for each type of record and specify the retention period. Knowing how long and how accessible the documentation needs to be allows the owner to define appropriate storage and retrieval criteria. This is important because for many records related to environmental issues storage times are lengthy. For example, under the English frameworks for controlling industrial pollution, the IPC and LAAPC regimes, some emissions not only require continuous monitoring of performance, but the records must also be kept for up to four years, and the information created when classifying substances must be kept for up to three years after the date on which the substance was supplied.

Records need not be piles of paper and large, heavy storage racks. There are many ways of keeping records without excessive paperwork. Consider the use of electronic storage of electronically generated material in long-term databanks as these do not clog-up current, active systems. There is also the use of microfilm and now CD storage and archive systems can 'read' a document and store it. Beware however that you only store appropriate materials in these ways. Some legal requirements in contracts require the original documentation to be kept. Figure 25.1 shows an example of environmental records procedure.

WHAT RECORDS SHOULD BE KEPT?

Legislation

- Pollution control requirements (e.g. IPC, LAAPC and the forthcoming IPPC in England);
- Emissions, including record of monitoring;
- Discharges, including to surface waters;
- Consents, for processes and activities;

Schlumberger

CHECKING & CORRECTIVE/ PREVENTIVE ACTION (continued)

RECORDS:

PROCEDURE OWNER: Mr A. Wright

Procedures for the identification, maintenance and disposition of records shall generally be in accordance with the procedures detailed in the Quality Management System and shall be the responsibility of the Quality Systems Manager. Records more specific to the Environmental Management System shall be dealt with as follows;

Information on applicable environmental laws or other requirements: Procedure Owner: Mr A. Povah: The Health & Safety and Environment Manager is responsible for this process. (Please refer to the previous section on Monitoring and Measurement)

Complaint Records: Procedure Owner: Mrs N. Smith: Complaints shall be generally dealt with as per the Customer Complaints Procedure (Quality Management System). The Customer Services Manager shall record all complaints pertinent to the Environmental Management System in the Customer Return Register and the Customer Complaints numbered file. She shall identify and notify the person within the company to whom the complaint is best addressed, that is either the General Manager or Commercial Manager direct, or the Technical Support Manager, the Health, Safety and Environment Manager, the Operations Manager, the Quality Systems Manager or the Systems Co-ordinator. Whomsoever is contacted, it is their responsibility to inform the Health, Safety and Environment Manager, who shall take note and ensure that appropriate Corrective Action is taken.

Training Records: Procedure Owner: Ms S. Cross: As detailed in the previous sectioned entitled Training, Awareness and Competence.

Product Process Information: Procedure Owner: Mr A. Wright: As detailed in the previous section entitled Operational Control.

Product Information: Procedure Owner: Mr G. Fothergill: The Commercial Manager shall provide such product information as is required by interested parties.

Inspection, Maintenance and Calibration Records: Procedure Owners: Mr A. Wright, Mr M. Poole, Mr A. Povah: Generally shall be in accordance with the Quality System procedure or as detailed in the previous section entitled Monitoring And Measurement.

Pertinent Contractor and Supplier Information: Procedure Owners: Mr D. Shaw, Mr M. Poole, Mr A. Povah: The Purchasing Manager shall be responsible for supplying relevant contractor/supplier information or it shall be supplied in accordance with established Quality System procedures or as detailed in the previous section entitled Planning. Information regarding subcontractors used in the Environmental System, (e.g. as analysts or waste disposers, etc) shall be retained and maintained by the Technical Support Manager or the Health & Safety and Environment Manager.

Incident Reports: Procedure Owner: Mr A. Povah: Records of all relevant incidents of an environmental impact nature shall be maintained by the Health & Safety and Environment Manager.

Emergency Response Plan: Procedure Owner: Mr A. Povah: As detailed in the previous section entitled Emergency Preparedness And Response.

Records of significant Environmental Impacts: Procedure Owner: Mr A. Povah: The Health & Safety and Environment Manager shall maintain records pertaining to all significant environmental impacts.

Audit Results: Procedure Owner: Miss J. Poston: The Systems Co-ordinator shall retain all records of Internal Environmental Audits.

Management Reviews: Procedure Owner: Miss J. Poston: The Systems Co-ordinator shall retain all records of Management Reviews.

ISSUE 2 - FEBRUARY 1997   Page 10

Fig. 25.1 Schlumberger's management of records, from their *Environmental Manual*

- Licences, for management of wastes;
- COSHH records on substances and assessments;
- Health and safety reports, especially of accidents and injuries; and
- Management controls that are relevant to environmental issues;
- Planning consents and related environmental assessment records.

ISO 14001

ISO 14001 has a list of documentation that will lead to record management requirements:

- Policy;
- Responsibilities, authority and interrelationships;
- Monitoring procedures and records;
- Communication and training procedures and records;
- Procedures for the identification of and access to regulations/register of regulations;
- Communications records;
- Aspect and impact evaluation procedures and register of
  - emissions;
  - discharges;
  - wastes;
  - contaminated land;
  - energy and resource use;
  - physical impacts, including noise; and
  - eco-system impacts;
- Considerations for abnormal incidents and accidents;
- Objectives and targets procedures and commitments;
- Environmental Programme including:
  - objectives and targets;
  - projects; and
  - new developments;
- Environmental management documentation;
- Emergency plans;
- Document control procedures;
- Controls for:
  - management responsibilities;
  - work instructions;

- process procedures;
- process performance monitoring;
- management approvals; and
- performance criteria;

- Non-conformance and corrective action for:
  - responsibilities;
  - procedures;
  - plans;
  - complaints and follow-up action
  - preventive actions; and
  - procedure changes;
- Records procedures and policies;
- Audit procedures and plans, including;
  - protocols; and
  - reporting;
- Review records;
- Supplier and contractor information;
- Product identification: composition and property data.

Checklist

? *Is your records management system comprehensive?*

? *Is there an audit trail? Can you find your way around the system?*

? *Are the records clearly laid out and readable?*

? *Is there linkage between the co-ordinating document and the departmental records?*

? *Are the records logical in date and process order?*

Communication hints

◆ Records are often regarded as the 'Cinderella' part of the system that follows all the other, more important activities. But when the assessor visits, it is your records of the management system that will bear the closest scrutiny to assess your compliance. Keep it simple and systematic.

◆ Readability should be paramount. Imagine that all the records will be subject to public scrutiny (many may be already, of course, through public registers).

◆ Only the necessary critical activity measurements should be passed up to senior management. They will want to know: what topics are important? Where are we now? Where should we be? What is the long-term outlook? Are there any abnormal things we should know?

◆ Have a special form for highlighting incidents and non-conformity records. Use brightly coloured paper to highlight the importance of such pieces of information.

26

ENVIRONMENTAL MANAGEMENT SYSTEM AUDITS

(4.5.4)

Objective

The goal is an established and maintained set of procedures to enable audits to be carried out.

ISO 14001 REQUIREMENTS

An organization has to establish and maintain programme and procedures for periodic EMS audits. Their purpose is to:

- determine whether or not the environmental management system conforms to planned arrangements for environmental management;
- determine if the organization has done a proper job in implementing and maintaining the EMS;
- provide information on the results of audits to management.

The organization's audit programme and its schedule has to be based on the environmental importance of the activity concerned and the results of previous audits. In order to be comprehensive, the audit procedures have to cover the audit scope, frequency and methodologies, as well as the responsibilities and requirements for conducting audits and reporting results.

DEFINITIONS

There are many definitions of environmental audits. Unlike other professions which use formal audits, environmental management is still evolving its own system of ethics and codes of practice. However, in terms of systems auditing, there are two clear definitions which apply to EMS audits. ISO 14011 defines an audit as:

> 'A systematic process of objectively obtaining and evaluating evidence to determine the reliability of an assertion with regard to environmental aspects of activities, events and conditions as to how they measure to established criteria, and communicating the results to the client.'

In other words, an auditor looks for evidence to show that an organization's EMS meets the requirements of the standard, and then has a look to see if the organization actually does what it says in its EMS documentation.

This definition reflects the historical concept of auditing – whether this is for health and safety systems, accounts, or quality management systems involving the systematic gathering of evidence against an assertion which an auditor can verify. These assertions are based on written EMS documentation, such as procedures.

The International Chamber of Commerce has also developed a commonly used definition for environmental audits, and the EMAS regulation has adopted this, albeit in a slightly modified form. EMAS defines an environmental audit as:

> 'A management tool comprising a systematic, documented, periodic and objective evaluation of how well environmental organization, management and equipment are performing with the aim of safeguarding the environment by (i) facilitating management control of environmental practices, and (ii) assessing compliance with company policies, which include meeting regulatory requirements.'

ROLES

The purpose of the requirement is to establish a regular and systematic evaluation of the environmental management system and the related environmental performance to ensure that these comply with ISO 14001 and are effectively implemented. This is a form of environmental audit, but with a specific focus on the management system. ISO 14001 and the EMAS Regulation draw parallels with ISO 9001 and the related series of standards for auditing. As a consequence, there are now three standards specifically aimed at environmental auditing, and the first to consider is ISO 14011, *Guidelines for environmental auditing – Audit procedures – Auditing of environmental management systems*. This note provides procedures for the conduct of EMS audits. It applies to all types and sizes of organizations operating an EMS, and establishes audit procedures that provide for the planning and conduct of an audit to determine conformance with EMS audit criteria.

The practices, protocols and procedures for an EMS audit are similar to those for a quality systems audit. The same care and attention to scope and the team selection, the same structured approach to information gathering and evaluating the findings, and the same care in identifying non-conformities in reporting are needed. At the conclusion of the EMS audit, the person responsible for the area or activity audited will have a clear indication of the completeness and effectiveness of the environmental management system in meeting the environmental performance requirements.

This last point can be cause for discussion. It is sometimes assumed that the environmental management system audit is only concerned with the completeness of the environmental management system and not the environmental performance. However, environmental management system audits are set up to determine whether the activities and the results comply with the specified requirements. How else do you know whether the environmental management system, if assessed to be complete, is actually effective? Effectiveness can be verified only by looking at the environmental results (the performance) and assessing whether they meet the policy, objectives and targets.

THE AUDITORS

Fair warning

In his play *The Homecoming*, Harold Pinter wrote that if you want to be a champion boxer, then you need to learn only two skills; how to defend yourself, and how to attack. A similar thing applies to EMS auditors, who need to know (i) about the technical, environmental issues relevant to the processes they are assessing, and (ii) how to carry out audits of formal management systems.

Although this may seem simplistic, in the early days of EMS auditors, there were many sorry tales of quality auditors who thought that an EMS was simply a QMS with the word 'environment' switched for 'quality'. Such auditors may have understood a lot about auditing, but lacked the technical knowledge to understand the processes they were auditing. At the same time, an environmental specialist lacking knowledge of auditing and systems would be unlikely to appreciate the often subtle differences between non-conformances and observations. Therefore an EMS auditor, whatever their background, is probably going to need a substantial amount of cross-training, both theoretically and in the field.

Many auditors have told us that the best auditing teams consist of traditional QMS auditors and environmental specialists. They learn from each other.

Requirements

Understanding that EMS auditors will be looking at environmental performance helps to identify what skills will be required by the audit team. Those familiar with quality system auditing may feel that they are competent to assess any quality system – whether for products, services, environmental management or health and safety systems compliance. You may feel that possessing industry-specific knowledge will be a sufficient qualification for an EMS auditor. After all, an industry expert would be able to identify whether a company's environmental policy omits a specific industry issue and is therefore not appropriate, or whether or not the objectives and targets that are set in the EMS meet the legal requirements for BATNEEC or industry practice. You may even consider that expertise in environmental issues is an essential requirement for an EMS auditor.

However, we have already said that all of these skills are important, but each is insufficient on its own. An experienced auditor must have an appropriate mix of auditing and industry-specific skills and be an expert on environmental issues. It is highly unlikely that one person will possess all these attributes (although it sometimes happens), so usually a team of professionals will work together. In large organizations, the relevant skills may be available in-house, or they may have to be procured from outside. In-house auditors must be independent of the department or function they are auditing.

AN INTEGRATED AUDIT

Given that the EMS is an integrated part of the management system, why do you need a separate audit procedure? Schlumberger, for example, has extended its audit procedures based on its quality management procedure to develop an auditing methodology which integrates quality, health and safety, and environment. Similarly, The Body Shop has an integrated approach to auditing known as 'Ethical Auditing', which encompasses health, safety, environmental, social issues such as animal testing and the way that employers treat their workforce and stakeholders. The integrated approaches which The Body Shop and Schlumberger use are not only more effective and efficient than single-issue audits, but also allow the companies to have a better overall picture of how different issues and processes interact.

Integrated auditing is thus a feasible and desirable option for many companies. It has the benefit of a single audit activity and avoids the duplication of costs and resources. However, it is a viable option only if your audit team has the correct mixture of skills to examine the EMS elements of the overall management system, and if your EMS, QMS and health and safety systems are completely and effectively integrated into the overall management system. For most organizations, compliance to environmental requirements affects relationships with legislative bodies, industry regulators, local communities, suppliers, purchasers and many more, a wider scope than a quality audit system. For many organizations, therefore, the EMS audit will be a separate activity.

THE AUDIT PROCEDURE

The method is not a meeting or a workshop, but a suggested form of protocol that should be followed. This may be used in a stand-alone audit of the EMS, or in a guide to your existing audit function to enable auditors to include EMS compliance with the other audit activities. Remember that the threads of the EMS must be woven throughout the overall management system.

The audits are intended to establish whether or not the environmental management activities conform to the environmental programme and are effective, and to establish the effectiveness of the EMS in fulfilling the organization's environmental policy. It is more than just the existence of a system in line with the standard. It is a test of the system's effectiveness in translating policy into improving performance. To test this, an audit plan has to cover seven factors:

1. The specific activities and areas to be assessed, including:
   - the organizational *structure*, roles and responsibilities;
   - the *procedures* to operate and administer the activities;
   - the *activities* and processes in the work area;
   - the operating procedures and *records*; and
   - the environmental *performance*.

2. The schedule for audit activity; audits being established on the basis of the significance of the activity and the result of previous audits.

3. Definitions of who is responsible for the audit activity in each area.

4. Definitions of the criteria for staff who carry out audits. Auditors must:
   - be independent from the areas being audited;
   - have some expertise in the relevant discipline;
   - be supported by specialists wherever necessary.

5. The protocol for conducting the audit, i.e., the order of events, collection of evidence and recording of findings.

6. The procedure for reporting the audit findings to those who are responsible for the audit area or activity and identifying those who are responsible for taking action on the reported deficiencies. The report should include:
    - EMS *conformity* or non-conformity with requirements;
    - EMS *effectiveness* in meeting objectives and targets;
    - *follow-up* of previous audit findings; and
    - conclusions and *recommendations*.

7. The procedures for *publishing* audit findings.

The key to success in establishing an EMS audit plan is to identify the owner of the activity and provide them with the management tools to implement the plans and procedures. From the departmental EMS workshop, you will have a programme of audit activity. That plan will also provide information on the skills required to carry out the audit successfully.

Selecting the audit team

The auditors must be independent of the area being audited. In large organizations there is a position dedicated to auditing activities, but in smaller organizations, it may be one of several responsibilities. In this case, one successful way to approach the audit is that function A audits function B, which audits function C, which audits function A. The protocols and procedures must be common. The audit programme can also be treated as a 'purchased service' from an outside agency, consultant or assessor. You may need an audit programme manager.

From knowledge of the area or activity to be audited, it is possible to draw up auditor criteria, and then establish a pool of suitably qualified people in the organization to draw on for the programme. You will need to ensure that the common protocols are understood by all the auditors you propose to use, so spend time reviewing these in a joint training session. As the audit programme progresses, you will need to review auditor performance to ensure confidence in the audit results.

Each audit team will have a *lead auditor*, a senior person responsible for a particular assessment and the *auditors*, the people making the assessments. The *programme manager* is responsible for the overall audit programme. There may occasionally be a sponsor of the audit other than the programme manager or the *auditee*, the person responsible for the area being assessed, and this third party is often called the *client*. Examples of clients may be an organization's customer or a prospective purchaser.

Checklist: EMS audit management considerations

? *Is there an internal audit capability?* You must have the capacity to audit the EMS system and the environmental performance of the organization.

? *What are the EMS standards you are auditing against?* You must have a standard against which to assess compliance. 'We have an EMS that meets the requirements of ISO 14001 and EMAS.'

? *Have you identified an audit programme manager?* This must be someone with necessary knowledge of EMS audit practices and procedures.

? *Have you identified the auditor skills you require?* They must be relevant to the requirements of the audit programme, activities and processes.

? *Do you have a pool of qualified auditors?* They must be appropriate to: the type of organization, have the relevant regulatory knowledge, personal skills, language skills, be independent.

? *Have you established a programme to ensure consistency in the audit?* You must train staff to ensure a common approach and mix and match teams so that consistency develops.

? *Have you a mechanism for evaluating the performance of the audit team?* You must ensure that the audits are appropriately carried out through some form of audit assessment.

Table. 26.1 indicates the main steps in the audit process to be considered by the audit programme manager.

Table 26.1 The main steps in the EMS audit process

Thinking	• Scope • Standards • Select lead auditor • Scan material
Planning	• Select team • Assign auditors • Plan audit • Establish documents
Doing	• Opening meeting • Accumulate evidence • Review evidence • Record findings
Reviewing	• Draft report • Review • Closing meeting • Final report

The key steps in the EMS audit

Scope: Establish the range or boundaries of the audit activity: where, what and when. There are benefits if the auditee and lead auditor can discuss and agree.

Standards: Establish the standards or the criteria that the assessment will use to seek evidence of compliance.

Select lead auditor: Choose the lead auditor and brief him or her on the scope, objectives and criteria of the audit.

Scan material: Review the scope to obtain information for selecting the team. Review the documented EMS for completeness and as an aid to planning.

Select team: In the light of the audit scope and EMS review, select the rest of the team.

Plan audit: Establish the areas and times to carry out the audit.

Assign auditors: Allocate the duties of the audit team.

Establish documents: Establish the assessment methods and working documents. Agree the plan with the auditee.

Opening meeting: Hold an opening meeting with the auditee, his or her management team and the audit team. Explain the scope, plan and method of the audit and set the time of the closing meeting.

Accumulate evidence: Collect the evidence by the methods planned. Be prepared to follow an audit trail where evidence indicates a non-compliance. Always ensure your auditors agree evidence of non-conformity with the auditees.

Review evidence and record findings: Establish the areas of non-compliance. These may be within the system, aspects of the performance or other points within the scope of the audit.

Draft report: Document the findings in a clear and concise manner, identifying non-compliant items with supporting evidence – validated by auditee.

Review: Analyze the findings with the auditee and obtain acknowledgement of the non-compliant items.

Closing meeting: Hold a minuted meeting with the auditors and auditee management teams. Ensure that they understand and agree with the results of the audit and its recommendations.

Final report: Prepare the final report and distribute to the manager responsible for the area, his or her manager and the environmental programme manager. Note that the auditee is then responsible for deciding on the necessary corrective action and implementation.

AUDIT FREQUENCY

The frequency of auditing the EMS will depend upon the factors of environmental performance risk. Areas of high environmental risk, complex processes and activities will be audited more frequently than administrative or support functions. In addition, consideration must be made of the result of previous audits which may indicate a need for an assessment of parts of the system where problems and significant evidence of non-conformance is found.

EMAS requires the whole organization should complete an audit cycle within a three year period. Some areas will be assessed annually if they meet the criteria indicated above where the nature and scale of activities demand a more regular scrutiny of the environmental management system performance.

AUDIT DOCUMENTATION

The records of audit findings, plans, non-conformance data and final reports form part of the environmental records management system. These must be retained to provide an adequate audit trail for external assessment and follow-up action by the manager responsible for the area assessed.

NON-CONFORMANCES

A non-conformance is defined as either a breach of the requirements of a standard, or a breach of the required procedures and instructions. Here are two definitions of a non-conformance:

> 'The result of the evaluation of the recollected audit evidence compared against the agreed audit criteria. The findings provide the basis for the audit report.'
>
> *ISO 14010.2*

> 'The non-fulfilment of specific requirements.'
>
> *ISO 8402*

As a general rule, there are two types of non-conformance – *major* and *minor*. A major non-conformance will inhibit certification. The following items all constitute major non-conformances.

- Failures to report a breach in legislation.
- Failures to record an incident.
- Failures to record when an organization has not met a specific objective or target.
- A failure to record a significant environmental effect.
- When an organization identifies a significant environmental effect, but does not do anything about it.
- When the organization misinterprets its own policy statement.

Checklist

Do you have a documented EMS audit procedure?

[?] *Do the procedures cover:*
- *review of the environmental management documentation*
- *activity review against the programme?*
- *assessment criteria to establish effectiveness?*
- *planning protocols?*

[?] *Do the audit planning procedures include:*
- *organization, procedures, activities, documents and environmental perform-ance?*
- *frequency of audits?*
- *responsibilities defined at all levels?*
- *personnel and skill requirements*
- *protocol for logging non-compliances*
- *measures for reporting?*
- *publishing plans?*

[?] *Do the protocols cover:*
- *the scope of the assessment?*
- *the assessment criteria?*
- *the standards?*
- *roles and responsibilities?*
- *team selection?*
- *outline planning?*
- *operating documents?*
- *the opening meeting?*
- *evidence gathering?*
- *recording the findings?*
- *reporting the findings?*
- *the closing meeting?*

Communication hints

Auditors are about as popular in some businesses as tax inspectors. The perception exists that the auditor is 'someone from Head Office come to catch us out'. Try to dispel this perception by using your communications system to clarify that the auditor's role is to facilitate improvement through objective assessment. At each phase ensure that the presentation of the audit activity is consistent with the concept of a healthy exploration of strengths as well as weaknesses.

Thinking: Communicate with the management of the area being audited early on, so that they feel involved in the scope and planning of the audit and the decision-making.

Explore fully the process and the outputs that will be generated to allay any fears of witch-hunt management.

Planning: Ensure that all those likely to be approached by the auditors are aware of the audit, its purpose and its approach. Aim at 'no surprises'.

Doing: Skilled auditors will always use an appropriate approach to assessments but the 'Show me ...' question can often elicit responses like, 'I am much too busy. See my subordinate', or even a demonstration of pride if it is going well. The auditors' style should be professional and open. A non-conformance, when identified, should be documented at the time and acknowledged by the departmental representative, always based on evidence.

Reviewing: The draft report review is an opportunity to ensure that the local management are aware of and agree that the audit report contents are factually accurate. It provides an opportunity for them to prepare the outlines of a planned response for the closing meeting.

The presentation of the meeting should begin with thanks for the co-operation that will have been received, a summary of the overall findings, with reference to specifics, if that is required, and a statement as to the auditee's status against the requirements of the standard. The presentation should conclude with recommendations for actions and priorities. You must allow some time for discussion to clear any misunderstandings and ensure that the recommendations are accepted.

The audit is an evaluation of the environmental management systems' performance, not the managers' performance. The report must therefore always be an accurate, objective view of what is found, not a performance appraisal of the staff involved.

CASE STUDIES

Schlumberger

Schlumberger has a very novel approach to EMS auditing. Instead of having a few people who audit an entire factory many of the staff actually do the audits. This reflects the management structure for the factories, which are divided into sections. Each section has specific responsibilities, which empowers the employees with ownership. So as well as implementing the working EMS on the factory floor, each section team also carries out auditing.

In real terms, this means a lot of people do a little auditing, and they audit other sections to provide objectivity. Schlumberger has found that this system is highly effective, as the breadth and depth of skills and backgrounds add a new dimension to the aspects and factors which the auditors investigate. The company also reports that many of the staff have become extremely enthusiastic about the whole system. 'If there is one thing which has changed the culture of the company, it is making the shop floor staff into internal auditors', says Tony Wright, Manager for Quality, Health, Safety and Environment. Allowing a shop-floor worker to audit the Managing Director, for example, creates a strong feeling of teamwork among the employees and is very beneficial for motivation. ▶

▶ The Body Shop

Like Schlumberger, The Body Shop has an integrated approach to EMS auditing. However, The Body Shop differs in that it used the same systems approach to look at other issues, such as animal rights and social issues.

The company uses its own in-house teams of auditors for internal audits, while relying on consultants for external verification of the system. Following its experience, the company has published a series of tips for auditing, called *The Seven Do's and Don'ts of Environmental Auditing and Disclosure* (Table 26.2).

Table 26.2 Seven dos and don'ts of environmental auditing and disclosure

Do get free/cheap advice wherever it is available: DIY manuals, local and central government departments, local and national business clubs, simple booklets and guides to the issues.	**Don't** assume that you have to be an expert. A great deal of environmental management and auditing is simply common sense. Networking and asking questions of similar business is the best way to avoid mistakes.
Do set up informal networks of internal supporters and environmental representatives to aid communications and internal campaigns.	**Don't** put too many resources into auditing if they are better directed at obvious priority actions and improvements – especially in the early days.
Do involve departments, managers and staff at every level, especially in policy formulation, internal goal setting, communications and training.	**Don't** forget that people want to be inspired by a vision; environmental activists are often happy to talk to business groups and companies committed to improving their environmental performance and participate in external campaigns.
Do set up an internal independent audit system or department and have them report to a main board director.	**Don't** forget to motivate, train and then re-motivate your managers, staff and volunteer networks.
Do use consultants for specific tasks, e.g., first review, audit verification, technical tasks (e.g., energy auditing). Always network with other businesses to find recommended consultants or local academic institutions for support.	**Don't** use consultants for general activities that are the proper responsibility of staff and managers, e.g., objective setting, resource allocation, co-ordination. If management cannot take these basics on board you are wasting your time.
Do consider adopting a formal standard for environmental auditing and management – but only when you're ready to commit.	**Don't** kill enthusiasm by introducing too many systems too early. Make it fun and don't be afraid to be controversial.
Do report formally and informally, publicly and internally. Stakeholder understanding is crucial to progress, as are targets and objectives for the future.	**Don't** be afraid of including both good and bad aspects of environmental performance: better that you draw attention to your faults than have your critics do it.

From The Body Shop's 'The Body Shop approach to Ethical Auditing', in their *Values Report 1995*

27

MANAGEMENT REVIEW
(4.6)

> ### Objective
> The goal is a report which summarizes the status of the organization's environmental management system and current environmental performance, reviews external and internal pressures for change and agrees an action plan for change.

ISO 14001 REQUIREMENTS

An organization's top management has to review the EMS periodically to ensure its continuing suitability, adequacy and effectiveness. The process has to ensure that the organization collects the necessary information to do this evaluation, and then document it.

As a result of the EMS audits, changing circumstances and the commitment to continual improvement, the management review has to look at the possible need for changes to the policy, objectives and other elements of the environmental management system.

MANAGEMENT REVIEWS

The purpose of the requirement is to ensure that senior managers responsible for the organization's EMS have the opportunity to assess the overall performance and the need to adapt any of its elements, from policy through to audit. For many organizations, the review is an opportunity to promote their environmental contribution publicly.

THE MANAGEMENT REVIEW MEETING

The key to reviewing the environmental management system is the regular management meeting that reviews the overall position. The meeting should include a *report* from the environmental programmes manager. The report should comprise the following:

- the results of audits and assessments;
- the actions taken on non-compliance;
- the progress of improvement plans and programmes;
- the performance of suppliers and partners;
- an overview of new and planned legislation;
- a review of public environmental issues;
- a summary of the concerns of the local community; and
- new environmental concerns from any area.

The report is planned as a regular, annual, agenda item on the Board or management executive meeting. Prior to the meeting you will establish the organization's current status, based on the information from the various functional or departmental assessments, and a review of the progress in improvement plans.

Pre-report workshop

Each senior manager or department/functional head should have the opportunity to report for a few minutes on developments, achievements and new challenges in his or her relevant business area. For example, the senior marketing manager might report on recent trends in the market place, what the competition is doing, or new opportunities being researched for 'greener' products with a marketing edge. The operations senior manager might report on new practices and processes that are being reported as BATNEEC or BEO and that need to be considered in the next round of investment plans. Other brief reports might also be made on relevant legislative developments, external community issues, corporate or promotional plans. You might summarize your perception.

After the workshop, prepare a draft report and circulate this to the environmental steering committee for agreement. The report will be based on the EMS, audit results and your workshop. Finalize the report and send it in advance of the Board meeting to the executive team members. Prepare a short summary presentation to capture the key elements of the report for the meeting.

Agenda for the meeting

1. Present the current position of the organization (environmental programmes manager).
2. Review by business areas (business unit managers).
3. Review of regulatory and legislative factors (legal department).
4. Report on current internal development plans (environmental programmes manager).
5. Report on external and community promotion plans (communications manager).
6. Conclusions and recommendations (environmental programmes manager).

THE PUBLICATION REQUIREMENTS OF THE STANDARDS

ISO 14001 requires organizations to publish their environmental policy, but not the audit results. However, many organizations do publish the audit results and review the information it provides.

The EMAS Regulation, however, requires the following information to be included in the public statement:

- name of the organization;
- name and location of the site – remember the Eco-audit Regulation is site based;
- brief description of the activities at the site (referring to annexed documents if necessary – allows for a standard company document to be used in support of the statement);
- name and address of the accredited environmental verifier who validated the statement attached;
- deadline for submission of the next validated environmental statement.

The following details must be annexed to the statement:

(a) A brief description of the environmental protection system.

(b) A description of the auditing programme established for the site.

(c) The initial validated environmental statement. The statement must include details of:
   - the activities concerned;
   - the environmental problems raised by these activities;
   - an inventory of emissions, of waste generation and of energy and raw material consumption;
   - the company's environmental policy, programme and objectives; and
   - the company's environmental performance).

Checklist

? *Is there a regular management review planned?*

? *Does the review cover*
  - *policy?*
  - *environmental management system?*
  - *audit results?*
  - *corrective action plans?*
  - *performance measures?*
  - *legislation?*
  - *outside factors?*
  - *investment?*
  - *training?*

Communication hints

◆ Ensure that the results of the audits and plans are agreed before the meeting to avoid any contentious issues.

◆ Publish the results, warts and all.

◆ Tell the truth.

◆ Focus on the facts.

CASE STUDY

Elmwood College

Since it started with its EMS, Elmwood College has developed a streamlined procedure for management reviews. Each review consists of a write-up of the internal audit results, coupled with an assessment of how well the college has achieved its objectives and targets. Each review is summarized in a tabulated form (Table 27.1).

This allows the college to write-up the review of environmental performance rapidly. The *Outcome* consists of a statement of the extent to which a *Target* has been achieved, while the *Commentary* will give an indication of future action, e.g., recommendations for further work. Once the review is complete, it is passed on to the College Principal who will base funding decisions on its recommendations.

At a strategic level, the review enables the college to re-examine its environmental policy, and explore any changes to the requirements of the system. The review also allows the college to set its objectives and targets for the following year. One of the most important functions of the review is that it provides a basis for staff, students and external parties to assess the college's environmental performance, as the review is available to anyone who wishes to see it.

Table 27.1 Environmental performance against set objectives

Objective and targets	Outcome	Commentary

Source: Elmwood College

PART

28

THE FINAL
IMPLEMENTATION REPORT

INTRODUCTION

In *Chapter 27* we looked at the management review of the EMS and related environmental performance. This final part of the book is intended to provide an approach to assessing the effectiveness of the project implementation through:

- the final report, and
- a self-assessment questionnaire.

See Figure 28.1 for a review of progress.

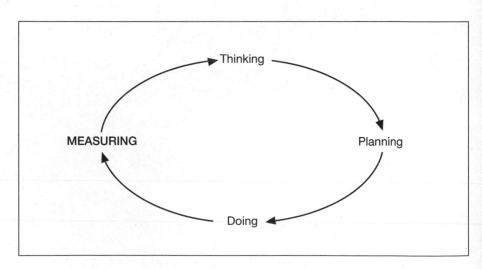

Fig. 28.1 Reviewing progress to plan and identify areas of improvement

> ## Objective
> To prepare a final report on the implementation of the environmental management system for senior management. Identify its achievements against the original plan and make recommendations on what to think about and plan for in any future activity.

THE FINAL REPORT

Your project measurement criteria will have been established at the start of the project and your regular reviews will have kept management appraised of progress to the plan. Now you need a final report. The report will not just comment on the progress of the project; it will also cover the end-product – the integrated EMS. The report should:

- identify areas where there are still gaps in the system design and performance against the standard;
- point towards areas where control limits can be tightened to reduce costs;
- indicate where wastes or impacts can be further reduced;
- identify improvement areas where you can now set more challenging targets from your new baseline;
- indicate where further focus on shared values, strategy, structure, staff, skills, systems, or style is needed.

The report should be based on an internal project review of the EMS in place by you and the project team, to give you information on current issues. It should include reference to the original project scope, plan and results. The internal project review can be based on the results of the self-assessment questionnaire (*see Chapter 28*). The remaining information will be in your project files.

THE INTERNAL PROJECT REVIEW

This review will be carried out by you and the project team at a regular meetings on completion of the EMS review. All members of the team should be invited to make a short presentation of their views of the project activity in their departments or functions. Each presentation should cover:

- key points of original plan;

- key points of actual progress;
- highlights – positive lessons learned;
- lowlights – things to be avoided in the future;
- recommendations for improvement.

Your presentation should follow the same format as above and include the results from self-assessment audits that you will have encouraged managers to undertake (*see Chapter 28*).

As the presentations are made, keep track of the key points on a flip chart in front of the project team. At the end of the meeting, review the contents of the charts to agree the key factors to form part of the final report.

After the meeting, prepare a draft report. Send this to the project team members for review and comment, and consolidate the comments into a final report.

Establish a review session on the executive management meeting, send out the report ahead of the meeting and prepare a brief 15–20 minute presentation on the contents. At the meeting, allow time for the presentation and some discussion on the recommendations for follow-up action.

A SELF-ASSESSMENT TECHNIQUE

Self-assessment techniques allow managers to take an objective look at their organization's status against the requirements of the standard. The usual methods of analysis employed by managers is a questionnaire or checklist that provides a useful indicator for the breadth and depth of the penetration of the environmental management system into the area under consideration.

A questionnaire which examines conformance with the requirements of ISO 14001 can be found in *Chapter 29*. This questionnaire allows you to work through the requirements of the standard and during your implementation programme, enables you to map your progress towards registration.

Note that if you have already carried out an initial environmental review, evaluated your environmental aspects and impacts, and determined your regulatory requirements, then you are about half way towards a successful implementation. Add to this any existing elements from a quality management system, or a scheme such as *Responsible Care®*, and you are well on the way to registration.

Lessons we have learnt
Formosa Plastics' ISO 14001 implementation experience

Many of the insights and experiences gained by Formosa Plastics in the course of implementing ISO 14001 are potentially applicable to other companies in the same situation:

- As one of the first companies in the US to achieve certification, Formosa had to overcome the psychological barriers caused by the amount of room that the standard leaves for interpretation, and by having to pursue conformance and implementation strategies with no knowledge or experience. Corporate staff's number one priority was to ensure consistent implementation through all facilities. Strong interpretative guidance from their corporate office and well-written procedures and training manuals were vital to make sure that their different plants interpreted and implemented the standard consistently.

- They found it very helpful to be able to build on their positive experience with implementing ISO 9002.

- In order to keep all the people necessary to implementing their EMS interested, involved and organized, they needed considerable organizational strength, muscle and salesmanship. Some of their methods of raising awareness and motivation included competitions, training exercises and internal marketing communications.

- Formosa found that environmental auditing could be carried out with the least possible disruption, leaving the audit and the process audited running efficiently, if they identified control points (analog quality control points). In practice, this means that you shouldn't audit waste stream segregation when a whole pile of waste is in the middle of being segregated and the segregators have their hands full, but should wait until it's possible to check through the documentation without disturbing an on-going process.

- They recognized early on that their biggest cost would be internal labour. Formosa limited their use of consultants to certain upfront advice and training sessions for corporate staff and auditors.

- Formosa emphasize the need for training in implementing an EMS. Training must be sufficient to ensure that plant personnel fully understand the standard and the management system, in order to implement it to the best possible effect and to be able to provide adequate answers to questions posed to them by auditors.

29

THE SELF-ASSESSMENT
QUESTIONNAIRE

INTRODUCTION

The self-assessment questionnaire (*see* Table 29.1) is designed for those involved in environmental management system implementation. It will allow you and your management team to check your progress against the requirements of the standard and identify areas for improvement. The questions are set in a linear scale using two extremes, between 'not yet started' to 'full compliance' with the specified requirements of ISO 14001. The questionnaire should be used as a desktop exercise using your best judgement on the status of the EMS implementation programme within your organization. Some checking may be useful if you are not clear where things stand, but this should be limited. The idea is to complete the questionnaire in a single work-session during a morning or an afternoon.

GUIDANCE FOR THE QUESTIONNAIRE

Each of the answers to the requirements for ISO 14001 can have five scores. To stand a chance of registration to ISO 14001, you must have a score of 4 for all the questions.

A=4 All elements are in place and integrated within every applicable part of the organization

B=3 Most the elements are in place

C=2 Some of the elements are in place

D=1 A few of the elements are in place

E=0 None of the elements is in place

Table 29.1 ISO 14001 Benchmark questionnaire

ISO 14001 Compliance test							

ISO 14001 Compliance test

			Score				
Q	Clause	Requirement	A	B	C	D	E

4.1 General requirements

| 1 | | Has your organization an established and maintained Environmental Management System (EMS), as required by the whole of Clause 4 in ISO 14001? | yes/no | | | | |

If you answer Yes to Question 1, go to the end of the questionnaire and score 256 points. If not, or you are not sure, then answer questions 2 to 35 before adding up your score.

| 2 | | Has your organization determined its baseline performance, e.g., through an Initial Environmental Review? | 64 | 48 | 32 | 16 | 0 |

4.2 Policy

| 3 | | Has your organization defined, documented and implemented its environmental policy? | 4 | 3 | 2 | 1 | 0 |
| 4 | | Does the policy include the following elements?
 • Provides the basis to set objectives and targets
 • Relevant to the organization's activities, products and services
 • Commit the organization to pollution prevention
 • Publicly available
 • Defined by top management
 • Commit the organization to comply with the law | 4 | 3 | 2 | 1 | 0 |

4.3 Planning

	4.3.1	**Environmental aspects**					
5		Have you developed procedures to identify and assessing the environmental aspects and significance of your activities, products and services?	32	24	16	8	0
6		Have you determined which aspects have significant impacts?	32	24	16	8	0

Table 29.1 (continued)

ISO 14001 Compliance test			Score				
Q	Clause	Requirement	A	B	C	D	E
	4.3.2	**Legal and other requirements**					
7		Have you established a procedure to keep you up-to-date with every law and regulation which applies to what you do?	4	3	2	1	0
	4.3.3	**Objectives and targets**					
8		Have you set out and documented your environmental objectives and targets?	4	3	2	1	0
9		When setting these objectives and targets, have you considered the following factors? ● Significant environmental impacts ● Legal and regulatory requirements ● Technological options ● Business, financial and operational requirements ● Views of interested parties ● Commit the organization to comply with the law	4	3	2	1	0
	4.3.4	**Environmental management programme**					
10		Do you have an environmental management programme to achieve your objectives and targets?	4	3	2	1	0
11		Does this programme include the following? ● A schedule to meet the objectives and targets ● Designated people responsible for the objectives and targets at each level in the organization	4	3	2	1	0
12		Do you have an electrical power efficiency programme?	4	3	2	1	0
13		Do you have an efficiency programme for gas use?	4	3	2	1	0
14		Do you have an efficiency programme for water use?	4	3	2	1	0

Table 29.1 (continued)

Q	Clause	Requirement	A	B	C	D	E
ISO 14001 Compliance test					Score		
15		Do you have a waste minimization programme? (solid, liquid, air)	4	3	2	1	0
4.4 Implementation and operation							
	4.4.1	**Structure and responsibility**					
16		Have you defined and documented the interrelationships, authority and responsibilities of the key personnel who manage, perform and verify work affecting the environment?	4	3	2	1	0
17		Have you appointed a management representative, who has a defined authority and responsibility to make sure that the EMS is established and maintained in compliance with the requirements of ISO 14001?	4	3	2	1	0
	4.4.2	**Training, awareness and competence**					
18		Do you have established and maintained procedures for communications, training, awareness and competence to make sure that employees at all levels in the organization are aware of: • the importance of compliance with your environmental policy • the potential effects of their activities on the environment, their roles and responsibilities • the potential consequences of departure from agreed procedures?	4	3	2	1	0
19		Do you have established and maintained procedures for identifying the training needs of your workforce?	4	3	2	1	0
20		Have you implemented a training programme for all key staff?	4	3	2	1	0

Table 29.1 (continued)

Q	Clause	Requirement	A	B	C	D	E
		ISO 14001 Compliance test					
					Score		
	4.4.3	**Communications**					
21		Do you have established and maintained procedures to receive, document and respond to communications from relevant interested parties concerning environmental impacts and management?	4	3	2	1	0
	4.4.4	**Environmental management system documentation**					
22		Have you produced an environmental management manual? Do you maintain it?	4	3	2	1	0
	4.4.5	**Document control**					
23		Do you have established and maintained procedures for controlling all documentation required by ISO 14001?	4	3	2	1	0
	4.4.6	**Operational control**					
24		Have you identified the functions, activities and processes which have the potential to affect the environment and are relevant to the policy, objectives and targets? Have you planned these activities to ensure that your organization performs these tasks under controlled conditions to minimize environmental impacts?	4	3	2	1	0
	4.4.7	**Emergency preparedness and response**					
25		Have you identified the potential normal, abnormal and emergency events? If so, then do you have an established and maintained procedure for dealing with emergencies?	4	3	2	1	0

Table 29.1 (continued)

ISO 14001 Compliance test							
				Score			
Q	Clause	Requirement	A	B	C	D	E
26		Have you developed an emergency plan, and does it contain the following elements? ● The services and people responsible for emergency responses ● Actions for different types of emergencies ● Data and information on hazardous materials, such as each material's potential impact on the environment ● Steps taken in the event of accidental releases ● Training plans and drills	4	3	2	1	0
4.5 Checking and corrective action							
	4.5.1	**Monitoring and measurement**					
27		Have you developed procedures, plus monitoring and measuring systems to verify compliance with specified requirements with legislation and track your performance against stated objectives and targets?	4	3	2	1	0
	4.5.2	**Non-conformance and corrective and preventive action**					
28		Have you defined the responsibility and authority for initiating investigations following a non-conformance, and corrective and preventive action in the event of non-compliance with specified requirements?	4	3	2	1	0
29		Have you established procedures for the investigation and corrective action in the event of non-compliance with specified requirements?	4	3	2	1	0
	4.5.3	**Records**					
30		Is there an established and maintained system of records to demonstrate compliance with the environmental management system requirements and the extent to which environmental objectives and targets have been met?	4	3	2	1	0

Table 29.1 (continued)

| | | | \u00A0ISO 14001 Compliance test | | | | | |

ISO 14001 Compliance test								
					Score			
Q	**Clause**	**Requirement**	**A**	**B**	**C**	**D**	**E**	
	4.5.4	**Environmental management system audit**						
31		Do you already have a management system in place (such as ISO 9001) and trained auditors to verify compliance with this management system?	4	3	2	1	0	
32		Do you have established and maintained procedures for EMS audits to determine that the environmental management activities conform to the programme and are effective in fulfilling the environmental policy?	4	3	2	1	0	
33		Have you an established and maintained plan for environmental management system audits?	4	3	2	1	0	
34		Do you have established procedures for reporting the results of environmental management systems audits to those responsible for the activity or area audited?	4	3	2	1	0	
4.6 Management review								
35		Has the organization's management reviewed the EMS adopted to ensure its continuing suitability, adequacy and effectiveness?	4	3	2	1	0	
		Totals						
		Grand total						

Example

Has your organization defined, documented and implemented its environmental policy?

4   Policy is relevant and fully integrated into the organization's management system.

3   Policy is in place but not fully implemented, nor meets all requirements.

2   Policy exists but does not address all the requirements and implementation has not started.

1   Policy exists in draft.

0   No policy exists.

Note: You must have all the elements in place to score highly. A policy must be relevant, understood, implemented and maintained throughout the organization. It must be publicly available, include a commitment to continual improvement in environmental performance and linked to the setting of environmental objectives and targets.

Notes on the scoring

All the questions except 2, 5 and 6 have a maximum score of 4. For Question 1, your score is multiplied by 16, while for Questions 5 and 6, each score is multiplied by 8 (*see* Table 29.1). This means that if you have carried out a thorough Initial Environmental Review (IER) and determined the environmental effects of your operations – together with their significance – then you are halfway to having implemented your EMS.

Table 29.2 Table of scores

Score	Comments
256	Excellent. If you are not registered to ISO 14001, then you should be well on the way to compliance. Do what you say you do in your environmental policy, and registration should be a formality. Then you could soon be joining the 400 or so companies in the UK and the 2200 world-wide which are already registered to ISO 14001.
200–250	Well done. You are nearly there. You have certainly established your baseline performance, determined your environmental impacts, and implemented nearly all the components required for a management system which meets the requirements of ISO 14001.
150–200	Score this high, and your EMS is taking shape. This is often the hardest point in implementing an EMS. You have put in a great deal of effort, yet it is incomplete and the benefits have yet to make themselves readily evident. However, keep going through this phase and you could be looking at registration – and financial savings – within a few months.
64–150	If you have completed an IER, determined your environmental impacts and developed your environmental policy, then you are halfway there. Now develop your objectives and targets, and the rest of your system should fall into place.
Up to 64	You have either completed a baseline-performance survey such as an IER, or have several elements of ISO 14001 already in place, for example, from an ISO 9000 management system.

30

EXTERNAL ASSESSMENT

Objective
To understand the process of registration, the steps within the process, and the benefits of external registration.

ISO 14001 REQUIREMENTS

The first clause of the standard says that you must have an environmental management system which complies with the requirements of the standard.

THE FINANCIAL AND ENVIRONMENTAL BENEFITS OF REGISTRATION

Implementing an EMS is one major step. Registration is another step and can be perceived as an extra expense. So why bother with it at all? Isn't it enough to simply implement and maintain an EMS to derive the benefits from it? The short answer is 'no', and during the research for this book, we found that many organizations reported three common reasons for this:

- External registration is an objective and independent assessment to show that you have met the requirements of an internationally recognized standard.
- The regularity of external assessments is an excellent incentive to maintain the system, to keep improving your environmental performance, and thus make even greater financial savings.
- Registered firms have reported both internal and external benefits, such as improved markets and better relationships with their workforces, regulators, stakeholders and customers.

In short, an impending external assessment is a prompt to maintain a system. This maintenance often starts with auditing, which in turn can reveal opportunities. Experience has shown that organizations then deal with any non-conformances and follow-up opportunities prior to the next assessment. Without this incentive, it would be all too easy to let a management programme take a lower priority – which can mean missed opportunities.

Many companies have also reported that the external assessors can be extremely helpful, because they bring a new pair of eyes to an organization, and often make observations which can help companies improve their performance, or identify new opportunities.

According to industry experience, however good you are, there is always some way in which you can improve. As you are so involved in what you are doing, it can be very easy to miss these opportunities, and this is where the external assessors can be so useful because they can identify areas which are easily overlooked from the inside. One industrial manager told us that he would be disappointed if the external assessors did not find any non-conformances during an assessment, as a non-conformance can tell you where you should be focusing improvements.

Tony Wright of Schlumberger Gas echoes this. The company registered to ISO 14001 through BSI Systems Assessment Services, and Wright says that the assessors were extremely supportive and helpful during this time. 'We involved BSI from the beginning, and through a series of pre-assessment visits, the assessors saw the development of our system from concept through to implementation. So when the final assessment came, we were able to iron out most of the bugs in a process which was seamless and stress-free,' he emphasizes.

One of the requirements for the design of BS 7750 in 1991 was the need for a standard against which compliance could be assessed and certified by an independent body. The success of the committee in designing such a standard was seen by the pressure to develop assessment and certification schemes from those companies in the pilot programme, from 1992 to 1994.

IT'S YOUR BUSINESS

What does certification of compliance mean for those wishing to attain ISO 14001 registration?

It may be useful to view ISO 14001 as a benchmark against which the EMS you have installed can be assessed. The benchmark sets out the elements of the system to be in place *inside* your organization. The first specification clause requires you to document *your* system and then ensure it is effective in operation. Figure 30.1 illustrates the relationship between the two.

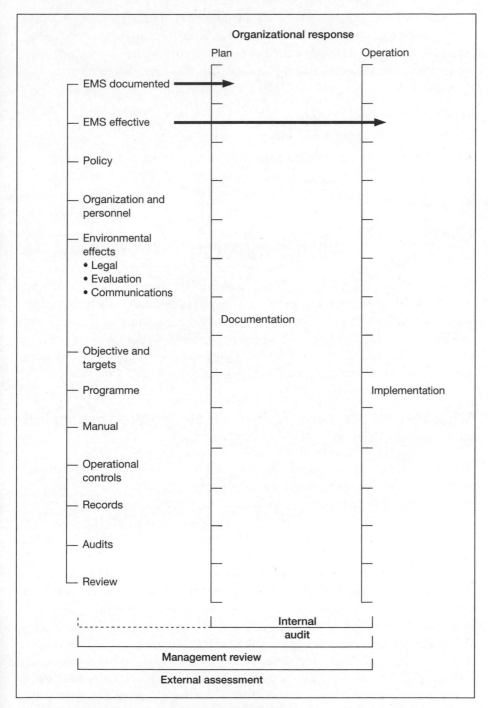

Fig. 30.1 ISO 14001 requirements and your business

You know your business, and the system must be integrated into your business, so it must be *your* system. ISO 14001 is a benchmark for assessment and review internally by an appropriately skilled assessor. But internal assessment, no matter how professional or competent the assessor, can always be viewed from the outside as lacking objectivity. So the benefits of independent assessment include:

- validation that you have got it right;
- a 'badge' to show the world at large;
- benefits from benchmarking against other registered companies;
- a yardstick to keep internal standards high;
- a goal for your staff to attain.

CERTIFICATION PROGRESS

For many companies, using BS 7750, and later ISO 14001, was enough. They had no desire to become registered, and the links to EMAS – which requires public declarations of performance – were not clear. This has now changed with the EC declaration of April 1997 which recognizes EN ISO 14001 as covering the elements of EMAS. Use of a bridging document is required – all this information is available in the *BS Handbook – A Guide to the ISO 14000 Series*.

What does the assessment body certificate indicate when applied to an EMS?

The EMS is assessed to a standard, ISO 14001, to deliver a specified environmental performance set by you as a result of policy and an analysis of your environmental aspects and legal requirements. Therefore the assessor will need to understand both the EMS and the consequent environmental performance to confirm compliance. Auditors will need additional training in environmental issues in order to become effective EMS auditors.

As your organization's environmental performance has a direct relationship to the policy, objectives and targets of the organization, is it expected that the certification body will act as arbiter to those elements of the system? Most certification bodies would say 'no', that it is the role of industry and legislation to define the levels of performance required. The certification body can provide assurance that systems are in place to meet ISO 14001, are operated effectively, and that the environmental performance meets the policy, objectives and targets.

Industry sector codes of practice have a role here to establish appropriate models of policy, objectives and targets to provide guidance to organizations and certification bodies.

What expertise is needed?

In addition to system assessment skills, it is clear that industry knowledge and environmental performance knowledge will be required in carrying out assessments to ISO 14001.

- **Industry knowledge** – for familiarity with the issues and special processes involved;
- **Environmental performance knowledge** – to ensure that test, measurement methods, and other practices are appropriate.

These mixed skills may be present in individuals, but it is more likely that a team will be needed to provide an appropriate mix. Industry will also require the assessment team to be a flexible part of an ISO 9000 assessment activity, so these skills are also needed.

How will external parties view certification?

How will outside organizations and individuals perceive the value of certification to ISO 14001 or EMAS? Will the Environment Agency or local authority inspectors view the certificate as providing evidence of legal compliance? Will ISO 14001 be deemed a Best Available Technique? Will the pressure groups and public regard the certificate as a valuable confirmation of commitment or as a 'rubber stamp' that adds little value to the environmental debate?

While it is too early to answer all these questions, there is now growing evidence that all external parties regard the development of ISO 14001 registration as a positive contribution to improving and benchmarking the environmental management status of organizations. It is recognized that it does not imply perfection, but that it is a significant step along the road to continual improvement of environmental performance.

ISO 14001 and EMAS

Appendix 1 gives a more detailed analysis of the current requirements of ISO 14001. In simple terms, the main difference during the assessment of EMAS is that the external verifiers require an Environmental Statement, and also assess the Initial Environmental Review. Otherwise, there is a great deal of commonality between the assessments of systems to ISO 14001 and EMAS, especially the ISO standard is now recognized as a core component of systems which comply with the requirements of EMAS.

On the other hand, more and more companies now recognize the value of open declarations of environmental performance, it is an essential part of establishing credibility in the eyes of the community. If you are not willing to publish your performance, the logic is that you have something to hide.

Therefore we can look forward to a future where assessed capability to ISO 14001 or EMAS, together with relevant public statements, provides the appropriate confirmation of compliance with the proposed regulation scheme requirements. For many companies, the stepping stones are clear (Figure 30.2); building on quality and health and safety systems, many organizations progress to ISO 14001 and then to EMAS.

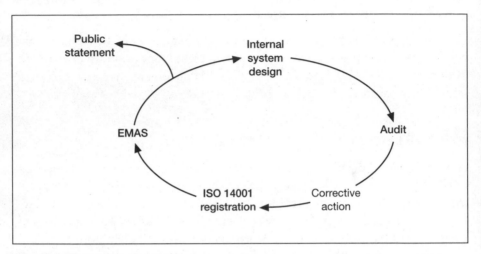

Fig. 30.2 The registration cycle

The Route to Registration – ISO 14001

In the next two sections, we will describe the process of registration to ISO 14001, followed by a look at the international guidelines for certified registrars. Registration takes place in two parts. Part 1 is a pre-assessment activity, while Part 2 is a three-phase assessment and if there are no major non-conformances, then the registrars will recommend registration for the organization they have been assessing.

The following descriptions will follow the BSI assessment process. This differs from many other registration bodies in that BSI has a pre-assessment, and the second part of the assessment is in three phases; many other registration bodies use a two-phase, instead of a three-phase assessment programme, combining the elements of the first and second phases.

Part 1: the pre-assessment

This activity consists of six parts (*see* Figure 30.3). The objective is to gather information so that BSI has a fuller understanding of your organization and its activities, as well as the state of your EMS. BSI can then plan the next part of the assessment, allocating the appropriate team members and focusing the right resources. The pre-assessment includes a pre-application questionnaire, which can provide valuable pointers for the assessment.

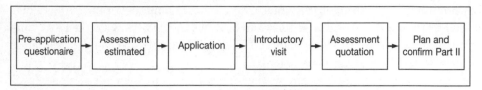

Fig 30.3 Part 1 of the assessment process – pre-assessment

Part 2: the three-phase assessment process

Figure 30.4 shows the three-phase assessment. Each phase covers the areas outlined, but the second phase is the real core of the assessment, because it focuses on the main driving forces behind the EMS – the environmental impacts and regulatory requirements. During the assessment, it is quite usual to find non-conformances. If the assessors find a major non-conformance during any phase of the assessment, then all these must be addressed and fixed before a registration body can recommend registration.

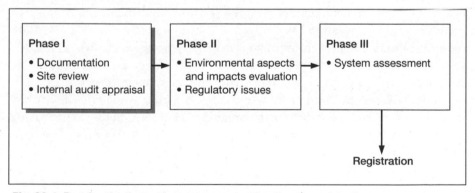

Fig. 30.4 Part 2 – the three-phase assessment leading to registration

Following a successful registration, continuing assessment occurs over a two-year cycle, typically with two assessment visits per year.

Who assesses the assessors?

Any body which wishes to assess organizations to ISO 14001 must meet strict criteria set out by independent bodies. In the UK, the organization which accredits British registrars is the UK Accreditation Service (UKAS), which in turn follows guidelines and criteria produced by the European Accreditation of Certification (EAC) Document G/5, published in August 1996. On a global level, 37 accreditation bodies – of which UKAS is one – are currently drafting uniform, international guidelines through the International Accreditation Forum (IAF), while ISO has worked with the same bodies to produce the ISO CASCO (the ISO Committee for Conformity Assessment) Guide 62, which provides uniform guidance for assessors of management systems.

For EMAS, the rules for accredited verifiers are set out at an international level through the European Union, while at national levels, each member state of the EU has an accredited Competent Body which evaluates and accredits each verifier. In the UK, the Competent Body is the Department of the Environment, Transport and the Regions (DETR).

CONCLUSION

In establishing an effective environmental management system in your organization, you have prepared the ground for future third-party certification. You will be able to guide the management team through that achievement with confidence.

At the start of the book, we indicated that the process of establishing an EMS is a change management process. As a result of the implementation of the programme, your organization has changed, but it does not stop here. ISO 14001 requires continual improvement of your management system, which is intended to lead to continual improvements in your environmental performance. The standard is written to take account of trends in requirements from legislation to community issues. By continually responding to these changing needs, and by involving everyone, everywhere in the organization in contributing to improving environmental performance, we are a step nearer to attaining our overall goal of sustainable development.

Real world tips for certification and verification

- *The initial assessment phases can be done as separate visits or as a continuous process.*

- *A verifier has much more leeway than an assessor in asking for specific changes that will satisfy them.*

- *Read assessors' findings carefully – they're giving you a clue as to the corrective action.*

- *Assessments and verifications are a learning process, sometimes for everyone concerned.*

- *Registration is a starting point, not a full stop.*

CASE STUDY

Formosa Plastics Corporation USA

FPC USA integrate their systems for H&S and environmental management in order to streamline these complementary management systems. The company achieved this through applying ISO 14001 to health and safety issues as well as environmental ones. While the certification body, BSi SA, only certified their EMS, the auditors agreed to provide observations of the H&S system, highlighting its problems, potential deficiencies and areas for improvement. Another way round this is to use BS 8800 as a guide for H&S systems, and then include this within the scope of an ISO 9000 system.

John Pastuck, who is now the manager of FPC Environmental Services, is in favour of formal certification to the standard because it brings added credibility. He states that there is a view which is sceptical towards organizations which self-declare, because there is industry experience to show that many members of the public assume that self-declaration it is just lip service.

Appendix 1
A QUICK TOUR OF ISO 14001

There are two useful sets of guidance for ISO 14001. The first of these can be found in the annexes to ISO 14001, while ISO 14004 explains the requirements for each clause in ISO 14001.

SCOPE

The standard ISO 14001 applies to any organization that wishes to:

- implement, maintain and improve an environmental management policy, objectives and targets
- demonstrate conformance with the policy, objectives and targets
- seek certification of its environmental management system, using an external organization
- make a self-determination and self-declaration of conformance with the standard.

All the requirements in the standard are intended to be used in your environmental management system. The extent of the application depends on the environmental policy of your organization, the nature of your activities and the conditions in which you operate.

The scope of an EMS is pre-determined by the processes carried out by the organization. If these have legislation applicable to them, or if they have any significant environmental effects, then such processes are by default included within the scope of the EMS.

DEFINITIONS

ISO 14001 includes a number of important definitions. The most significant are outlined in the following text.

(i) Continual improvement

The process of enhancing the organization's environmental management system, in order to achieve improvements in the organization's overall environmental performance. These improvements are to be in line with the organization's environmental policy. The improvements need not take place simultaneously in all areas of activity.

(iii) Environmental aspect

An element of an organization's activities, products or services that can interact with the environment. A 'significant' environmental aspect is an environmental aspect which has, or can have, a significant environmental impact.

(iv) Environmental impact

Any change to the environment as a result of an organization's activities, products or services. Such change is an environmental impact whether it is adverse or beneficial, and whether it is caused by the organization in whole or in part.

(v) Environmental Management System (EMS)

The part of the organization's overall management system responsible for the environmental policy. Its areas of responsibility include organizational structure, planning activities, responsibilities, practices, procedures, processes and resources for developing, implementing, achieving, reviewing and maintaining the environmental policy.

(vi) Environmental Management System audit

A verification process to determine whether an organization's EMS conforms to its EMS audit criteria. The process is to be systematic and documented, and is to obtain and evaluate evidence objectively. The process of the audit includes the communication of its results to the organization's management.

(viii) Environmental performance

Measurable results of the environmental management system, related to an organization's control of its environmental aspects. Results are based on an organization's environmental policy, objectives and targets.

(ix) Environmental policy

A statement by the organization of its intentions and principles in relation to its overall environmental performance. The statement provides a framework for action and for the organization to set its environmental objectives and targets.

Clause 4.1 General requirements

This states that the organization is to *establish and maintain an EMS*, while the rest of Clause 4 goes into the details.

Clause 4.2 Environmental policy

This is the organization's *declaration of its intent* to the actions necessary to:

- comply with environmental legislation
- continually improve its environmental performance.

The environmental policy must:

- be defined by top management
- be appropriate to environmental impacts
- be committed to improvements
- commit resources
- be committed to compliance with environmental law and other requirements
- provide a framework for setting/reviewing objectives and targets
- be documented, implemented, maintained and communicated
- be publicly available.

Clause 4.3 Planning

Clause 4.3.1 Environmental aspects

Your organization must identify which of its activities, products or services have, or can have, a significant environmental impact. This means that you need to consider all your processes, determining if these have any environmental impacts, and whether these impacts are significant or not. There are lots of methods of determining significance, such as risk analysis. Your organization also has to establish and maintain the procedures necessary for identifying environmental effects and their significance.

The aspects related to your organization's significant environmental impacts must be considered when setting environmental objectives, i.e., the most significant will act as primary driving forces in setting the objectives. You need to keep any information on environmental aspects up to date.

Clause 4.3.2 Legal and other requirements

Your organization must establish and maintain a procedure so that legal and other requirements relevant to its environmental aspects can be identified and accessed. This will be closely linked to the register of environmental aspects, as each process identified can have both environmental aspects and legislative requirements.

This clause also requires the organization to identify any applicable regulations, codes of practise and other corporate requirements.

Clause 4.3.3 Objectives and targets

Your organization must formulate its objectives and targets. These must be established and maintained throughout it. The organization must also consider the following when objectives and targets are established/reviewed:

- legal and other requirements;
- significant environmental aspects;
- technological options;
- financial, operational and business requirements;
- views of interested parties;
- objectives and targets consistent with environmental policy (including a commitment to pollution prevention).

Clause 4.3.4 Environmental management programme(s)

This clause requires your organization to designate responsibility for achieving objectives and targets, and the means by which they are to be achieved. The programme shall also be kept up to date, and the organization must specify a timeframe by which it is going to achieve the objectives and targets.

Clause 4.4 Implementation and operation

Clause 4.4.1 Structure and responsibility

Your organization's management shall also provide essential resources for:

- human and specialized skills;
- technological aspects;
- financial aspects.

Your organization's top management must appoint specific representatives, who shall have defined roles, responsibilities and the authority to:

- ensure that the organization meets its EMS requirements;
- report on EMS performance to top management as a feedback procedure.

Clause 4.4.2 Training, awareness and competence

Each member of staff with an environmental role or roles must know how to do his or her job. The standard requires the following:

- Training requirements must be identified.
- These needs shall be appropriate to the personnel.
- The personnel shall be aware of the necessary procedures.
- The personnel shall know and understand the importance of conformance with the EMS, policy and procedures.
- Each member of staff shall know the significant environmental impacts of his or her work activities.
- The staff shall know and understand the environmental benefits of improved personal performance.
- The organization needs to train staff for their roles/responsibilities in relationship to the environmental policy.
- The organization's staff must be aware of the consequences of departure from specified operating procedures.
- Any personnel performing tasks which can cause a significant environmental impact shall be competent on the basis of appropriate education, training and/or experience.

Clause 4.4.3 Communication

Communications are the links which make the EMS operate effectively, therefore the organization must establish and maintain procedures for:

- internal communication
- receiving, documenting and responding to relevant communication from external interested parties
- external communication on significant environmental aspects.

The organization shall consider processes for external communication and record its decision.

Clause 4.4.4 EMS documentation

The standard requires that the organization shall establish and maintain information to:

- describe the core elements of the management system and their interaction
- provide direction to related documentation.

EMS documentation is similar in its hierarchy to QMS documentation, and takes the following form:

Level 1 – *Environmental Manual*
Level 2 – *Environmental Procedures*
Level 3 – *Working Practices.*

Clause 4.4.5 Document control

Your organization must control documents in such a way that:

- they can be located
- they are kept up to date and approved for adequacy by authorized personnel
- current versions of relevant documents are available where they are needed for the effective functioning of the EMS
- obsolete documents are prevented from being used unintentionally
- any obsolete documents retained are suitably identified.

All the documentation must be legible, dated (with revision dates), readily identifiable, and kept in an orderly manner for a specified period. The organization must also establish and maintain procedures and responsibilities for the creation and modification of documents.

Clause 4.4.6 Operational control

This section of the standard relates to the control of operations and activities associated with identified significant environmental aspects. The organization must identify operations which lead to the control of environmental impacts, and it must ensure that they are carried out under specified conditions by:

- establishing and maintaining documented procedures to cover situations where their absence could lead to deviations from the environmental policy, objectives and targets;
- stipulating operating criteria in these procedures;
- establishing and maintaining procedures related to their identifiable significant environmental aspects;

- communicating relevant procedures and requirements to suppliers and contractors.

Clause 4.4.7 Emergency preparedness and response

Abnormal situations can have highly significant environmental impacts, e.g., spillages of chemicals which find their way into rivers. So the organization must have procedures to identify and respond to accidents and emergency situations, and to prevent or mitigate the environmental impacts that may be associated with them.

After the occurrence of accidents or emergencies, the organization must review its emergency preparedness and response procedures, and revise them where necessary. The organization shall also periodically test such procedures where practicable.

Clause 4.5 Checking and corrective action

Clause 4.5.1 Monitoring and measurement

Without monitoring and measuring, there cannot be effective control of a process. Therefore you need to monitor and measure the key characteristics of its operations and activities that can have a significant environmental impact:

- establish and maintain documented procedures for this process;
- record information to track performance, relevant operational controls, and conformance with the organization's objectives and targets;
- calibrate and maintain monitoring equipment;
- retain records of the calibration and maintenance process, according to the organization's procedures;
- evaluate its compliance with relevant environmental legislation and regulations.

Clause 4.5.2 Corrective and preventive action

You need to establish and maintain procedures for defining responsibility and authority for:

- investigating non-conformance with the requirements of the EMS;
- taking action to mitigate any impacts caused by non-conformance;
- initiating and completing corrective and preventive action;

- corrective/preventive action taken to eliminate the causes of actual and potential non-conformances shall be appropriate to the magnitude of the problems, and proportional to the environmental impact encountered;
- changes in the documented procedures as a result of corrective and preventive action implemented and recorded.

Clause 4.5.3 Records

Records are the physical evidence that organization has implemented an EMS, and that the EMS is effective and demonstrates conformity. So the organization must establish and maintain procedures to identify, maintain and dispose of records (including training records and the results of audits and reviews).

Any environmental records must be legible, easy to identify and trace to the activity, product or service involved. The organization must also keep the environmental records so that they are readily retrievable and protected against damage, deterioration or loss. Their retention times shall be established and recorded.

Clause 4.5.4 Environmental Management System (EMS) audit

The organization must establish and maintain a programme and procedures for periodic EMS audits to be carried out, in order to:

- determine whether or not the EMS conforms to planned arrangements for environmental management (including the requirements of ISO 14001), and has been properly implemented and maintained;
- provide information to management on the results of audits.

The organization's audit programme (including any schedule) shall be based on the environmental importance of the activity concerned and the results of previous audits.

(ISO 14011 describes the way in which the organization should carry out audits of its EMS.)

Clause 4.6 Management review of the EMS

At intervals, your organization's top management must review the EMS to ensure its continuing suitability, adequacy and effectiveness, and the evaluation has to be based on the information collected in the management review process. You need to document the review.

In the light of results, changing circumstances and your organization's commitment to continual improvement, the management review must address the possible need for changes to elements of the EMS.

Appendix 2
ISO 14011: ENVIRONMENTAL MANAGEMENT SYSTEM AUDITS

INTRODUCTION AND SCOPE

ISO 14011 provides some useful guidance for the conduct of EMS audits. It applies to all types and sizes of organizations operating an EMS, and establishes audit procedures that provide for the planning and conduct of an audit of an EMS to determine conformance with EMS audit criteria.

The normative references for this auditing procedure are:

ISO 14001:1996 Environmental Management Systems – Specification with guidance for use
ISO 14010:1996 Guidelines for environmental auditing – General principles
ISO 14011:1996 Guidelines for environmental auditing – audit procedures – auditing of environmental management systems
ISO 14012:1996 Guidelines for environmental auditing – Qualification criteria for environmental auditors

EMS AUDIT OBJECTIVES, ROLES AND RESPONSIBILITIES

4.1 Audit objectives

The first step of an audit is to define its objectives, for example:

- to determine conformance of an auditee's EMS with the EMS audit criteria
- to determine whether the auditee's EMS has been properly implemented and maintained
- to identify areas of potential improvement in the auditee's EMS
- to assess the ability of the internal management review process to ensure the continuing suitability and effectiveness of the EMS
- to evaluate the EMS of an organization where the desire exists to establish a

contractual relationship, such as with a potential supplier or a joint-venture partner.

4.2 Roles, responsibilities and activities

4.2.1 Lead auditor

The lead auditor has to do the following:

- determining the scope of the audit
- ensuring audit efficiency/effectiveness, conduct and completion of the audit, within the audit scope and plan approved by the client
- obtaining relevant background information
- determining whether the requirements for an environmental audit, as given in ISO 14010, have been met
- forming the audit team, planning the audit
- directing the activities of the audit team in accordance with the guidelines of ISO 14010 and 14011
- communications with the client/audit team
- resolving problems and conflicts
- communicating non-conformances/recommendations

4.2.2 Auditors' responsibilities and activities

The auditors in the audit team must:

- follow the directions of and support the lead auditor
- plan and carry out the assigned tasks objectively, effectively and efficiently within the scope of the audit
- collect and analyze relevant and sufficient audit evidence to determine audit findings and reach audit conclusions regarding the EMS
- prepare working documents under the lead auditor's direction
- document individual audit findings
- safeguard documents pertaining to the audit and returning such documents as required
- assist in writing the audit report.

4.2.3 Audit team

The following factors apply to the audit team:

- qualifications, e.g., as given in ISO 14012
- type of organization, processes, activities or functions being audited
- the number, language skills and expertise of the individual audit-team members
- any potential conflict of interest between the audit-team members and the auditee
- requirements of clients, and certification and accreditation bodies
- technical expertise.

4.2.4 Client's responsibilities and activities

The client's responsibilities and activities are as follows:

- determining the need for the audit
- contacting the auditee to ensure the auditee's full co-operation and initiating the audit process
- defining the objectives of the audit
- selecting the lead auditor/auditing organization
- providing appropriate authority and resources to enable the audit to be conducted
- consulting with the lead auditor to determine the scope of the audit
- approving the EMS audit criteria
- audit plan approval
- receiving the audit report and determining its distribution.

5.1 Initiating the audit

5.1.1 Audit scope

The client and the lead auditor determine the extent and boundaries of the audit. Any subsequent changes to the audit scope require the agreement of the client and the lead auditor. The resources committed to the audit should be sufficient to meet its intended scope.

5.1.2 Preliminary document review

This is carried out by lead auditor at the beginning of the audit process. The organization's documentation includes environmental policy statements, programmes, records or manuals for meeting EMS requirements. This stage uses all appropriate background information.

If the documentation is inadequate for the audit, then the lead auditor has to inform the client, and no additional resources should be expended until the audit team has received further instructions from the client.

5.2   Preparing the audit

5.2.1 Audit plan

The plan has to be flexible, encompass the objectives, scope and audit criteria, and identify the following:

- the working and reporting languages of the audit
- reference documents
- expected time and duration for major audit activities
- the dates and places where the audit is to be conducted
- units to be audited
- the relevant functions and/or individuals, identify the high priority areas of the auditee's EMS elements
- the procedures for auditing the auditee's EMS elements
- audit-team members
- the schedule of meetings to be held with the auditee's management
- confidentiality requirements
- report content and format, and the expected date of issue and distribution of the audit report
- document retention requirements.

5.2.2 Audit-team assignments

Each audit-team member must be assigned specific EMS elements, functions or activities to audit, and the lead auditor must then issue instructions on the audit procedure.

Assignments should be made by the lead auditor in consultation with the team members concerned, and the lead auditor can make changes to work assignments during the audit, to ensure optimal achievement of the audit objectives.

5.2.3 Working documents for the auditors' investigation

These include the following:

- forms for documenting supporting audit evidence and audit findings
- procedures for checklists used for evaluating EMS elements
- records of meetings.

Working documents are to be kept at least until the audit is completed. Confidential or proprietary information should be suitably safeguarded by the audit-team members.

5.3 Conducting the audit

5.3.1 Opening meeting

At the opening meeting, the lead auditor must do the following:

- introduce the members of the audit team to the auditee's management
- review scope, objectives, plan and agree on the audit timetable
- provide a short summary of the methods used to conduct the audit
- establish official communication links between audit team/auditee
- confirm that the resources and facilities needed by the audit team are available
- confirm the time and date of the closing meeting
- promote the auditee's active participation
- review relevant site safety and emergency procedures for the audit team.

5.3.2 Collecting audit evidence

The evidence must be sufficient to enable the auditors to determine that the EMS conforms to the audit criteria. The auditors must collect evidence through interviews, examination of documents and observation of activities and conditions which indicate non-conformity to the EMS audit criteria. The auditors shall verify interview information by supporting information from other sources (such as observations, records and results of existing measurements).

5.3.3 Audit findings

Having conducted the audit, the lead auditor shall oversee and direct the following:

- review all evidence to determine non-conformities
- document non-conformities in a clear, concise manner, supported by audit evidence.
- audit findings should be reviewed with the responsible auditee manager, with a view to obtaining acknowledgement of the factual basis of all findings of nonconformity.
- audit findings of conformity may also be documented if included in the agreed scope, but the auditors must take due care to avoid giving any implication of absolute assurance.

5.3.4 Closing meeting

The closing meeting with the management and those responsible for the functions audited takes place after collection of the audit evidence, and before the preparation of the audit report. The auditors must do the following:

- present audit findings to the auditee, in such a manner as to obtain their clear understanding and their acknowledgement of the factual basis of the audit findings
- resolve disagreements, if possible before the lead auditor issues the report.

Final decisions on the significance and description of the audit findings ultimately rest with the lead auditor, though the auditee or client still may disagree with these findings.

5.4 Audit reports and document retention

5.4.1 Preparation of audit report

The audit team has to prepare the audit report under the lead auditor's direction. He or she is responsible for its accuracy and completeness, and the topics addressed should be those determined in the audit plan. Any changes desired at the time of the report's preparation should be agreed by the parties concerned.

5.4.2 Content of audit report

The minimum contents of the audit report are:

- the identification of the client and the organization audited
- the agreed objectives, scope and plan of the audit
- the agreed criteria, including a list of reference documents against which the audit was conducted
- audit dates, identification of the auditee's representatives, and audit-team members
- statement of the confidential nature of the contents
- the distribution list for the audit report
- summary of audit process including any obstacles encountered
- conclusions.

5.4.3 Distribution of audit report

The lead auditor should send the audit report to the client, while the distribution of the report is determined by the client. Any additional distribution of the report outside the auditee's organization requires the auditee's permission.

Remember that an audit report:

- remains the sole property of the client
- is confidential
- must be issued within the agreed time period in accordance with the audit plan.

5.4.4 Document retention

The auditors must retain all working documents and draft and final reports pertaining to the audit. The retention period is by agreement between the client, the lead auditor and the auditee, and in accordance with any applicable requirements.

Appendix 3
THE ISO 14000 SERIES

Standard

ISO 14001 – EMS: A Specification with guidance

ISO 14002 Environmental Management Systems – Guidelines on special considerations affecting small and medium enterprises

ISO 14004 – EMS: General Guidelines on Principles, Systems and Supporting Techniques

ISO 14010 – Guidelines for Environmental Auditing: General Principles

ISO 14011 – GEA: Auditing of EMS

ISO 14012 – GEA: Qualification criteria for environmental auditors

ISO 14015 Environmental Assessment of Sites and Entities (EASE) working draft Summer 1997

ISO 14020 Environmental Labels and Declarations – General Principles

ISO 14021 Environmental Labels and Declarations – Environmental Labelling – Self Declaration – Environmental Claims – Terms and Definitions

ISO 14022 Environmental Labels and Declarations – Environmental Claims – Self Declaration – Environmental Claims – Symbols

ISO 14023 Environmental Labelling – Self Declaration – Environmental Claims – Testing and Verification Methodologies

ISO 14024 Environmental Labels and Declarations – Environmental Labelling TYPE 1 – Guiding Principles and Procedures

ISO 14025 Environmental Labels and Declarations – Environmental Labelling TYPE – Guiding Principles and Procedures

ISO 14031 Environmental Performance Evaluation – Guidelines

ISO 14040 Life Cycle Assessment – Principles and Framework

ISO 14041 Life Cycle Assessment – Life Cycle Inventory Analysis

ISO 14042 Life Cycle Assessment – Impact Assessment

ISO 14043 Life Cycle Assessment – Interpretation

ISO 14050 Environmental Management – Terms and Definitions Standard.

Appendix 4

AIG CONSULTANTS ENVIRONMENTAL AUDIT – PRE-SURVEY QUESTIONNAIRE

1. General information

1.1   Contact details of Organization

1.2   Contact details of Parent Organization

1.3   Organization's core business?

1.4   Core business of Parent Organization?

2. Site history

2.1 Current occupier's operations

2.1.1   How long has current process been operated?

2.1.2   Have the current occupiers made any major modifications? If so, then what?

2.1.3   Have the current occupiers used the site for any purpose other than present activity? If so, then what?

2.1.4   Have any areas been used by occupiers for disposal of waste, except incineration?

2.1.5   Have any audits/surveys been carried out on the site in the last two years? Give details.

2.1.6   Please supply plans of site, pipe runs, location of warehouses and other storage facilities, drainage systems.

2.2 Previous owners/occupiers

2.2.1 Name any previous occupiers of the site.

2.2.2   Was a pre-acquisition audit conducted at the time of purchase/lease of the site?

2.2.3   Was the site developed to current use from green-field area?

2.2.4   What was the activity of previous occupiers? Details of all trading/manufacturing activities should be provided here from the original site development.

2.2.5 Has the site been used at any time to dispose of waste? If so, specify the type of waste, how treated, and method of disposal if known.

2.2.6 Has there been any significant releases or spillages of toxic materials on the site. If so, then was a clean-up carried out? Please describe any measures taken.

3. External factors

3.1 Neighbouring risks

3.1.1 Please provide a map or plan of the site and local area showing nearest townships and local rivers, canals or other waterways.

3.1.2 What are the approximate numbers of inhabitants in the immediate vicinity (up to one km radius)?

3.1.3 Please provide details of any particularly sensitive or hazardous industries which are in the immediate vicinity.

3.1.4 Are there any nature reserves?

3.2 Geology, hydrology and meteorology

3.2.1 What is the constitution of the area on which the site is located?

3.2.2 What is the approximate depth to groundwater in the area?

3.2.3 Is there any known abstraction of groundwater for site operations or other purposes?

3.2.4 What are the drainage arrangements for rainwater, and groundwater (site drainage plans are required)?

3.2.5 Are there any other factors which may interfere with normal drainage routes (mine-workings, railway tunnels, underground pipelines, reclaimed ground)?

3.2.6 Is the site prone to flooding ? If yes, give details of any recent floods at the site.

3.2.7 Has the location suffered from any earth tremors or earthquakes?

3.2.8 In what direction is the prevailing wind?

3.2.9 What is the average rainfall in the area?

4. Environmental management environmental policy

4.1 Does the site operate to an environmental policy ? If so, is there a corporate or site specific document?

4.2 In each separate part of the plant, are there written objectives to be fulfilled to meet the overall policy standard?

4.3 How are the site environmental objectives brought to the attention of employees?

4.4 How are the site environmental objectives brought to the attention of contractors?

5. Organization for environmental protection

5.1 Are the responsibilities of senior managers/directors written into job descriptions? What are their responsibilities ?

5.2 Is there a manager allocated to each of the following (if applicable); air pollution; liquid effluents; waste collection and disposal?

5.3 Is there a management group/working party which considers environmental protection? If so, how often does it meet?

5.4 If an airborne release occurs, is there a formal procedure for action?

5.5 In the event of a release which has/could gain the attention of the public/media, is there an Immediate Notification Procedure?

5.6 Are new projects and equipment assessed for their environmental impact ? Against what standards are they assessed?

5.7 Are the pollution costs of existing processes known, either for each stream or for the process as a whole?

5.8 What, if any, is the planned expenditure for pollution minimization during the next year?

5.9 If a statutory or advisory limit on an emission (noise, air, etc.) is exceeded, do formal procedures exist to correct the emission?

5.10 Are all incidents which are potentially environmentally damaging investigated to determine the cause and action necessary? Who carries this out and who ensures that actions are taken?

5.11 Is there a central register of all raw materials, intermediate/ product/waste hazards for emergency services in the event of an onsite event?

6. Compliance with environmental law

6.1 Atmospheric discharges

6.1.1   Does the site discharge gases and/or vapours to atmosphere? List the emission points. If no, go on to the next section.

6.1.2   Is the site activity subject to licensing or consent from the Regulatory Authority in respect of air emissions?

6.1.3   Are the flow rate, temperature and composition of each relevant stream known? List them.

6.1.4   Does the process involve any of the processes or chemicals requiring registration under the Health and Safety (Emissions to Atmosphere) Regulations 1983? List them.

6.1.5   For each of the items listed under the previous clause, has a works registration been issued by HMIP (HMIPI in Scotland)?

6.1.6   Are any measurements taken, and records maintained of discharges to atmosphere?

6.1.7   Does any process emit substances defined as noxious or offensive? List them.

6.1.8   Have any complaints for odour nuisance been received in the last two years? If yes, detail complaint and remedial action taken.

6.1.9   Does the site operate a furnace, power house or boiler ? If no, go on to 6.1.13.

6.1.10 Does the furnace, power house or stack have a grit or dust arrestment facility? What type?

6.1.11 If an emission of black or dark smoke can occur periodically, are the emissions within the Dark Smoke Regulations?

6.1.12 Do the Clean Air (Emission of Grit and Dust from Furnaces) Regulations 1971 apply? If exempt, provide details.

6.1.13 Has the site been prosecuted for any infringement of air quality regulations? (Local Authority or HMIP)

6.2 Liquid effluents

6.2.1   Does the site discharge effluent to a water plc operated treatment plant?

6.2.2   Has a consent in respect of discharges been granted? Detail.

6.2.3   Are discharges monitored? At what frequency?

6.2.4   Is a charge made for the effluent treatment?

6.2.5   Are comparisons of actual suspended solids, COD and flow made with those specified in the charges tariff? Provide details of these values and total annual charge.

6.2.6 Has a water balance ever been calculated?

6.2.7 Does the site discharge effluent to waters controlled by the NRA (River Purification Board in Scotland)?

6.2.8 Is the discharge in, or does it later flow through, an environmentally sensitive area? (e.g., SSSI)

6.2.9 Does the effluent contain any 'Red List', 'Black List 1' or 'Grey List' substances? List them.

6.2.10 What steps are taken/will be taken to minimize substances in effluent?

6.2.11 Does the site storm water discharge to controlled water in a separate manner to the trade effluent?

6.2.12 Has a consent been given? Detail.

6.2.13 Is storm water monitored? How frequently?

6.2.14 Can toxic or flammable materials be accidentally discharged via the storm main? Has such an incident occurred in the past two years? Provide details.

6.2.15 Provide details of any prosecutions for illegal discharges of effluent or spills to waterways.

6.3 Waste

6.3.1 Provide an estimate of the quantity and quality (types) of waste generated on site.

6.3.2 Are any classified (industrial/special) wastes generated?

6.3.3 Are any controlled wastes disposed of on site? Please give details. Is a site licence required?

6.3.4 Is there an individual charged with responsibility for co-ordinating and controlling the use of waste contractors?

6.3.5 Are 'waste brokers' used?

6.3.6 Does the waste contractor use a third party haulage firm? If so, is the haulier registered for waste transport?

6.3.7 Does a fully documented system operate for transfer of waste from site to final disposal including all intermediaries? Describe the route which the wastes flow.

6.3.8 Have the waste contractors facilities been inspected by site staff? If so, were you satisfied that the facilities are suitable for your wastes and that other wastes disposed of at the facility are compatible?

6.3.9   Are records kept concerning the use and selection of waste contractors?

6.3.10   Are complete consignment notes kept on wastes shipped?

6.3.11   Has there been any litigation concerning disposal of wastes generated on the site? Please detail.

6.4 Noise nuisance

6.4.1   Detail any complaints received regarding noise from the site.

6.4.2   Have noise measurements been taken:
         (a) On site;
         (b) At the site boundary? Provide details and results.

7. Storage

7.1 Hazardous materials (including fuel) – non-bulk

7.1.1   Provide details of suppliers, inventory of stored materials and safety data sheets to show physical, chemical and toxic properties with particular reference to environmental impairment.

7.1.2   Provide a plan of storage area(s) with details or storage arrangements, constructional details (ventilation and protection of electrical apparatus), and separation distances from boundaries and buildings.

7.1.3   What is the storage area(s) floor construction type (e.g., concrete)?

7.1.4   Is there any spillage containment with bunds and/or interceptors? In both storage and unloading areas? Detail.

7.1.5   What provision is there to contain fire-fighting water? Are the emergency services aware of the types of materials stored?

7.1.6   Is the storage activity subject to licensing, consent or permit by a Regulating Authority? Please specify where appropriate.

7.2 Bulk storage

7.2.1   Are bulk storage areas bunded? Describe construction.

7.2.2   List bulk storage facilities indicating age and whether they are above or below ground.

7.2.3   How are the vessels inspected? How frequently?

7.2.4   Does the EC Directive on Major Hazards (CIMAH) apply to the site? Provide details of the substance involved. Has a Safety Case been submitted to the Health and Safety Executive?

7.3 Intermediaries and finished products

7.3.1   Are there any special requirements for storage of intermediaries and finished products?

8. Transport

8.1   Does the plant operate its own freight transport?

8.2   Is the haulier a member of a recognized association?

8.3   Have there been any incidents which have resulted in environmental impairment? Please give details.

9. General

9.1 Political

9.1.1 Are there any active pressure groups in the area? Have they shown an interest in the site?

9.1.2   What is the attitude of residents, press and authorities to the environmental performance of the site?

9.2 Special substances

9.2.1   Is there any asbestos on site? Please provide details.

9.2.2   Do any of the electrical appliances on site contain PCBs? Please specify.

10. Other points of interest in relation to environmental impairment

10.1   Please provide details of any issues which may be considered germane in relation to environmental impairment.

INDEX